Pearl of the Desert

Pearl of the Desert

A History of Palmyra

RUBINA RAJA

OXFORD
UNIVERSITY PRESS

OXFORD
UNIVERSITY PRESS

Oxford University Press is a department of the University of Oxford. It furthers
the University's objective of excellence in research, scholarship, and education
by publishing worldwide. Oxford is a registered trade mark of Oxford University
Press in the UK and certain other countries.

Published in the United States of America by Oxford University Press
198 Madison Avenue, New York, NY 10016, United States of America.

CIP data is on file at the Library of Congress
ISBN 978–0–19–085222–1

DOI: 10.1093/oso/9780190852221.001.0001

1 3 5 7 9 8 6 4 2

Printed by Sheridan Books, Inc., United States of America

Contents

Acknowledgments

This book is about the oasis city of Palmyra in the Syrian Desert and the archeology and history of the site, especially in the Roman period when the city flourished as the result of its role in the caravan trade. It is from this period—the first three centuries CE—that the vast majority of our material and written sources stem. However, the book also touches on Palmyra before the Roman period, as well as after the city's sack in 272 CE and again in 273 CE, and it traces developments over the years, extending from the events of the Umayyad period, through to the arrival of the first European tourists and the tragic eruption of civil war in the twenty-first century. This material forms a vital part of any discussion about Palmyra, since people lived in the city long before Rome, and they continued to dwell there in the centuries after. For this reason, this book differs from many other accounts of Palmyrene history. Nor does this book study Palmyra in isolation: in Antiquity, the city was at the heart of international trading networks and were caught between the empires of Rome and Parthia, while in modern times it has become enmeshed in international politics, as well as global debates about the trade and protection of cultural heritage. It is therefore my aim here to offer an overview of Palmyra that places the city at the heart of vibrant, often-shifting networks.

I could not have written a book such as this without standing on the shoulders of many other scholars who have been researching and writing on a variety of topics concerning Palmyra for decades. They include Nathanael Andrade,[1] Kevin Butcher,[2] Lucinda Dirven,[3] Peter Edwell,[4] Michal Gawlikowski,[5] Udo Hartmann,[6] Emanuele Intagliata,[7] Ted Kaizer,[8] Fergus Millar,[9] Maurice Sartre and Annie Sartre-Fauriat,[10] Eivind Seland,[11] Andrew M. Smith III,[12] Michael Sommer,[13] and Jean-Baptiste Yon.[14] I am lucky to know and value them all as mentors and colleagues. They inspired my own interest in Palmyra, and without their work, I could not have written a new account of Palmyra's archeology and history, adding my own perspective based on my research undertaken over the last ten years.

The book covers several themes, including the historiography of the rediscovery of the site, the urban development of the city, the funerary sphere,

Palmyrene religion and its material expressions, trade, Palmyrene social constructions, the historical framework within which Palmyra developed, and key events that influenced the city. However, it is not meant to be exhaustive on all aspects, and I therefore direct interested readers to the literature on various topics that I reference in both the endnotes and the bibliography. Several books and articles, some of which are mentioned above, have been written about the archeology, history, and general development of Palmyra in recent years, and these can be used as supplementary reading for this book.

I have also drawn repeatedly here on the research undertaken by the Palmyra Portrait Project, which I have directed since 2012 and which comprises what is now known to be the largest corpus of funerary portraits to stem from a single location in the Roman period. This collection contains more than 3,800 limestone portraits found in tombs and they depict the Palmyrene elite. The careful study of these representations has opened up new perspectives on Palmyra and its society as well as providing a wealth of data on which we can draw to drive forward new discussions about the city's development across almost 300 years of flourishing urban life. It is the combination of the unique evidence available to us from the first three centuries CE, together with the new understandings of society generated by the Palmyra Portrait Project since 2012, and the developments in Syria across a decade of civil conflict, that justifies the writing of this book.

The book is aimed at students of archeology, classics, and history, scholars with an interest in the Roman Near East, and anybody engaged in debates about material culture and cultural heritage as well as an interested general public. In providing an overview and presentation of known evidence, together with new data, I hope that this work will emphasize Palmyra's importance to the archeology and history of both the Near East and the Roman world, and that it can serve as a basis for knowledge in a day and age when visiting the site itself is rendered extremely difficult.

The book has been made possible through support received from many sides and over numerous years. I am deeply grateful to the Carlsberg Foundation for supporting my research since 2012 and for making both the Palmyra Portrait Project and its strong research team possible. In facilitating the project, they have also made it possible to produce this book. Without the continuous support of the Carlsberg Foundation, I could not have undertaken such focused research on Palmyra. Numerous publications have come out of the Palmyra Portrait Project, and a full list can be found at FIGSHARE.[15] I also offer my gratitude to the Danish National Research

Foundation, who presented me with the opportunity to establish the Centre for Urban Network Evolutions at Aarhus University in 2015 (DNRF grant 119). This grant has allowed deeper research on urban matters than would otherwise have been possible. I also thank the ALIPH, Augustinus, and Carlsberg Foundations for granting me recent support for two further projects focusing on Palmyra: one on Archive Archeology and the archive of Harald Ingholt, and one on circular economy and urban sustainability in Antiquity, which takes Palmyra as its point of departure. These projects have allowed new research on entirely different aspects of Palmyrene history and archeology. The Danish Institute in Damascus funded the printing costs for the color illustrations.

I thank the Institute for Advanced Study, Princeton, for granting me membership in 2019 and for the funding provided by the Hetty Goldman Membership Fund, which allowed me to expand my research on Palmyra. In particular, I thank Professor Angelos Chaniotis for his engagement with my work during my stay. A further thank you goes to Professor Emeritus Glen Bowersock and Professor Emeritus Patrick Gehry, both of whom provided useful input on papers that I delivered while in residence at the institute. Gratitude also goes to the J. P. Getty Museum and the Getty Research Institute for granting me a visiting museum fellowship in the summer of 2018, which enabled me to do preparatory work for this book. In this connection, a special thank you goes to Dr. Kenneth Lapatin and to Dr. Jeffrey Spiers at the J. P. Getty Museum for supporting my work, as well as to Jim Cuno, president and CEO of the Getty Trust, for his interest in my research.

Particular thanks are owed to the Ny Carlsberg Glyptotek and its staff, since I have been welcomed to its collections with open arms and doors since 2012. I thank the former directors of the Ny Carlsberg Glyptotek, Flemming Friborg, and his successor Christine Buhl Andersen, for their support. Furthermore, I give particular thanks to curator Anne-Marie Nielsen, as well as to head of collections Dr. Rune Frederiksen, for their time and support whenever I needed to visit the collections over the years. The special exhibition *The Road to Palmyra*, held at the Ny Carlsberg Glyptotek in 2019 and which I co-curated with Anne Marie Nielsen, gave me much inspiration for various themes in the book, and my work for the publication of the collection catalogue in 2019 gave me an opportunity to delve deep into the history of every single item in the museum's Palmyra collection. In this connection, I would also like to thank Bert Smith and Christopher Hallett for discussing aspects of Roman period portraiture with me while I worked on the catalogue as well as during the exhibition itself, when we visited the exhibition together.

A heartfelt thank you goes to Mary Ebba Underdown, daughter of Harald Ingholt, who on several occasions shared knowledge with me about her father's work in Palmyra and beyond. A large thank you is also due to Harold and Phil Underdown, as well as Nadine Lemmon, for their help in providing me with further information about Ingholt's work in Palmyra during the 1920s and '30s. I am hugely grateful to the wider Ingholt family for sharing both their knowledge and their documents with me and for granting me rights to publish these over the last years.

Without the commitment, professionality, and hard work of the assistant professors, post docs, research assistants, PhD students, and student helpers involved with the Palmyra Portrait Project over the years, it would have been impossible to compile the large database project from which parts of this book also emerged. Therefore, a large thank you goes to assistant professor Dr. Olympia Bobou, post doc Dr. Amy Miranda, research assistants Jesper Vestervang Jensen (MA), Ditte Johnson (MA), Nathalia Breintoft Kristensen (MA), Dr. Julia Steding, and Rikke Randeris Thomsen (MA) for their diligent and thorough work on the Palmyra Portrait Project database. I also thank the former post docs involved in the project, Dr. Annette Højen Sørensen, Dr. Tracey Long, and Dr. Signe Krag, for their dedication, and for immersing themselves so wholly into the Palmyrene material with me throughout the consolidation phase of the project.

I would also like to thank colleagues and friends within the field of Palmyrene studies, all of whom contributed to making my understanding of Palmyra broader and deeper. These include, in no particular order of importance, Nathanael Andrade, Eleonora Cussini, Michal Gawlikowski, Maura Heyn, Ted Kaizer, Jørgen Christian Meyer, Annie Sartre-Fauriat, Maurice Sartre, Eivind Seland, and Jean-Baptiste Yon. Thanks are also owed to my many colleagues who have shared their knowledge through workshops and conference publications over the years but who are too numerous to mention here, although many of them are cited in this book. I also thank Michael Blömer, Achim Lichtenberger, and Søren M. Sindbæk for their collegial input to my research over the last many years. My studies of urban societies in the East have profited from discussions with all of these people, as well as with several other colleagues working on the Near East. I would also like to offer my gratitude to the anonymous readers for their immensely helpful and insightful comments.

A tremendously large thank you goes to Stefan Vranka at Oxford University Press, New York, for his willingness to work with me on a variety of Palmyra—and Near East-related—projects and for his immense patience with delays in the work. He has been an inspiration to work with and the most patient, knowledgeable, and detail-oriented editor one could have wished for. Further huge thanks must go to assistant professor Dr. Olympia Bobou and center administrator Christina Levisen for their careful editing and proofreading in the early stages of this manuscript and to Dr. Rosie Bonté, who helped turn the manuscript into the book it needed to become. Dr. Eva Mortensen has done a brilliant job compiling the index. I am deeply grateful to them all. Without the help of all the people mentioned here, this book would not have been produced this smoothly.

Finally, my heartfelt thanks go to my family, my husband Stephan and our children, Andreas, Hannah and Bernhard, for not only mentally—but also physically—"letting me go" and allowing me several months of concentrated research time away from home without any of the demands of normal everyday life. Their understanding means more to me than can be expressed in words.

I dedicate this book to Mary Ebba Underdown and the people of Syria. May the coming years bring peace to the country.

Aarhus, Denmark, March 2021

Abbreviations

AE	*Année épigraphique* (Paris: Presses universitaires de France, 1888–).
ACO	Schwartz, Eduard (ed.). *Acta conciliorum oecumenicorum*, 4 vols. (Berlin: De Gruyter, 1914–1940).
CIL	*Corpus Inscriptionum Latinarum* (Berlin: Berlin-Brandenburgische Akademie der Wissenschaften, 1853–).
CIS	*Corpus Inscriptionum Semiticarum* (Paris: Reipublicæ Typographeo, 1881–1962).
Dura	Final Report V.1 = Welles, Charles Bradford, Robert Orwill Fink, and James Frank Gilliam. *The Parchments and Papyri*, vol. 5.1, *The Excavations at Dura-Europos Conducted by Yale University and the French Academy of Inscriptions and Letters. Final Report* (New Haven: Yale University Press, 1959).
Dura Prelim.	Report VII/VIII = Rostovtzeff, Michael Ivanovitch, Frank Edward Brown, and Charles Bradford Welles. *The Excavations at Dura-Europos Conducted by Yale University and the French Academy of Inscriptions and Letters: Preliminary Report of the Seventh and Eighth Seasons of Work, 1933–1934 and 1934–1935* (New Haven: Yale University Press, 1939).
IDR	*Inscripţiile Daciei Romane* = Inscriptiones Daciae Romanae (Bucharest: Bucureşti Editura Academiei Republicii Socialiste România, 1975–1988; Paris: De Boccard, 2001).
IG	*Inscriptiones Graecae* (Berlin: Berlin-Brandenburgische Akademie der Wissenschaften, 1887–).
IGLS	*Inscriptions grecques et latines de la Syrie* (Paris: Geuthner, 1929–).
IGR	Cagnat, René et al (eds.). *Inscriptiones graecae ad res romanas pertinentes*, 3 vols. (Paris: Leroux, 1901–1927).
IGUR	Moretti, Luigi. *Inscriptiones graecae urbis Romae*, 4 vols. in 5 parts (Rome: Istituto Italiano per la Storia Antica, 1968–1990).
ILS	Dessau, Hermann (ed.). *Inscriptiones Latinae Selectae*, 3 vols. (Berlin: Weidmann, 1892–1916).
I.Portes	Bernand, André. *Les Portes du désert. Recueil des inscriptions grecques d'Antinooupolis, Tentyris, Koptos, Apollonopolis Parva et Apollonopolis Magna* (Paris: Éditions du Centre national de la recherche scientifique, 1984).

OGIS   Dittenberger, Wilhelm. *Orientis Graeci Inscriptiones Selectae*, 2 vols. (Leipzig: Hirzel, 1903–1905).

PAT   Hillers, Delbert R., and Eleonora Cussini. *Palmyrene Aramaic Texts* (Baltimore: Johns Hopkins University Press, 1996).

RIB   Collingwood, Robin George, and Richard P. Wright. *Inscriptions on Stone*, vol. 1, *The Roman Inscriptions of Britain* (Oxford: Clarendon Press, 1965).

RMD   *Roman Military Diplomas* (London: Institute of Classical Studies, School of Advanced Study, University of London, 1978–2006).

SEG   *Supplementum Epigraphicum Graecum* (Leiden: Brill, 1923–).

1

The Archeology and History of Palmyra

Palmyra is a city famous for its situation, for the richness of its soil, and for its agreeable springs; its fields are surrounded on every side by a vast circuit of sand, and it is as it were isolated by nature from the world, having a destiny of its own between the two mighty empires of Rome and Parthia, and at the first moment of a quarrel between them always attracting the attention of both sides.[1]

—Pliny the Elder

Palmyra is a place wreathed in legend. Tales about the site have been passed down from Antiquity—many initially set down by authors who, like Pliny, had never visited Palmyra and thus cannot be considered wholly reliable[2]—and the city has continued to fascinate, providing a source of inspiration over the centuries for operas, books, poems, tapestries, and paintings. Yet despite its almost mythical status, Palmyra is also a real location, home to a vivid past, tangible archeological finds, and ongoing ideological importance.[3] It is the aim of this book to look past the legends that enshroud the city and to shed light on what we truly know about this iconic center.

Known in Antiquity—and still today in modern Arabic—as Tadmor, Palmyra is located in an oasis in the middle of the Syrian Desert, approximately equidistant between the banks of the River Euphrates and the shores of the Mediterranean Sea (Fig. 1). The city sits in a pass created from a range of hills that branches out from the Anti-Lebanon mountain range to the northeast.[4] This route leads to the Syrian city of Homs and continues to the Mediterranean coast. East of Palmyra lies the steppe desert, which ends only with the Euphrates River. There is also a natural route that leads in the direction of Damascus and passes the mouth of the Efqa Spring, while to the north of the oasis is a higher desert plateau, cut through by two valleys (or wadis—channels that are dry except in the rainy season).

Pearl of the Desert. Rubina Raja, Oxford University Press. © Oxford University Press 2022.
DOI: 10.1093/oso/9780190852221.003.0001

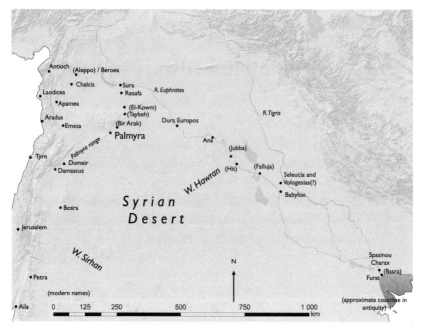

Figure 1 Map of Palmyra and the region (Courtesy of Eivind Heldaas Seland. Base map copyright ESRI 2014).

Before the events of the last troubled decade and the outbreak of a tragic civil war in Syria in 2011, Palmyra was the most visited archeological site in Syria. The city was named a UNESCO World Heritage Site in 1980, and it attracted thousands of visitors every year. Tourists keen to experience the monumental ruins often set off from Damascus, crossing the desert to experience the city rising to meet them from the desert ground, much as it must have greeted approaching visitors some 2,000 years ago. Despite the massive destruction that has taken place in Palmyra since the outbreak of the civil war, the ancient site still exists; but in 2013, as the Syrian conflict escalated, it was placed on the UNESCO list of World Heritage Sites in Danger.[5] The risk still facing Palmyra provides an urgent reminder that cultural heritage is too often used as a target in times of conflict, and that our common history can be all too readily destroyed.

Pliny the Elder's well-known quote about Palmyra, taken from his *Natural History*, plunges the reader *in medias res* with regard to the geography and history of the city. At the time that Pliny was writing, Palmyra was in its Roman imperial heyday, a time of bounty that saw the city flourish. This growth, however, came to an abrupt halt when the city was sacked, with dev-astating results, by the Roman emperor Aurelian in 272 CE and again in 273 CE. Although Pliny never visited Palmyra, he provides a concise description of the city's location as well as the wider political implications of this geo-graphical position in the first century CE, using information that was likely derived from the writings of other ancient authors.[6] Despite his brevity, Pliny's text offers a crucial insight into what was deemed important about Palmyra in the ancient world.

Tellingly, Pliny's description focuses not only on the city of Palmyra but also on its wider hinterland; these two elements of Palmyrene society and its survival are so closely entwined that it is virtually impossible to study either in isolation.[7] Palmyra demanded a managed hinterland in order to survive and sustain itself, and the essential and symbiotic relationship be-tween the city and its surroundings is testified to by documents produced throughout the Roman period, among them numerous inscriptions from the city and the famous Tax Tariff of 137 CE.[8] The latter item is a monumental structure of local limestone (height: 200 cm, or 79 inches; width: 640 cm, or 251 inches) on which was carved a bilingual inscription of the tax tariff; it provides important details on various aspects of trade and is discussed fur-ther in Chapter 2.[9] The stone bearing the tariff inscription was erected on the city's main street opposite the Sanctuary of Rahbaseireh, a location that was very prominent in the urban landscape. The purpose of the tariff was to re-solve conflicts between local traders and tax collectors,[10] and it features both the city's old regulations on Palmyrene trade and the new regulations that replaced them. These were inscribed in the local Palmyrene Aramaic dia-lect as well as in Greek, demonstrating clearly that these laws were intended not only for Palmyrene local society but also for visitors and trade contacts. However, the information carved on the Tax Tariff is concerned exclusively with trade that came through the city itself and therefore does not offer detail about any trade extending outside the city and its immediate hinterland.[11]

Pliny's mention of the fields surrounding Palmyra reminds us that de-spite its desert location, the city was in fact encircled by arable land (Fig. 2). This could have been achieved only through what must have been an inten-sive management of water resources, perennial or seasonal, throughout the year.[12] Palmyrenes had a reputation for being good tradesmen and soldiers, particularly archers, but they must also have been excellent water engineers. Pliny writes about the life-giving springs of Palmyra. The source of the fa-mous Efqa Spring was in the city itself (Fig. 3), while there were several other

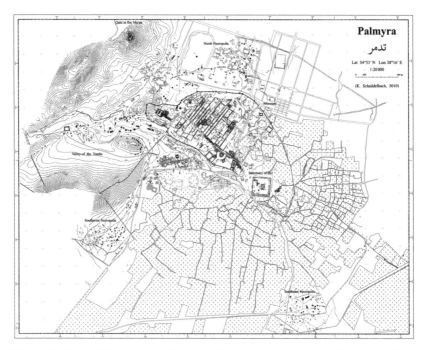

Figure 2 Map of Palmyra and the immediate surrounding area (Courtesy of Klaus Schnädelbach).

Figure 3 The old Efqa Spring, seen from the north (Rubina Raja and Palmyra Portrait Project, Ingholt Archive at Ny Carlsberg Glyptotek).

springs in the surrounding area.[13] These provided water for general usage both in the city and its hinterland, but drinking water was apparently derived from other sources, and the Palmyrenes, at least in the Roman period, relied on water being brought into the city by aqueducts.[14] Water is the most precious resource in the desert, and it is likely that the Palmyrenes spent much time and energy ensuring they had a stable supply, especially in the Roman period when the city's population exploded.

Despite these springs and fields, Palmyra, as Pliny noted, was nonetheless isolated, an oasis surrounded by desert. However, while Pliny describes "a vast circuit of sand," the desert around Palmyra is not the traditional dunes that might be seen in, for example, the Sahara but is instead a landscape of varied, and partially mountainous steppe. Modern Arabic contains two terms for desert: *sahra* describes sandy deserts, while *badiya* is used for the deserts that the Bedouin inhabit, and where it is possible to find pasture and water for animals.[15] The badiya desert receives rainfall every year in the winter and spring, between November and May, and it can even be quite lush at certain times of the year.[16] This type of desert allows for a variety of agricultural activities as well as for animal husbandry, and we know from the Tax Tariff that this was certainly the case around Palmyra.[17] Because the steppe around Palmyra is mountainous to a degree,[18] wadis are found in the hinterlands of the city. The two wadis found to the north of the city are known in modern times as Wadi as-Suraysir and Wadi al-ʿEid, and these intermittently fill with water for short periods after heavy rain falls, even creating dangerous flash floods on occasion. These two wadis meet approximately 1.3 km (0.8 miles) east of the Efqa Spring, where they rejoin the spring's waters before entering a depression to the southeast.

The land around the city is dotted with settlements and villages. These would have served to keep the city supplied with essentials but would have been wholly dependent on the city as a venue where the villagers could sell their produce.[19] Some Palmyrene art also stems from the settlements of the hinterlands, indicating that they were not just places in which people worked but were considered important enough in their own right to adorn.[20] Votives were also established in these locations, which would seem to indicate that the character of the settlements might have been more permanent than has often been assumed.

While it is now clear that Palmyrene territory covered a much broader area than was previously thought, it is still not entirely clear how and to what degree these lands were managed across the year, how land ownership was

administered or divided between the city and private owners, or how ownership developed over time.[21] New estimates of the extent of the city's territory
in the Roman period indicate that it covered an area extending some 75 km
(47 miles) to the northwest of the city up to Khirbat al-Bilas; 65 km (40 miles)
to the west-southwest, up toward the borders of the territories of Sura and
Resafa in the northeast, and toward the River Euphrates to the southeast.[22]
As such, and with the exception of potential outposts along the Euphrates,
the territory of Palmyra was wholly situated in the northern part of the region that is now termed Badiyat ash-Sham, or the Syrian Desert.[23] An understanding of this geographical context is crucial since it helps reveal the way
the ancient Palmyrenes exploited their land and used the region for overland
transportation connected to the caravan trade. We therefore have to envisage
a complex and sophisticated use of territory, which was based both on public
and private landownership, as well as on a population that was partially sed-
entary but also partially or semi-nomadic.[24]

Crucially, in his description of Palmyra's location, Pliny emphasizes that
while the city was remote, it was nonetheless in constant contact with regions
to both east and west throughout the Roman period. Moreover, he comments
that Palmyra had "a destiny of its own," caught as it was in a special position
between Rome and Parthia. This was in many ways true. Palmyra was a city
situated in what may be termed a no man's land, a field of political trajectories
on the borders of other empires' territory that could adjust quickly to changing geopolitical circumstances. This made Palmyra vulnerable to changes
in the dynamic political situation, but it also offered the advantage of negotiating with both sides and taking advantage of shifting power structures.[25]
Palmyrene society, thus had to be more nimble than many other places in the
ancient world, quick to adapt and to take advantage of change.

While Pliny does not specifically mention Palmyrene trade connections,
we know that the city made its fortune in the first three centuries CE through
developing and successfully maintaining trade networks as well as via its political and military connections.[26] However, although Palmyra formed a key
node on a global network, Palmyrene society remained locally based, with
strong local traditions—for example, in sculpture, which can be traced for
at least 300 years in the archeological record.[27] It is this seeming discrep-
ancy between the society's global orientation and its simultaneous focus on
local traditions that makes Palmyra so fascinating to study. This contradiction, during the first three centuries CE, forms the main focus of this book.
However, excursions will also be made to both earlier and later periods and

to the wider debate about the cultural heritage of the site in the wake of the Syrian civil war, since the city's medieval and modern developments all contribute to the remarkable history of this mesmerizing place.[28]

Ancient Tadmor—Palmyra before Palmyra

Pliny is the earliest writer to refer to the city using the Latinized name Palmyra; the ancient name for the site was Tadmor (*tdmr*), and this was probably a word with pre-Semitic roots. It is likely that the native place-name Tadmor, like its Greek and Latin variants, was derived from indigenous terms for the palm trees in the oasis that were so important to the settlement.[29] As a named locality, the site had existed for millennia before the region was brought under Roman rule.[30] Remains testify to activity in this area from as long ago as 50,000 BCE, during the Middle Paleolithic.[31] More substantial evidence for habitation in the oasis comes from the Neolithic period, dating as far back as the seventh millennium BCE.[32] Some of the earliest human activity in the area can be found east of the Efqa Spring, where the two wadis meet, and where a tell grew over several millennia to a height of approximately 7 m (23 ft). This was the site of the iconic Temple of Bel, the earliest known phase dedicated in 32 CE, before it was destroyed by ISIS in 2015. It is assumed that a central place of worship was located there in prehistoric times.[33]

The name Tadmor first appears in sources that date to the first half of the second millennium BCE, and several early documents mention people coming from Tadmor, among them a tablet from Cappadocia (in modern Turkey) and two other documents in Akkadian from Mari (in modern Syria).[34] These written sources go hand in hand with the archeological evidence from the site,[35] making it clear that there was some sort of known, named settlement at the Efqa Spring in the second millennium BCE. According to the Book of Chronicles in the Old Testament, a Tadmor in the steppe was fortified by King Solomon.[36] However, this is largely understood by historians to be a misinterpretation of the place Tamar ("Palm"), a city located in Judah, which is mentioned in the First Book of Kings as a site at which Solomon undertook building activities.[37] It is therefore very likely that the two Tadmors had nothing to do with each other. Nonetheless, the author of the Chronicles seems to have had Tadmor in the Syrian Desert in mind when writing; this point suggests that the site was known to people when the Book of Chronicles was being compiled in the fourth/third centuries BCE.[38]

We can know little about the extent or nature of this settlement in the second millennium BCE. However, documents written in Mari at this time do refer to Tadmoreans being attacked by nomads, which would seem to indicate that the Palmyrenes themselves were, in contrast, known as a largely settled people. It also suggests that people from Tadmor traveled abroad and, importantly, that they drew the attention of the king of Mari, potentially indicating that the settlement and its wider surroundings at this time fell under the domination of this city-state.[39] However, while these early sources shed a glimmer of light both on Tadmor's existence and its sufficient standing to merit reference, they leave no hint that the oasis settlement had at this time become an important node for regional trade.[40] It would seem, therefore, that Tadmor became central to the large-scale, organized caravan trade only in the early Roman period. Moreover, and like so many other locations in the Near East, the archeological sources reveal little about the period from the Late Bronze Age to the end of the Iron Age.[41]

As far as we know, Palmyra was not refounded under Seleucid rule, in contrast to many other cities in the region in the wake of Alexander the Great's conquest of the East, which began with his invasion of the Achaemenid Empire in 334 BCE.[42] This meant that while veterans from Alexander's army were settled in other sites in the region and received land there, this did not take place in Palmyra. This absence of an influx of Greek veterans might in fact have influenced Palmyra's development more strongly than has hitherto been acknowledged, as it meant that Palmyrene society would have stayed far more "local," and less exposed to outside influences than many other towns and cities in the region. The written evidence from the Hellenistic period (generally dated 323 BCE–31 BCE) that alludes to Tadmor/Palmyra is often judged as unreliable and imprecise by scholars in their accounts of what sort of place Palmyra was.[43] There is, however, both archeological and written evidence suggesting that the city existed in some form during the Hellenistic period and that it might have been of some significance.[44] Not much is known about the extent of the urban site before the early Roman period, partly because archeological work at the site has largely concentrated on the Roman period.[45] What little evidence is available to us comes either from focused attempts at discovering the Hellenistic period or from discoveries made during excavations that were in fact aimed at finding other things.[46] As such, it is difficult to draw any conclusions about the general development of the city, the size of its society, or the scale of its monumentalization in the Hellenistic period.[47]

In this respect, Palmyra differs little from other sites across the Near East where the Hellenistic period is difficult to identify, although we know from some archeological evidence, written sources, and historical events that the region was already intensely urbanized at this time.[48] Indeed, the relative lack of Hellenistic material from Near Eastern sites has been a key focus of scholarly debate, leading to two schools of thought: the first suggests that the Near East suffered from a type of cultural amnesia, with a profound break between the Greek heritage and influences from the East, while the second emphasizes that it is possible to trace a strong cultural continuity in the region.[49] In recent years, before the outbreak of the conflict in Syria, research had revealed further Hellenistic remains in Palmyra appearing to show some support for the latter argument, undermining the theory that adheres to cultural amnesia.[50] Despite extensive research, including geo-physics, however, this material remains scarce; it largely comprises evidence for a water supply, mudbrick walls for houses, and an early defensive wall made of mudbrick, together with small finds such as pottery, glass, and other objects.[51] Although our knowledge about Hellenistic Palmyra thus remains limited, these finds might indicate that the region is richer in Hellenistic finds than has hitherto been thought, and it also lends support to the idea of cultural continuity.[52]

Palmyra Under Roman rule

By the time Rome had conquered the East during the campaigns of Pompey the Great in the mid-60s BCE, Palmyra must have been a city proper (Fig. 4).[53] Urban development in Palmyra really became established in the late first century BCE, and due to reorganizations of the urban spaces during the early Roman period, we may assume that much archeology from earlier periods has been lost.[54] It is possible, however, that Hellenistic Palmyra was not located in the same site as the Roman city.[55] Archeological evidence recovered in the area of the Temple of Bel suggests that the site saw activity from the early second century BCE and into the early Roman period.[56] Furthermore, brief references in written texts provide a small amount of information about Palmyrenes in the Seleucid period, although the reliability of these sources remains disputed.[57] Much in common with other settlements of the Near East, it is difficult to grasp the extent to which Palmyra was developed in this period, but the settlement undoubtedly existed.

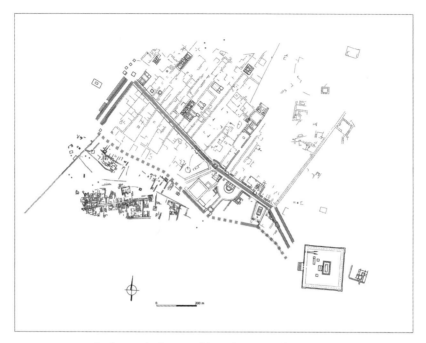

Figure 4 Map of Palmyra (After Gawlikowski 2019, pl. 2, courtesy of Michał Gawlikowski).

Any study of Roman Palmyra has to acknowledge the broader political and geographical context of both the city and its broader regional location. Despite its setting in the Syrian Desert, Palmyra was no disconnected island but was rather a node, an important player in the interregional infrastructure that connected East and West, and it had held this role long before the Romans truly turned their attentions eastward.

The creation of the Roman province of Syria, in 64 BCE was preceded by a number of key events with which Roman interests in the region were deeply entangled.[58] Mark Antony first turned his sights on Palmyra in 41 BCE, and the Greek historian Appian of Alexandria (c. 95–c. 165 CE), although writing almost two centuries later, reported that the city's inhabitants fled east, toward Parthia.[59] During the period of the Roman civil wars, which to a large extent played out in places far from Rome, the Near East held huge strategic importance.[60] This continued until the very last days of the Roman Republic: after the Battle of Actium, in 31 BCE, King Herod the Great set out by ship to catch up with Octavian (later known as Augustus), who had resoundingly defeated Mark Antony and Cleopatra.[61] Despite having previously offered strong backing to Mark Antony and Cleopatra, Herod met Octavian in Rhodes, where he pledged his support to the new political power in Rome, and in doing so, offered a wholesale reversal of his previous policy.[62] Herod was obviously convincing enough in his professions of loyalty to Octavian that he was allowed to rule the province of Judaea. There, Herod met with great success—at least from a Roman perspective—and his influence is perhaps a key reason that Roman rule become so well-established in the region.[63] The agreement made between Herod and Augustus came to impact the world on a global scale over the next 300 years.[64]

Under Augustus, inscriptions from Palmyra inform us about citizens calling themselves Palmyrene and Tadmorean, which suggests that the organization of the city and its civic identity must have been firmly established by this time.[65] However, it was only after the general consul Germanicus's expedition to Syria in 17–19 CE that Palmyra was entirely integrated into the Roman administrative framework. This development is testified to in both the city's public inscriptions and in its urban development more generally.[66] In keeping with wider patterns in the region, it was at this time that the city also began to develop monuments; the Sanctuary of Bel received attention, for example, and the first tower tombs were constructed.[67] Like other regional centers, such as cities in the Decapolis, Tetrapolis, and on the Levantine coast, Palmyra also stands as a prime example of the cities in the region that benefited directly from the Pax Romana—the long period of peace that began under Augustus. As a result of this new stability, the city experienced an economic upturn, allowing its inhabitants to invest in urban embellishment.

It is in this period that Palmyra truly emerges from the archeological and written sources and becomes a tangible location that we can envisage and explore. Urban development at the site began in the late first century BCE and continued throughout the first three centuries CE. During these years, the city grew and flourished, and became adorned with public and private monuments, sanctuaries, and the numerous monumental grave towers that still overlook the city today (Fig. 5).[68] Much of the archeological evidence from the city stems from the first three centuries CE and includes the thousands of funerary portraits for which Palmyra is famous.[69]

Figure 5 Aerial view of Palmyra from the 1920s (Rubina Raja and Palmyra Portrait Project, courtesy of Mary Ebba Underdown).

Palmyrenes at Home and Abroad

The region of Greater Syria came under Roman domination with the invasion of Pompey the Great in the 60s BCE, and it stayed there for the centuries that followed, until the Romans were defeated by the Sassanians in the late third century CE.[70] During this period, Palmyra developed, grew, and was very much shaped as a product of the Roman Empire and the stability brought by the Pax Romana.[71] Nonetheless, Palmyra and its hinterlands were also in constant interaction with other areas, and in particular those regions to the east such as the Parthian and Sassanian empires.[72] The presence of these empires intermittently underpinned Palmyrene concerns about their links to Rome and ultimately played a role in the rebellion headed by Zenobia in the late third century CE—an event that is discussed in more detail in later chapters—and which, for a short time, made Palmyra a major player in the politics of the East.

In addition to written sources that refer to Palmyra, the city is home to a rich heritage of both archeology and epigraphy (the writing of inscriptions), which testifies to the city's history and development in the Roman period as well as, to a degree, in later periods. At its largest extent, the city covered an area of approximately 120 hectares (0.5 square miles), but only a limited part of this has been investigated archeologically.[73] The population seems to have been significant, at least in the Roman period.[74] Palmyrene society was organized into a number of tribes or groups who held power in the city.[75] A total of fourteen tribal names are known from our written sources,[76] of which four main tribes comprised the utmost elite. It is, however, possible that we mainly come across these four tribes in the ancient sources because they were established during the Roman period as an artificial construction. It appears that under Roman influence, the civic body of the city was organized differently than it had been previously, and it is therefore difficult to understand the complexities of Palmyrene social organization before the Romans.[77] However, society was certainly structured in groups. From the Roman period onward, it is possible to identify in inscriptions the implementation of terminology used elsewhere in the Roman East for civic structures within Palmyra. Local Palmyrene society was dominated by the male upper class. While women are also mentioned in inscriptions as being benefactors and owning property,[78] Palmyra was very much a patriarchal society, and we have no evidence that women held any official positions in civic or religious life.[79]

We know little about the early development of Palmyra, and it remains unclear when exactly the city came into existence architecturally.[80] However, the material evidence indicates that the middle of the first century BCE was a period of active building.[81] The main street of Palmyra ran from the area in front of the monumental Sanctuary of Bel and went through the center of the city. This street, as might be expected in this period, was lined with the most important building complexes of the city: the theater, other sanctuaries, and the agora as well as numerous public, civic, and honorific monuments.[82] In some other important aspects, however, the cityscape of Palmyra was quite unique. The columns that flanked the main street, for example, were mounted with consoles on which statues of important Palmyrenes were displayed. Almost none of these statues survive, but the inscriptions—which are often bilingual, composed in both Palmyrene Aramaic and Greek—tell us whom these now-lost statues honored and why.[83] While honorific statues were a well-known phenomenon in the Graeco-Roman world, it is quite unique to Palmyra that statues were positioned on these consoles half way up the columns.[84] Numerous other statues were displayed on bases standing on street level, and together these would have made Palmyrene public space a truly dense sculptural environment. This would have reminded all spectators of the importance of the elite, who carried out beneficial works for the city in the tradition of Greek *euergetism* (doing good for society).[85] Almost all of these monuments and sculptural art were made of local limestone, which came from quarries around the city.[86] Any marble found in the city would have been imported, either as raw stone blocks or as finished or semi-finished products; the Near East had no marble quarries, and the stone would have come from other places, such as quarries in Asia Minor, Greece, or Italy.[87]

The sanctuaries of Palmyra have yielded significant insights into the importance of religion to the life of the city. Palmyrenes worshipped a string of deities, male as well as female. Palmyra's main sanctuary was that of Bel, which had an enclosure (*temenos*) measuring approximately 205 m by 205 m (673 ft by 673 ft) with a temple located in the center. The temple was unusual for a Roman temple in that its main entrance was along one of the long sides of the building.[88] Other known sanctuaries from Palmyra include those of Baalshamin, Allat, and Nabu, while several others are mentioned in the written records but have not yet been archeologically verified.[89] Much has been written about the religious life of Palmyra, but despite the fact that many deity names and physical sanctuaries are known, actual religious beliefs and practices remain something of an enigma to us.[90] Our main sources of information about the structure of religious life are inscriptions, representations of Palmyrene deities and priests, and the so-called banqueting tesserae, tiny clay tokens with impressions on them, as well as the sanctuaries themselves.[91] As in so many other places in the Near East, it is likely that religious life would have involved communal ritual dining; this is testified to by both the banqueting tesserae and by the banqueting halls found in some of the sanctuaries.[92] At these feasts, the gods would have been honored, and food, paid for by the banquet's sponsors, would have been served. Although the banquets were religious events, they were equally important as social events at which people would mingle, and the donor would be celebrated as a good citizen and a devout follower of the gods.

Palmyra is known for its monumental cityscape, but it is equally celebrated for its rich cemeteries (*necropoleis*). More than 500 tombs have been found in Palmyra.[93] The famous tower tombs hover around the city, casting long shadows in the sand. These tombs, which were the first monumental buildings to house burials in Palmyra, were introduced in the first century CE.[94] Before this period, single-shaft graves were the common way to bury the deceased. Later, underground tombs (*hypogea*) were introduced, and so were the temple or house tombs, although this latter type of burial monument was for the utmost elite families in the city.[95]

Crucially, it was not only in public areas that Palmyrenes crammed their spaces with representations of individuals. The funerary sphere was also densely inhabited with limestone representations of the men, women, and children of the Palmyrene upper class.[96] It is a little-known but extraordinary fact about Palmyra that the city hosts the highest quantity of funerary portraiture from the ancient world outside of Rome, with more than 4,000 extant examples (Fig. 6).[97] These works—funerary stelae depicting full-figure representations, more-than-bust-portrait reliefs (so-called *loculus* reliefs), banqueting reliefs, and sarcophagi—were produced over a fairly restricted period of time, namely, the first to the late third century CE. It seems that the tradition of portraiture was firmly established in Palmyra by the late first century BCE—a relatively early date compared to sculptural evidence from the

Figure 6 Loculus relief depicting a priest, 200–220 CE. Ny Carlsberg Glyptotek, Copenhagen, IN 1033 (Photo: Ny Carlsberg Glyptotek, Copenhagen/Anders Sune Berg).

wider region.[98] This Palmyrene portrait habit was certainly influenced by the knowledge of Graeco-Roman portraiture in the region and beyond, but we know little about the dissemination of such trends to Palmyra.[99] Nonetheless, early Roman Palmyra could well have been a nodal point for diffusing the renewal of the portrait tradition in the East.[100] While Palmyrene sculpture may not present a peak in the development of sculpture in the Roman Empire in general, the sheer number of works created within the relatively short time frame of just 300 years gives us unique possibilities for understanding how Palmyrene art developed in this period, a situation that remains absolutely unique for the ancient world. The funerary sculpture has survived to a much larger extent than sculpture from the domestic and public spheres, largely because these pieces were located inside the graves, which protected them from weathering, as well as making them difficult to remove.

Palmyrenes were truly integrated into the Roman imperial system, but at the same time, they adhered closely to their own strong, local traditions. This is underlined not least through their local language, their own dialect of the Semitic language Aramaic, which is today termed Palmyrene Aramaic.[101] Palmyra has been called the only truly bilingual city in the Roman Near East.[102] It is remarkable how the epigraphic evidence from Palmyra allows us to get closer to the choices made by Palmyrene society in various situations. The inscriptions, which stem from various spheres (civic, private, funerary, and religious), provide fascinating insights into the choices that Palmyrenes made according to where they (most often the elite) were displaying themselves. The public sphere hosts a wealth of bilingual inscriptions that were composed in both the local Palmyrene Aramaic dialect and in Greek, and in some cases, the inscriptions are even trilingual, with the addition of Latin. This use of additional languages in public stands in stark contrast to the inscriptions from a funerary context; there are well over 1,000 inscriptions from this sphere, written almost exclusively in Palmyrene Aramaic.[103] Meanwhile, inscriptions relating to people's private lives—which are comparatively few in number—demonstrate knowledge and use of both local and foreign languages. The way languages were used in Palmyra leaves the clear impression that its people knew exactly how and when they wanted to employ different languages as well as the different cultural implications they invoked through their choices.

The usage of different languages within Palmyra also points more widely to the city's connections with its surroundings. Palmyra has been called the last stop on the Silk Road, and the city was certainly a node for trade in the Roman period, although it was by no means the only one.[104] Indeed, the notion that there was a single entity known as "the Silk Road" should be disregarded; the Palmyrenes were not in charge of passing on goods from A to Z, but rather formed just a part of a far more complex network of trade that extended to the Far East. The trade that passed through the city of Palmyra was under the control of, and coordinated by, the local elite, the Palmyrene male-dominated upper class.[105] Camel caravans ended in Palmyra, and this was where the goods that they carried were reloaded to other means of transportation, for example, donkeys, which could better tackle the mountainous regions to the west.[106]

Palmyra's male elite was not only involved in the overland trade: we know that Palmyrenes were also involved in seafaring and that elite merchants had networks that expanded far beyond the desert region. It was this international trade that made Palmyra so wealthy in the Roman period.[107] As discussed in more detail in Chapter 4, Palmyrenes are mentioned in inscriptions in Egypt, Rome, North Africa, the Indian Ocean region (the modern Gulf area), and as far away as Britain.[108] They acted as traders, Roman officials, and soldiers; Palmyrene archers, in particular, were renowned for their skills and were employed in the Roman army. They were stationed, among other places, in the border town of Dura-Europos on the Euphrates.[109] It has also been suggested that Palmyrene archers feature on one of the reliefs on Trajan's column in Rome, in testament to the fact that they served the emperor during his Dacian Wars.[110]

Palmyra was a rich and wealthy city in the first three centuries CE. Based on the research undertaken since the early nineteenth century, we are now in a position to see beyond the myths that shroud the city and to identify more clearly the complexities and realities of Palmyrene society. As discussed in more detail below, it was a city with strong local traditions, but it was also a place that was home to a people capable of adapting to an often-shifting political and military context. It was a city on the boundary between world empires, which is profoundly communicated in the architecture and art of the city;[111] but it was far more than a remote oasis city that owed its existence to the Efqa Spring. Indeed, Palmyra was home to a society that was highly aware of its fragile physical situation, located in the hard environment of the steppe desert and sandwiched between strong imperial powers.[112]

The Fall of Roman Palmyra

A pivotal turning point in Palmyra's history was the devastation of the site in 272–273 CE by Roman troops under the direction of the emperor Aurelian. The city never recovered from the blow. Before Aurelian's brutal sack of the city, Palmyra had, by virtue of its growing wealth, risen to become an important player on the global scene, balanced between the struggling empires of Rome and ancient Persia. The Palmyrenes had learned to negotiate their place in a part of the world that was in constant flux; power structures often shifted depending on the rulers in charge as well as on economic, climatic, and social factors. This all changed with Zenobia.

Today, Zenobia is the most famous inhabitant of Palmyra, even though she represents only a small intermezzo in the city's rich, long, and complex history. Even before the rediscovery of Palmyra, Europeans were fascinated by Zenobia and her rebellion against the Romans, despite the fact that it ultimately ended in disaster. She is the lens through which Europeans long perceived the Orient as a region of wonders, adventures, and romance, coloring historiographical traditions about the city.[113] Many of these accounts, however, bear little relation to the actual historical events, for which evidence is extremely scarce. What we do know of Zenobia is that she appears to have seized power of a larger region in the Near East after she began ruling Palmyra on behalf of her under-age son, Vallabathus.[114] Although she ruled for only a short time, between 267 and 272 CE, she managed to capture Egypt and expand Palmyrene territory into large parts of ancient Anatolia (modern Turkey). And we know that her strategy was to cost her the Palmyrene Empire.

Until Zenobia's defeat in 272 CE, it was not clear which course history would take. Zenobia's expansion of Palmyrene territory essentially cut the Romans off from the routes to the East, and their trade, as well as military interests, was threatened. A successful expansion of Palmyrene territory would have changed the geopolitics of the time. However, with the sack of the city, Palmyrene society was devastated. Palmyra was plundered, its monuments destroyed, and public and private buildings and spaces stripped of their wealth. The city itself contracted to enclose less than half of the area that it had covered in its heyday, while Palmyrene society was torn apart and the inhabitants murdered or scattered into the city's hinterlands, where they most likely resumed a pastoral and nomadic way of living.[115] The trade that had previously made Palmyra so rich and powerful was diverted along other routes.[116] Although Palmyra survived on a much smaller scale, it never truly recovered.[117] Therefore, the first three centuries CE represent the period that gives us the most extensive material evidence from the site.

We do not know what happened to Zenobia after Aurelian's sack of Palmyra. It is possible that she died in Palmyra, or perhaps she was taken to Rome, where she was displayed as the emperor's booty and kept prisoner until her death, as is claimed in the fourth-century CE *Historia Augusta*.[118] This work is one of the main Western sources for our knowledge about Zenobia, but it is also deeply unreliable. It gives a wonderful, although in all probability wholly fictional description of her, which is almost certainly inspired by male writers' expectation of what an eastern female leader should look like at this point in time:

> Her face was dark and of a swarthy hue, her eyes were black and powerful beyond the usual wont, her spirit divinely great, and her beauty incredible. So white were her teeth that many thought that she had pearls in place of teeth. Her voice was clear and like that of a man.[119]

While this description paints a vivid picture of Zenobia, through which we can almost imagine her white teeth glowing and hear her clear and strong voice ringing out in passioned defense of her actions, the reality is that we have little information about her appearance.[120] There are no visual representations of Zenobia stemming from Palmyra, and indeed our only contemporary renderings of her come from coins that were struck in Alexandria while Egypt was under Palmyrene rule, a point discussed in more detail in Chapter 4. Nonetheless, it is most typically the description from the *Historia Augusta* that we see reflected in later imaginings of Zenobia, particularly in European literature, music, and paintings produced in the seventeenth, eighteenth, and nineteenth centuries (Plate 1).[121]

Today, Zenobia and her failed bid for control in the Near East is so well known that for many, her name is virtually synonymous with the word Palmyra. Any study of the city, however, reveals that there is far, far more to Palmyra than Zenobia. There is a wealth of archeological and epigraphical material not only from the first three centuries CE but also from Late Antiquity and the Islamic periods. It is true that this might not capture the imagination in quite the same way as romanticized legends about the city's tragic queen. However, the material record reveals to us a site that housed an immense amount of cultural knowledge and diversity in a location that, while seemingly desolate and isolated, continued to represent an important hub in the middle of the Syrian Desert, halfway between the River Euphrates and the Mediterranean Sea.[122] Palmyra, as seen from the city's own perspective, was a place "in between" as well as in the center—a place that was deeply rooted in local traditions and yet in constant interaction with other regions, cultures, and people over millennia.[123]

Palmyra and Its Rediscovery

After Palmyra was sacked in 273 CE, the city was reduced to a Roman frontier town and housed a garrison. With the coming of Christianity to the region, it also became the seat of a bishop, and it remained an episcopal see until the end of Late Antiquity and the Arab invasion.[124] During the Christian and early Islamic period, churches, and later a mosque were constructed in the city.

In the post-classical period, Benjamin of Tudela (1130–1173) is the earliest known European to have claimed to visit Palmyra.[125] He was a Spanish Jew and a rabbi who visited a wide range of cities across Europe, Asia, and Africa in the twelfth century. He wrote an account of his travels, *The Travels of Benjamin*, in Hebrew, which was later translated into several other languages. Benjamin was particularly interested in Jewish societies. His travel account tells us little about the archeology of the regions through which he passed, but it nonetheless provides an important historical description of the Near East. Thereafter, no European is recorded as visiting Palmyra until the seventeenth century, at which time the Italian missionary, Pietro della Valle (1586–1652) traveled in the vicinity of Palmyra in both 1616, and 1625, although he did not set foot in the city. He was followed by the Frenchman Jean-Baptiste Tavernier (1605–1689), who likewise saw the ruins from a distance in 1630.

In 1678, an attempt was made by a group of British merchants to visit Palmyra, but they were held up in the desert by Bedouins; they only achieved their goal some years later, in 1691, when they made a second attempt and spent four days at the site. In 1751, James Dawkins (1722–1757) and Robert Wood (1717–1771) visited Palmyra and became the first to publish an extensive description of the site accompanied by drawings and etchings.[126] This publication became famous throughout Europe, and their visit was immortalized in a well-known painting from 1758, which depicts the two men at the moment of their discovery of Palmyra (Plate 14). The image has become iconic, but it also offers a timely reminder of the profoundly Orientalized view of the East that was so prevalent among Europeans at the time. The men are dressed in white togas and European style riding boots, while surrounded by their local entourage dressed according to local styles and Ottoman fashion. After Dawkins and Wood, a string of Europeans visited the site, and Palmyra quickly became a must-visit destination, added to the itinerary of all serious travelers, adventurers, and early tourists visiting the Near East. Palmyra began to gain a legendary status due to its monumental ruins set in front of the backdrop of the impressive oasis (Plate 2), and both the Sanctuary of Bel—considered in the eighteenth century to be a Sanctuary of the Sun—and Palmyra's massive grave towers featured prominently in early drawings of the city. They reminded every visitor and reader of Palmyra's long history as well as its lost wealth, which was displayed through these intriguing architectural complexes.[127]

Even before Palmyra became a popular destination to visit, the city gained legendary status in the European arts, becoming a particularly fashionable subject of literature and music during the Renaissance. By the seventeenth century, long before the site's ruins were known to Europeans, the city and its queen, Zenobia, were nonetheless icons of the Orient. As noted earlier, much of the reason for this interest, and for the images projected onto Palmyra and its queen, must lie with colorful but unreliable sources such as the *Historia Augusta*, which effectively built up a mirage in the minds of educated Europeans. Tellingly, in the past decade, and since civil war has broken out in Syria, the deeds of Queen Zenobia have once again become prominent, connected not just to a renewed interest in scholarship in the region but also to the political symbolism of Syria's president Bashar al-Assad. A statue of Zenobia was recently erected in Damascus as a sign of the power of the state. However, the events that led up to Zenobia's rise to power still remain relatively unexplored as part of the wider narrative of Palmyrene history.

In the late nineteenth century, visits by Western travelers to Palmyra became more common, and as the number of visitors to the site grew, the art of Palmyra also began to attract attention. It was in the 1880s that the earliest collections of Palmyrene art in Europe came into being, established at the Museé de Louvre in Paris and the Ny Carlsberg Glyptotek in Copenhagen.[128] In particular, the rich funerary art from Palmyra's numerous monumental graves was exported to Europe and later to America. Today, items from ancient Palmyra can be found in many private and museum collections.[129] It

was not until the early twentieth century, however, that organized archeological research was undertaken, beginning with a German team who
explored parts of the site.[130] From the period of the French Mandate (1923
to 1943) until the present, an immense amount of archeological research
has taken place in Palmyra. Much of the early work was done by the French,
but since then, researchers from the United States, Austria, Britain, Japan,
Germany, Norway, Italy, Poland, and other countries—often in collabo-
ration with Syrian colleagues and authorities—have conducted fieldwork
in Palmyra. Many of these research results are available in either their preliminary or final publication form. The bibliography on Palmyra is rapidly
increasing, and much information is available about the site, although no
complete overview of the literature on Palmyra is currently available.[131]

Palmyra in a Modern Age

Ancient Palmyra was located in a region through which many people passed
but few visitors stopped for long, and where society was characterized by a
strong focus on long-lasting local traditions, many of which can be traced
in the archeological and written sources. However, the Palmyrenes were
also dependent on building and maintaining strong connections with the
world around them. They paid particular attention to their trade relations,
sought to control coordination of trade in the region, and were very aware
of events that took place in the world around them. It is to a certain extent
these discrepancies—a society that was extremely local and traditional and
yet keenly focused on the outside world—that make the city and its people so
fascinating to study. The allure of ancient Palmyra, the pull that it exerts over
people, remains even today, in a modern age of globalization. The survival
strategies employed by an oasis city and its hinterlands over two millennia
ago may seem strange or irrelevant to twenty-first-century readers. But when
we consider how quickly a globalized world can encounter severe problems,
as shown in the 2020 pandemic, it brings to the forefront both the vulner-
ability of globalization and the similarity of threats that have faced both
modern and ancient societies. Diseases, shifting power structures, failing
infrastructures, and climate change would have had just as significant an
impact on Roman Palmyra as they do on communities today, and the comparison makes us ask even more pressingly: how did ancient societies cope
with diverse and sudden change? How did a society such as Palmyra tackle

plagues, wars, economic recessions, and fluctuating access to water over three centuries? While I do not pretend that this book will offer solutions to global issues, it is certainly my intention to bring forward the importance of studying the past as a way to better situate ourselves in the present and to understand the millennia-long globally connected world of which we are all a part.

Over the years, several books have been published in numerous languages that explore Palmyra, dealing with evidence from the city, covering specific aspects of society, detailing the lives of individuals, or focusing on the importance of the city within the Roman world. So why another book on this famous oasis city situated at the Efqa Spring in the middle of the Syrian steppe desert, and why now? In 2011, conflict broke out in Syria, and in 2015, the Islamist group ISIS seized the city and destroyed a number of ancient monuments, drawing massive international attention to the site. The unrest in Syria has drawn Palmyra, as well as a string of other cultural heritage sites, into a wider global debate about how to protect cultural heritage in zones of armed conflict. It has also fueled fierce debate about how to stem the trade in cultural heritage objects from illegal excavations, as artifacts continue to make their way onto the art market despite international regulations. As civil strife continues unabated in Syria, it has become ever more pressing to communicate Palmyra's narrative as a unique oasis city to students of archeology and history as well as a concerned general public.

In the last ten years, Palmyra has been variously used as a symbol of resistance by Syrian rebels, as a sign of power and a site of violence to demonstrate the authority exercised by ISIS in a destabilized region, and as a mark of the supremacy of the Syrian state, with different agents all appropriating and exploiting the fame of this renowned site to publicize their own views and beliefs. Most recently, both UNESCO (United Nations Educational, Scientific, and Cultural Organization) and Russia have taken an interest in Palmyra and in monopolizing a potential rebuilding of the site after the destructions and looting. We are thus standing at yet another threshold in Palmyra's long history, in which the past—as happens so often—is reinvented and reappropriated by several parties for their own purposes. This is one reason for raising awareness of what Palmyra can teach us about the need to protect cultural heritage. Despite international borders, cultural heritage belongs to the world and should be cared for by us all; disseminating knowledge is one way to heighten awareness and encourage us to think of how to preserve such priceless sites.

The tragic and ongoing conflict in Syria, combined with the exciting new research occurring within the Palmyra Portrait Project, means that a timely new account of the city is merited. It is the aim of this book to explore aspects of Palmyrene society that are different from those usually offered in historical accounts of the site—to see the society through funerary sculpture.

I am convinced that basic research is one important way in which we may bring more qualified knowledge to a broader audience. Through documentation and evidence, we heighten opportunities to learn about the future through the past, underlining the importance of the humanities in times of crises. Since 2012, the Palmyra Portrait Project, headed by the author, has collected as comprehensive a corpus as possible of Palmyrene funerary sculpture. At present, the corpus holds more than 3,800 limestone portraits produced locally in Palmyra between the late first century BCE and the sacking of Palmyra in 272/273 CE.[132] These portraits shed new light on Palmyra's complex history and reveal to us a city of the Near East that was at once a provincial Roman period center with strong ties to Parthia and yet also home to a material culture that was often entirely non-provincial, indicative of a strong and continuous local identity. While the city was in some ways located at the outer edge of the Roman Empire, the body of portraits examined shows clearly that Palmyra and its inhabitants did not consider themselves to be peripheral to anything. Rather, the city's population displayed in numerous ways that they held themselves to be quite central to the world they inhabited. As Pliny suggested, the city followed "a destiny of its own," and this trend can now be traced, via the portraits, throughout the Roman period.

Palmyra in the Syrian Desert remains a fascinating site. It can help us understand the ways in which developments impacted the site over thousands of years and how the local society interacted with the surrounding world. At the same time, the devastating war currently going on in Syria reminds us that elements of cultural heritage are often targets in conflicts and that their destruction is exploited to destroy people's hope for a better future.

2

Urban Island or Node in a Network?

The World of the Living

Although Palmyra was an oasis city situated in the middle of the Syrian Desert, it was not, and has never been, an isolated place.[1] Oases have always served as connecting points. What can be said to be different about Roman Palmyra in comparison with other cities of the period, however, is that Palmyra appears to have risen to prominence as a focal point relatively quickly, both in the region and more widely. This rapid rise in fortunes was due not only to the city's location and its control over vital resources such as water, but also because of the involvement of the Palmyrene elites in land and marine trading networks. Palmyra's male elite were actively involved in the organization of the trade and were thus able to shape the ways it was conducted, effectively centering Palmyra as the pivotal point around which trade took place, both locally and farther afield, especially to the East.[2] This chapter explores Palmyra as a living city, a place where individuals lived and worked, in order to examine both the city's individual nature and its setting in the wider ancient world.

Social Structure

The discussions that surround the development of Palmyrene society from the late first century BCE until the city's fall in 272 CE, and which are connected in particular to questions about the population's ethnic heritage (were they Arab, for example?) and background (was this originally a nomadic or semi-nomadic population that had gradually become sedentarized?) are many and complex.[3] Moreover, on the basis of the available evidence, these are questions for which we cannot reach any clear answers. Smith was most likely right when he stated that "in most of the Roman Near East, those whom we encounter in the desert may be best described as both seminomadic, in that they move between pastoral landscapes but generally within

Pearl of the Desert. Rubina Raja, Oxford University Press. © Oxford University Press 2022.
DOI: 10.1093/oso/9780190852221.003.0002

prescribed territorial limits, and pastoralists or agro-pastoralists, since they also tend to engage in some agricultural production, however limited."[4] In recent years, research into the Palmyrene hinterland, largely undertaken by a Norwegian survey project, has demonstrated that land use was probably far more complex than has previously been thought. There is clear evidence that the landscape was dotted with complexes of varying sizes, used either perennially or on a seasonal basis for both pastoral and agricultural purposes, and supported by an extensive water-management system in many places within the hinterland.[5] Such findings indicate that at least certain elements of Palmyrene society were mobile and would have moved between areas that could not be reached on a daily basis from the city center, and of course, some of the population must also have been permanently based in the hinterland. However, estimates of the population size of Palmyra remain uncertain; in 1999, for example, Savino suggested that between 40,000 and 60,000 people lived in the city of Palmyra in the second century CE, with a further 250,000 based in the hinterland.[6]

Palmyrenes were deeply involved with the organization of the caravan trade, and this was a significant source of wealth for many.[7] Not only did the wealth deriving from the caravan trade spur the monumentalization of Palmyra, a trend that is discussed in more detail below, but it also led to the mobilization of armed forces by Palmyrenes to protect the caravans—units that later went on to serve in the Roman army in various places of the empire, such as at Dura-Europos.[8] The monumental Palmyrene Tax Tariff of 137 CE, mentioned in Chapter 1, provides a wealth of information about the organization of trade in Palmyra, both from 68–69 CE when the tariff edict of Mucianus was applied, and after.[9] A decree from the Palmyrene council from the 130s CE served as a basis for the Tariff of 137 CE, which describes a typical eastern Greek city in which the council makes the decisions (without the popular assembly).[10] Both the earlier tariff and that of 137 CE also give insights into the changing status of Palmyra within the Roman Empire.

The Palmyrene Tax Tariff, today in the Hermitage Museum in St. Petersburg, is one of the most famous pieces of evidence from the city, and it is the best-known source on the socioeconomic situation in both Palmyra and the wider region in the first and second centuries CE (Fig. 7). However, it focuses only on trade coming through Palmyra as well as in and around the city—not on long-distance trade as such. The purpose of the tariff was to regulate trade in Palmyra and its inscription on the monument provides

Figure 7 Palmyrene Tax Tariff, 137 CE. State Hermitage Museum,
St. Petersburg, ДВ-4187 (Courtesy of Vibeke N. Nyborg).

us with rich detail about key elements of day-to-day trading activity, such as
the fees for loading and transferring goods between caravans, or the prices
for a number of goods, both imports and local produce. Moreover, the tariff
not only sheds light on the development of local regulations but also offers
important insights into Palmyra's status within the Roman province of
Syria, It gives information about the laws and property regulations that impacted Palmyra's various population groups, as well as about the city's civic
structure.[11] While the Tax Tariff shows a bilingual document composed in
Palmyrene Aramaic and Greek, the city's two main languages, Greek seems
to have been the prevailing language within the document—and indeed in
Palmyrene commerce and governance more generally.[12]

The sources available to us largely tell us about the upper layers of society,
and more specifically, about the male segment of society. Despite the rich
evidence from the city, we can therefore only get glimpses of the people who
dwelt in Palmyra through the so-called cessions texts (legal texts), through
tracing workshop traditions in the locally produced portraits of the city, or
through other more or less disconnected finds.[13] What is clear, however, is
that the family unit was at the very heart of Palmyrene society and that local
traditions surrounding family affiliations persisted throughout the Roman

period.[14] Palmyrene society was based on a tribal structure in the broadest sense of the word, which can perhaps best be described as constellations of extended families[15]—discussed in further detail below—and society was based on kinship relations that operated in both close and extended forms. Branches of the same family were connected through the family name and could be traced genealogically across several generations. These familial connections can be identified in the monumental graves of the city—in the tower tombs; the large underground tombs, or hypogea; and the so-called house or temple tombs.[16] As will be discussed further in Chapter 3, these monuments were used to house the deceased of Palmyra's elite families. Nonetheless the images used on these tombs, which depict still-living family members alongside their deceased loved ones, underline the importance of family ties and a long genealogy. The often-generic inscriptions found in the graves confirm this picture.

Palmyrene society was patriarchally structured.[17] Elite male Palmyrenes were often the heads of large families.[18] They funded urban monuments and religious activities such as banquets, and often constructed monumental family tombs on which they could be displayed together with members of their closest family.[19] They held responsibility for familial wealth, which was built on yields from the hinterland and involvement in trade, and they made all economic decisions related to these fortunes. These elite men were active in the city's religious life (with the role of religion discussed in more detail later in this chapter); many held priesthoods and civic offices as well as taking part in the organization and financing of the caravan trade. They held such roles both within Palmyra and more widely, suggesting a clear ability and desire to integrate themselves firmly into the Roman imperial system and beyond it.[20] In many ways, the behavioral pattern of those who held power and influence in Palmyra is comparable to that identified in other Roman cities of the East, where the notion of doing good for one's society (*euergetism*) was considered particularly important to represent oneself—and be perceived by others—as a good citizen (Fig. 8).

However, certain behavioral traits in this group were also apparently unique to Palmyra. For example, the office of priest in Palmyra seems to have been deeply dependent on family structure.[21] The large number of Palmyrene priests represented in sculpture across the funerary, public, civic, and religious spheres, numbering almost 500, together with the thousands of depictions of priests on the so-called banqueting tesserae, show that Palmyra had the largest group of priests of any place in the ancient world.[22] While

Figure 8a Public female sculpture. National Museum of Damascus, Damascus, C4021 (Rubina Raja and Palmyra Portrait Project, Ingholt Archive at Ny Carlsberg Glyptotek, PS 1131B).

Figure 8b Public male sculpture. National Museum of Damascus, Damascus, C4024 (Rubina Raja and Palmyra Portrait Project, Ingholt Archive at Ny Carlsberg Glyptotek, PS 1129C).

this at first might appear odd, the reason for this high number of priests might in fact be quite pragmatic; it indicates that Palmyrene priesthoods were structured quite differently from priesthoods in the Roman world and suggests that Roman religion as a whole had little influence on the regulation of Palmyrene religious life.[23] Palmyrene priesthoods appear to have been inherited or passed on to male members within families or perhaps tribes more broadly, as shown by the visual representations on especially lavish sarcophagus lids (Fig. 9).[24]

We know little about the everyday life of elite women in Palmyra.[25] This is also true of children as well as ordinary people, freedmen, and slaves, none of whom have left the same kind of traces in the archeological and written sources as Palmyra's elite men.[26] We have some evidence for both freedmen and slaves in Palmyra, and these groups would have formed an integrated part of society in the Roman period.[27] Despite the trade and travels of the male elite, it is also certain that many Palmyrenes would have been bound to chores close to, or within the city. Women, children, freedmen, slaves, and many ordinary men would in reality have stayed within the city and its environs for much or all of their lives. The agricultural activities that were necessary for the city and its people, including cultivation of the surrounding lands, pastoral activities, the general management of the hinterland, and ensuring a stable water supply to Palmyra, would all have demanded substantial organization and labor.

Figure 9 Sarcophagus lid with banqueting scene, 200–220 CE. National Museum of Damascus, Damascus, 4946 (Courtesy of DAI Damascus).

What Palmyrene women did and exactly what role they played in Palmyra outside of the domestic sphere is unclear. Women are, however, prominently represented in the city's funerary sculptures, with female portraits making up about 30 percent of the entire corpus.[28] Within these images, women are not only represented as wives and mothers but often also as individuals in their own right, elite women who belonged to important Palmyrene families. In the early portraits, women are often shown with spindles and distaffs, a motif seen across the Roman world that connects them with a domestic setting. In later periods, from the later first century onward, women are often depicted with lavish clothing, elaborate headdresses, and much jewelry to underline their social status, despite the fact that these portraits could be accessed exclusively within the private graves.[29] Nonetheless, the domestic attributes that women are given in portraits, their appearances with their children, and the fact that they are most often veiled—only giving glimpses of the wealth that they possessed—would seem to indicate that the female realm of influence was largely restricted to a domestic context or possibly to the organization of their family's businesses.[30]

Palmyrene women are not generally known to have taken part in public or religious life by holding official positions. The one obvious exception to this is Zenobia, as discussed later. However, women did participate to some extent in both public and religious life and should not be overlooked as an important factor in Palmyrene society. This is indicated from some inscriptions and iconographic representations, where they are shown in a few fragments of religious reliefs as spectators—albeit entirely veiled—to religious processions[31] and honored with inscriptions in public spaces.[32] Women also appear as donors of votives, sometimes together with their children, as shown by representations on some small altars found in Palmyra (Fig. 10).[33] In addition, we know from some inscriptions that women could own property.[34]

A significant amount of statuary has been found in Palmyra, but this mostly comes from funerary contexts. Relatively little has survived from the public sphere, due largely to the weathering of the local limestone, reuse of imported materials such as marble and bronze, and general wear, tear, and destruction, all of which has taken place over millennia.[35] However, we do know that women were also represented in the public space and that some even had honorific statues set up for them (Fig. 8). One example of this stems from what we may term secondary evidence and comes from the grave of a certain Hairan. Here, paintings of honorific statues of Hairan

Figure 10 Altar with a standing female and boy, early first century CE. Ny Carlsberg Glyptotek, Copenhagen, IN 1080 (Photo: Ny Carlsberg Glyptotek, Copenhagen / Anders Sune Berg).

and his wife feature on the walls at the sides of their family's burial niches, indicating that their original statues stood somewhere in the public space in Palmyra. There are also actual examples of honorific statues of women that have survived.[36]

Children of the elite also feature in Palmyrene funerary and religious art. Over 200 representations of children appear in the funerary sculpture. Often they are shown together with their parents or other family members.[37] However, they were also represented in their own right in smaller than life-size full figures on stelae, which were used to cover burial niches in the tombs.[38] It is also clear that Palmyrenes did not simply consider their children as familial attributes; a number of double reliefs exist that depict mothers grieving for their adolescent or adult children by exposing their upper chest to reveal scratches above the breasts—a sign of mourning in Antiquity.[39]

Tribes and Terminology

From the evidence available to us, it would appear that Palmyrene society consisted of a prominent elite, which persisted throughout the Roman period, together with traders, farmers, and slaves. From the later second century onward, people attached to the Roman army could also be added to this list. However, the elite clearly stand most prominently in the evidence. It also appears that Palmyra's relative isolation in the Syrian Desert contributed to the ongoing development of a strong and closed local society that retained a clear emphasis on its own traditions, as testified to by the funerary and religious spheres.[40]

The bulk of the evidence for the terminology used in the Roman period stems from the public inscriptions and the funerary inscriptions, as well as the tiny so-called banqueting tesserae.[41] The term *Phd* was used to indicate the tribe. Often the longer phrase *dy mn phd bny X*, meaning "who is of the tribe and the sons of," was shortened to *bny X* or to *dy mn bny X*, as is often seen on banqueting tesserae.[42] This indicates that the subgroups that underpinned the four main tribes also held importance, at least within the local framework of Palmyrene society. The longer phrases might have given people direct access to very specific information that could be decoded in the local context. Potentially this was more important than the tribal information, which might have been implied through the abbreviated phrases. The Greek term for tribe, *phyle*, occurs in five instances in Palmyra. Likewise, the Greek term *eggenes X*, born of the same race as or a natural descendent of X, can also be found in inscriptions from 179 CE onward.[43]

Smith correctly emphasizes familial relations as the most prominent kinds of relationships mentioned in the inscriptions of Palmyra. This is closely connected to the fact that the vast majority of the inscriptions stem from the funerary sphere, where they were displayed in closed-off family tombs in which there was no need to mention networks other than familial connections. These would have been clear to the family itself, and they would often also be stated on the exterior of the graves, in the now-almost entirely disappeared founder reliefs.[44] Palmyrenes were fully able to switch between the various spheres of their lives and integrate the information that was necessary to decode messages and inscriptions in a given situation.

This ability to distinguish between social settings and to apply different kinds of language according to the setting can clearly be seen in an inscription dating from 52 CE. This is a dedicatory inscription that was found reused in a later context in the Temple of Baalshamin, and it gives a long description of a female donor's familial ties.[45] The inscription can be translated as follows:

> Amtallât, daughter of Baraâ, son of Atenatan, who is of the daughters of Mîtâ, wife of Taîmâ, son of Belhazaî son of Zabdibêl, who is of the tribe of the *bny m'zyn*, dedicated a column to the god Baalshamin.[46]

In this instance, in which the inscription forms part of a clear public and religious dedication, it was fully appropriate to give such detail, and it would seem that there was in fact a desire to underline the importance of one's familial ties on both the paternal and the maternal sides of the family. This inscription also shows the importance of studying the inscriptions and their use of family terminology within their broader social contexts.

Smith lists 98 known uses of *bny* and 17 instances in which *bny* (15) or *phyle* (2) are used, and it now seems secure that these terms deal with tribal affiliations.[47] As mentioned earlier, sources from the second half of the second century CE tell us about the four tribes of the city, who were not mentioned before this time.[48] It is likely that these four tribes incorporated a higher number of underlying tribes—at least fourteen, if not nineteen. There have been many discussions about the four tribes of Palmyra; according to one interpretation, they were the most important aristocratic groups within the city, and another line of argument concludes that they formed the civic governing body of Palmyra.[49] The introduction of four tribes, which effectively subsumed a much higher number of tribal groups, is not easy to explain.[50] There seems to have been a reorganization of some type within Palmyrene society in the Roman period, but whether this restructuring changed anything in the private spheres of Palmyrene life is less certain.[51] The evidence from funerary settings, at least, does not suggest this, and a majority of scholars believe that this restructuring did not actually change the original tribal structure of Palmyrene society but rather was simply a social public organization of these families into broader groups.[52] As such, the creation of four tribes might instead once again reflect the ability of Palmyrene society to adapt with great agility to changing circumstances. We know that the four new tribes were connected to four main sanctuaries within the city, and it might well be that the institution of the tribes was connected to the need to secure financing and thus provide some kind of private or tribal sponsorship for these sanctuaries. This hypothesis, however, remains speculative. Over time, it is evident that there was flexibility in the terminology connected to families and tribes in Palmyra, and that words changed over time. Even so, it is clear from the way the Palmyrenes expressed themselves in their inscriptions that they saw themselves as being connected to families within a variety of both smaller and larger networks. Moreover, they were content to employ different ways to express these relationships, adapting language according to the social sphere in which they operated, whether funerary, religious, or civic.

The Veneer of Society

A key area of debate when discussing Palmyrene society has been whether or not it can be termed a Greek city.[53] Central to this debate is the question of whether the use of Greek language within Palmyra was deeply integrated into all aspects of public, everyday life, or whether it should rather be considered a veneer, merely coating a society that was in fact far more locally based.[54]

Palmyra was not a city founded in the wake of the Hellenistic expansion.[55] Certainly, for Alexander the Great and his army there would have been no reason to fortify the site or to install veterans in this remote desert location, which had little to offer in terms of gaining control over the region or ensuring military stability. As such, the extent to which Palmyra can be considered truly Greek at its core is far more difficult to grasp than at sites such as Gerasa in the Decapolis region (located some 400 km/250 miles southwest of Palmyra, in modern Jordan), which was a Hellenistic refoundation.[56] This information strongly suggests the way earlier periods of the site's development should be viewed. It has become clear over the last decades that there is far more evidence dating from the Hellenistic period in Palmyra than has hitherto been understood.[57] Even so, it is extremely difficult to give precise responses to questions about when and to what extent Palmyrene society was nomadic or semi-nomadic, or the degree to which Palmyrene society was under Greek influence.[58]

Nonetheless, there can be no doubt that Palmyrene society did become increasingly influenced by Greek culture—even when the city came under Roman rule.[59] Recently a new perspective has been offered on this multifaceted process, which can be traced well into the second century CE, in Nathanael Andrade's book on local identities in the Roman Near East. The book takes a fresh look at Palmyra in the Hadrianic period and argues for a close connection between the city's bilingualism and its local identity.

Andrade suggests that the Palmyrenes were able to express their own particularities by combining several languages, for example, Greek and Palmyrene Aramaic.[60] While Palmyra might therefore be considered the only truly bilingual society of the Roman Near East, the nature of this bilingualism demands assessment.[61] Did most Palmyrenes speak both the local Palmyrene Aramaic dialect and Greek? This cannot be assumed, since Palmyrene Aramaic was used almost exclusively in the funerary sphere.[62] And culturally how are we to contextualize the several hundred bilingual inscriptions that were set up in the public spaces of Palmyra? We know that Greek was used extensively in such locations, as seen, for example, on the bilingual Tax Tariff, as well as on many honorific inscriptions.[63] Nonetheless, the usage of Greek in a funerary context was very limited and can be dated almost exclusively to the second half of the second century CE.[64] Latin, meanwhile, was seldom used at all in Palmyra; it appears in only five funerary inscriptions, all of which are connected to non-Palmyrenes.[65] At the same time, numerous Safaitic inscriptions have been found in Palmyra's hinterlands, thus establishing the presence of yet another dialect in the city's immediate surroundings.[66] It would seem, then, that those who lived in Palmyra and its territory embraced more than just knowledge of Palmyrene Aramaic and Greek.

As mentioned in Chapter 1, we know little about Palmyrene society before the turn of the first millennium, and the vast bulk of our evidence stems from the second century CE onward. However, this evidence does reveal to us a city at the peak of its development. We do not know how many people lived in the city at this time,[67] nor can we realistically say how many people traveled to Palmyra for the purposes of trade. Might it have been a relatively low number? Is that what we find reflected in the material evidence, despite the several hundred bilingual inscriptions that exist from the public sphere? Was Palmyra, despite its ability to integrate into the wider traditions of the Roman East, in fact very much a local society, based on local traditions that were centered around the tribal structure of the city and the familial relations within the city?[68] The evidence certainly points in this direction, not least the vast amount of material and inscriptional evidence from the funerary sphere.[69]

Palmyra's Monumentalization

Urban development across the Near East intensified in the first century CE, spurred on by the Pax Romana and the increased political stability in the region after the Battle of Actium in 31 BCE.[70] As a result, it suddenly became possible for societies to invest in the embellishment and expansion of their built environments, which was an important factor in both everyday living and in promoting the city and its status among other settlements in the region.[71] Nonetheless, Palmyra appears to have differed from the way many other urban sites in the Near East developed and expressed themselves.[72] It does not seem to have been laid out according to any kind of overall plan, for example, nor did it seem to engage in competition with other centers through the minting of civic local coinage, one of the prime media used by cities to communicate their identity and importance to the wider world.[73] These differences might well have been because of the location of the site, which was relatively far away from other urban centers. Palmyra, positioned at a distance from other settlements and far from both rivers and sea, was even for its own region quite peculiar, and it was very probably considered isolated—if occasionally of strategic importance—before its emerging wealth in the early Roman period.[74] Crucially the city was located in a steppe desert, with a hinterland that was controlled, managed, and exploited by people who had known the land intimately for generations, and when the city began to develop, it was largely driven by local support from the region's partially nomadic tribes.

During the Roman period, Palmyra was embellished with a range of monuments that were inspired by the same Graeco-Roman building traditions that we can also identify in many other cities across the Roman world. An unplanned center that grew organically over the centuries, Palmyra sprawled outward, and several monuments were located along its main street (Fig. 4). Monumental and smaller temples, sanctuary spaces, public spaces such as baths, a theater, and an agora with a *bouleuterion* (a council house) were built, and it is possible that a basilica was also constructed, although this is not entirely clear from the layout of the building remains. Over time, the streets of Palmyra were paved and lined with columns; this was an ongoing work, and stretches of some streets appear never to have been finished. Monuments such as the so-called Triumphal Arch and the Tetrapylon were also constructed, and these tied together otherwise disparate elements of the city. Importantly, it was in this same time period that Palmyra's several hundred monumental graves were constructed.

The urban monumentalization of the Roman period must have demanded the existence of some sort of civic organization since both the planning and financing of building projects must have been in place before work began.

We can therefore assume that the earliest monumental building projects in Palmyra reflect an already existing civic administration and an established way of organizing the financing of projects, whether through public funds or private benefactions.[75] While plans of Palmyra have been created over the years, with the first urban plan of the site made in 1926 and updates ongoing since then, no complete overview of the city's development has yet been made, and indeed the exact extent of the city still remains unknown.[76] It seems, however, most likely that it covered around 120 hectares at its largest. The 2010 map by Schnädelbach is the most precise urban plan available to us today, though a more recent map, created by Gawlikowski in 2019, has added important features.[77] While Palmyra was evidently not the product of careful urban planning, one particular monumental building complex nonetheless clearly stood out and dominated the site, namely, the Sanctuary of Bel. This was an extremely large sanctuary with a vast temenos (enclosure) that incorporated the Roman-period temple. This monumental temple complex would certainly have been constructed alongside other monuments in the settlement, including private dwellings, and it is not improbable that other public and sacred buildings were also built, although if this is this case, these have not (yet) been evidenced in the archeological record.[78]

As noted, little is known about the extent of the urban site in Palmyra before the early Roman period, not least due to the difficulty of identifying extant Hellenistic remains. The remains that prevail in the Palmyrene landscape today stem from the first to third centuries CE. From the 1920s onward, when large-scale archeological projects were initiated during the French Mandate in Syria, many of the originally Roman-period monuments were stripped of their later post-Antique phases. The most prominent example is the Sanctuary of Bel, where the temenos housed an entire small village and the temple had been converted into a fortress in the medieval period; these two elements were wholly demolished to recreate the complex as it would have been in its Roman-period phase, a point that is discussed in Chapter 6.

The Religious Life of Palmyra

Palmyrene religious beliefs and the deities that were worshipped in Palmyra have been the subject of intense scholarly discussion for several decades, although Ted Kaizer's 2002 monograph still constitutes the standard work on this topic.[79] The city's religious life was focused around both local deities and the cults of foreign gods, which were often adapted to better fit with Palmyrene culture.[80] The Sanctuary of Bel was the main sanctuary for all Palmyrenes, but four tribal sanctuaries also existed in Palmyra, each connected to one of the four main tribes introduced to the city in the second century CE.[81] Numerous other deities would in addition have been worshipped alongside the gods that we find reflected in Palmyra's religious architecture.[82] Inscriptional material offers further insights into this complex and rich religious life, as do banqueting tesserae (Fig. 11). These tiny clay tickets, which were used to gain entrance to religious feasts held in the banqueting halls and courtyards of the city's sanctuaries, hold rich iconographic and inscriptional evidence that offer insights into the many deities, male and female, who were worshipped in the city at various points in time.[83] Palmyrene religious practices were first and foremost oriented at a very local level. While we know that Palmyrenes worshipped outside of Palmyra and made dedications both to their own gods and to the deities of other societies when they traveled, within the city it seems that religious beliefs remained primarily focused on local deities.[84]

The main local gods of Palmyra were Bel (lord), Yarhibol (the lord of the spring), Aglibol (the calf of the lord), and Malakbel (the messenger of the lord). The latter three are known only from Palmyrene contexts and must be considered entirely local deities, whose cults were followed long before the first epigraphic evidence was produced in the second half of the first century BCE.[85] The earliest inscription testifying to religious activity in Palmyra records an honorific statue that was dedicated by priests of Bel in 44 BCE.[86] This inscription indicates that the name of the former indigenous god, Bol, had by this time changed into the Mesopotamian-influenced name Bel (lord).[87] An honorific inscription, found within the Sanctuary of Bel and dating from 45 CE, celebrates the individual who apparently dedicated the site to Yarhibol, Aglibol, and Bel, in 32 CE. Another inscription from the same site, evidently produced during the first half of the first century CE, reveals that this sanctuary was also referred to as "the house of the gods of the Palmyrenes"; this name suggests that the four tribes of the city could all be brought together through a joint place of worship.[88] In connection with the reorganization of Palmyra's tribes during the Roman period, four tribal sanctuaries can be identified: these were the Sanctuary of Atargatis; the so-called Sacred Garden, which was home to Aglibol and Malakbel; the temple of Arsu; and two further sanctuaries, namely, those of Baalshamin and Allat, which served one tribe alternately.

Figure 11a–b Tessera with a reclining priest and a seal impression. Ny Carlsberg Glyptotek, Copenhagen, IN 2771 (Photo: Ny Carlsberg Glyptotek, Copenhagen).

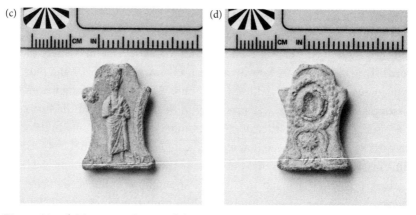

Figure 11c–d Tessera with a standing priest and a seal impression. Ny Carlsberg Glyptotek, Copenhagen, IN 3206 (Photo: Ny Carlsberg Glyptotek, Copenhagen).

Several other places of worship are also known from Palmyra, among them the Sanctuary of Nabu, the shrine dedicated to Shadrafa and Du'anat, and the recently discovered temple to Rabaseire, all of which are sanctuaries located within the city.[89] Just outside the city, to the southwest, a small temple is located on top of the Jebel Muntar. This was dedicated to Bel Hammon and Manawat, both of whom were worshipped there alongside the Palmyrene

Figure 11e–f Tessera with a reclining priest, servants mixing wine as well as seal impression. Ny Carlsberg Glyptotek, Copenhagen, IN 3208 (Photo: Ny Carlsberg Glyptotek, Copenhagen).

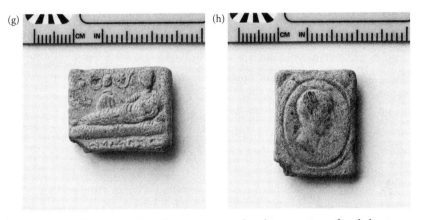

Figure 11g–h Tessera with reclining priest and seal impression of male bust. Ny Carlsberg Glyptotek, Copenhagen, IN 3213 (Photo: Ny Carlsberg Glyptotek, Copenhagen).

god Malakbel and a female deity, incorrectly referred to on an inscription as Benefal.[90] This example of a foreign goddess stands alongside the mention of other deities as evidence for the assimilation of Roman and Mesopotamian gods alongside local cults in Palmyra. It points to the fact that religion in Palmyra was practiced in a dynamic environment that was quick to adapt to local, regional, and Roman imperial structural changes.[91] As mentioned

above, priesthoods within Palmyra appear to have retained their local structure throughout the Roman period and were not influenced by Roman domination in a significant way. This shows the ability of Palmyrene society to
adapt to a changing cultural environment while simultaneously continuing
to follow local traditions within their wider social framework.

The Sanctuary of Bel

It is unsurprising that some of the earliest remains found in Palmyra from
the Hellenistic period stem from the area around the Sanctuary of Bel (Plate
3). Here, building structures dating from the third to the first centuries BCE
have been discovered beneath the later temple of Bel.[92] These, however,
have not been explored fully, since they lie under the later Roman-period
temple. The Sanctuary of Bel was the city's main sanctuary.[93] It was later
used as a church, a mosque, and then a fortress in the 1930s, but during the
early years of the French Mandate, these phases of the site were removed,
and the temple was restored to its appearance during the Roman period. The
temple's architecture has been studied in detail by Seyrig, Amy, and Will.[94]
Sculptural, architectonic, and epigraphic fragments that belong to the earlier
Hellenistic phases of the temple have all been found in the area around the
later Roman temple.[95] Such finds suggest that the earlier underlying structure or structures were demolished before the Roman-period temple was
constructed. Recently, further remains dating to this earlier period have
been published. Three columns to the east of the temple might have belonged
to a larger building that has been interpreted as a banqueting hall from the
sanctuary's Hellenistic phases, based on their relatively low location in relation to the Roman-period remains.[96]

The earliest Roman-period phase of the Bel temple seems to have been
contemporary with Palmyra's incorporation into the Roman province of
Syria in 18/19 CE, and this corresponds well with the general picture that we
can construct of a city increasing in prosperity and with a keen interest in
integrating itself into the Roman Empire.[97] The temple itself took over a century to construct. Although a 1975 publication about the site states that it
was finished by 32 CE,[98] we know today that it was in fact not completed until
the end of the first century CE;[99] it was the northern adyton (the innermost
sanctuary or shrine) that was consecrated in 32 CE. We can also tell from epigraphic evidence that the temple was financed by several different sponsors.

The long process of construction raises questions about the economy of the site in this period; it was not uncommon for building projects to take place over several generations, or even never to reach completion.

The Bel temple had a Greek ground plan that in many respects closely imitates the Artemis temple from Magnesia, which we know was planned by the Greek architect Hermogenes.[100] The temple, in principle a classical pseudoperipteros temple, was Roman Palmyra's most monumental building and it was obviously the city's most sacred focal point. However, there were several features that set the Palmyrene temple apart from its Greek predecessor in Magnesia. The main entrance was located along the temple's one long side, while at each short end, there were niches, so-called adyta, in the temple's raised cella, within which cult images were displayed. Ionic half-columns were visible on both short sides where one could have imagined openings. The roof was flat, and staircases led up to the roof where it is assumed that rituals might have taken place. The rectangular temenos, constructed in the last quarter of the first century CE, around 80 CE, was vast; it measured 205 x 210 m (672 x 698 ft) and covered an area of approximately 43,000 m^2 (463,000 sq ft). The construction of the temenos demanded a remodeling of the temple, the foundations of which had been exposed when the area was leveled for the temenos square. A podium was thus constructed around the steps of the temple, and a ramp was added in front of the monumental entrance to the building, which gave the temple a very significant look. The porticoes of the temenos were lined on all sides with double colonnades of the Corinthian order, but these were not set up at the same time, and it seems that the higher portico, opposite the temple's entrance to the west, was never completed.[101] The columns were fitted with the typical consoles or brackets that were found everywhere in the public spaces in the city and on which statues could be displayed. While the temple and temenos were almost aligned, the sanctuary itself did not align with the rest of the city, which suggests that the temple was built on top of a much older, pre-existing sanctuary that had existed before the city began to develop.[102] Indeed, even the early Roman phases do not seem to align with the sanctuary's orientation.[103]

The temenos also held several other monuments, all located in front of the temple's monumental entrance. These included a monumental altar, a banqueting hall with adjoining kitchen structure, a square monument with niches, and a lustration basin (for purification rituals).[104] A ramp has been identified in the northwest corner of the temenos, which led from the outside of the temenos under its wall into the sanctuary space. This could have been used for leading sacrificial animals into the temenos, as well as for processions. It is estimated that the banqueting hall was able to hold more than 100 guests.[105] Ritual dining would have taken place in this hall, and this notion is given further credence by the numerous banqueting tesserae found in the area, including some in the hall's drains.[106] It is possible that many more guests might have participated in the ritual banquets, for which they might have been placed in the porticoes of the large temenos. Both the tesserae and iconographic evidence from the temple suggest that while the Sanctuary of Bel might have been a place of worship for the city's main god, it was also a center of cult for other deities.

The city of Palmyra held several other sanctuaries. West of the Sanctuary of Bel, the Sanctuary of Arsu has been located, although little of this temple remains. Further shrines were also situated on this road, which followed the ancient wadi.[107] Other sanctuaries were located outside the city center, in areas where tombs were also constructed. These included a sanctuary that was connected to the Efqa Spring and dedicated to Yarhibol, the spring's protector. This sanctuary, however, is known only through inscriptions, and no archeological evidence for it has yet been found. Other important sites of worship included the Sanctuary of Allat, originally an Arab goddess, and that of Baalshamin, who was an ancient Syrian weather deity. Both these temples stood in courtyards with porticoes. The Sanctuary of Baalshamin was replaced by a more centrally located sanctuary, and the older sanctuary has left no archeological traces. However, that of Allat is still visible. It holds a central shrine that is just large enough to have contained the cult image of the seated goddess.[108]

Some sanctuaries are known primarily through epigraphic sources. This is the case for one of the tribal sanctuaries, the so-called Sacred Garden of Aglibol and Malakbel.[109] It is also true of the temple dedicated to Rabaseire, mentioned in the Tax Tariff dating to 137 CE, and located across from the Agora.[110] A sanctuary dedicated to either Astarte or Atargatis (or perhaps to both deities) is similarly mentioned only through inscriptions.[111] A Caesareum, a sanctuary dedicated to the Roman emperor or emperors, is mentioned in an inscription from 171 CE.[112] We know that cultic activity was connected to the Efqa Spring, and this activity has also been linked by some with a sanctuary for the solar god Yarhibol.[113]

The Temple of Nabu

The Sanctuary of Nabu is located southwest of the Sanctuary of Bel.[114] Nabu was a local deity of Mesopotamian origin, often assimilated with the god Apollo. Several inscriptions from this sanctuary mention Nabu, but dedications to other deities have also been found, as is often the case in Palmyrene sanctuaries.[115] The Elahbel and Belsuri tribes are the most frequently mentioned donors in the epigraphic evidence from this temple.[116] There was an earlier sanctuary in the same location, but a new temple surrounded by colonnades was constructed in the first or second century CE.[117] A temple was located in the center of a trapezoidal courtyard that measured approximately 70 x 40 m (230 x 39 ft). The main entrance to the sanctuary was on the south side, facing away from the main street, but there was also a door that allowed access from the north; this held vegetal decoration as well as seven busts of deities.[118] It is likely that an important cause of changes to the sanctuary was the layout of the main street, especially as the former court-yard had been more regular in shape.[119] The new courtyard had columns with Doric capitals and consoles for statues, both features that are well known from other complexes and the main street.[120] The sanctuary had a propylon (entrance complex) with a colonnaded hexastyle facade with Corinthian columns. A set of rooms on each side of the entrance could be accessed from the outside. Within the sanctuary was a small peristyle temple, measuring 6 x 12 m (20 x 39 ft) and with Corinthian columns. It featured a staircase into which an altar was integrated. The staircase led up to the peristyle, which was added in the second century CE. Several parts of the temple's decoration are preserved, and these show a variety of elements such as rosettes, lion-head spouts, and a single fish, as well as heads, one wearing a nimbus crown, which had been attached to the column capitals.[121]

A square monument, potentially dating to the second century CE, stood in front of the temple. This featured columns on each corner, which mea-sured 4.3 m (14.1 ft) on each side, and supported a roof under which reliefs depicted deities and Palmyrene priests making sacrifices. This monu-ment might have functioned as another altar or alternatively as a *hamana* (shrine).[122]

The Temple of Baalshamin

The Sanctuary of Baalshamin was dedicated to a Semitic weather and fertility deity, but a range of other deities are also mentioned in inscriptions and offerings within the sanctuary.[123] The sanctuary consisted of several colonnaded courtyards. The well-known temple from this site, which is now destroyed, was added in the early second century CE. The sanctuary was connected to the tribe of the Bene Ma'ziyan, and this connection is further emphasized by graves belonging to tribal members from the pre-Roman period that are located in and around the sanctuary.[124] The sanctuary has various phases from the first quarter of the first century CE onward, with the initial phase consisting of a set of courtyards.[125] In 67 CE the sanctuary was changed radically with the addition of colonnaded courts.[126] It was also at this point that a dining hall in the southeast part of the so-called great court was dedicated.[127] Further alterations were made in the late first century, in the shape of peristyles and a central court.[128] The Corinthian tetraprostyle temple dedicated in 130/131 CE was financed by Malè, also known as Agrippa Yarhai.[129]

The Temple of Baalshamin (Plate 4) was, in many ways, quite peculiar. It featured Corinthian columns on the inside of the cella walls, and cornices that were crowned by merlons. It also had windows set into each long end of the temple.[130] The small adyton, which was 8 m (26 ft) in depth, was decorated with aedicular facades with detailed moldings.[131] Single and double columns, as well as pilasters with Corinthian capitals, were set on high pedestal bases.[132] Niches decorated with shell designs, floral imagery, and griffins were located on the eastern walls facing the entrance.[133] The main entrance to the central part of the temple was flanked by rooms, and the cella has an aedicular roof shaped as a semi-circular exedra over the large central back wall niche, to which a relief, no longer extant, had been attached. A sculptural element, which predated the temple architecture and which must have come from a different structure, served as the lintel for the niche opening. It represents a central eagle with wings spread, flanked by two smaller eagles on each side, a rosette, and the bust of a deity with a nimbus.[134]

The Temple of Allat

The Temple of Allat was located in the northwest of the city, in the area of the later Camp of Diocletian.[135] As elsewhere, other deities were worshipped in this sanctuary alongside the goddess Allat. Inscriptions found at this site show dedication to the Arabic gods Rahim and Shamash.[136] One dedicatory inscription from 115 CE, made by a member of the Bene Ma'ziyan, also refers to an earlier family member named Mattanai, who was the donor of the original cult image in Allat's hamana. This mention of an ancestor suggests that the sanctuary's earliest datable phase was in the first century BCE.[137] The first hamana was a structure without windows, and it measured 7 x 5 m (23 x 16 ft).[138] A monolithic altar stood in front of the entrance. A niche was set into the west wall in the first century CE; this most likely housed the image that we know was dedicated by the Mattani. From the mid-first century CE onward, inscriptions tell us about the dedication of porticoes, which formed a courtyard measuring 46 x 29 m.[139] A hamana was constructed to the west. Development of the sanctuary continued at least until the middle of the second century CE.[140] Further constructions were also undertaken, and two smaller buildings or monuments were found in the northwest corner of the courtyard and in front of the eastern entrance to the sanctuary. It is possible that these structures were used for altars or for housing further cultic images.[141]

During the second century CE, the temple underwent profound change as the hamana became part of the cella of the new tetraprostyle temple of the Corinthian order, dedicated by a Taimarsu.[142] The new temple measured about 18 x 9 m (59 x 30 ft), and internal decorations included pilasters on the exterior walls.[143] The roof of the temple was left open, which is indicated by drainage channels, and somewhere in the temple, the Athena Parthenos statue, made from imported Pentelic marble, was erected.[144] This status is an iconic piece, shown to incorporate traits from several different Athena Parthenos types; it must have been imported in a finished state and set up in the sanctuary.[145] This sanctuary was destroyed during the sacking of Palmyra in 272 CE, but it was reconstructed sometime afterward, when it was incorporated into the military Camp of Diocletian. The cult statue, which had survived, was also reused.[146] Lime kilns constructed in the fourth century CE indicate that the sanctuary had fallen out of use by this time.[147]

The Temple of Arsu

Arsu was the god of the desert and protector of caravans, and he was connected to the tribe of the Bene Mattabol.[148] The sanctuary was one of Palmyra's four main tribal sanctuaries, and has been identified as such through an inscription dating to 144 CE.[149] Arsu's sanctuary has been identified archeologically through an altar with an inscription dedicated to the god that dates to 63 CE. The altar was discovered during excavations that uncovered the foundations of a temple, which was located in a courtyard surrounded by porticoes with rooms.[150] In this sanctuary were found what has been interpreted as an entire series of banqueting tesserae featuring representations of Arsu.[151]

It is clear that significant emphasis was placed on the constant development and upkeep of sanctuaries in Palmyra. Chronologically, the process of embellishing the sanctuaries appears to have intensified in the middle of the first century CE, and this continued into the second century CE and beyond. The four tribal sanctuaries were undoubtedly focal points. However, other deities were also worshipped at these locations, and both the epigraphic and archeological evidence clearly point to the existence of sanctuaries that were dedicated to a string of other deities. Palmyra's religious life can thus be seen as rich and varied—a clear reflection of the complexity of wider Palmyrene society.

Infrastructure

During recent excavation work in Palmyra, parts of the city's early street network were investigated in connection with the re-excavation of the site where the second-century Tax Tariff originally stood.[152] This work revealed what appears to be the earliest paved road in the city, constructed around the middle of the second century CE; the stretches that have been uncovered were paved with flagstones. This road was in fact laid out along the course of the Wadi as-Suraysir, which ran through the Valley of the Tombs (Wadi al-Qubur) through Palmyra. In Antiquity, this wadi coincided with the path that joined the oasis from the west. The wadi was dammed at the head of the valley at an unknown point in time in order to prevent seasonal flooding in parts of the settlement. Today the level at which this early street is located is some 3 m to 4 m beneath the present level of the plain.[153] Gawlikowski concludes that this early street, which was 12 m (39 ft) wide, would have formed the main street in Palmyra.[154] There are no visible traces of wheeled transportation in the paving, and so the excavators have concluded that the street must have been used exclusively by pedestrians and not by either wheeled traffic or camels, since the flagstones would not have been suitable for them. The identification of such a pedestrianized zone in the center of Palmyra underlines the expansion process that the city underwent and the growing need for an urban space that could be used exclusively by inhabitants and visitors. A space like this was also very important for representative purposes, with many of Palmyra's main monuments and complexes constructed along this road. The paved road divided the earlier settlement on the southern side of the plateau from the later Roman city to the north.

Colonnaded streets were a feature widely encountered in the East. Scholars have approached these constructions in different ways, with an in-depth study of their origins conducted at other sites from across the region.[155] While there certainly might have been a number of different reasons that led to the construction of these public spaces within cities, one particular reason seems to have been paramount: colonnaded spaces made the public space uniform and allowed for decoration of the urban spaces in the areas through which the highest number of people passed on a daily basis. They also provided optimal spaces that could be used by the civil elite for self-representation and self-promotion. In this latter area, Palmyra excelled.

As noted, the street network of Palmyra was evidently not planned from the outset and conceived of as a whole. The colonnaded street appears to have had three sections, with the first stretch from the mid-second century CE, and the last stretch constructed in the third century CE.[156] There are, however, distinct differences in the techniques used to construct the various parts of the colonnade.[157] Moreover, it appears that none of these sections was ever fully finished.[158] Palmyra's main street was about 1.2 km (0.75 miles) in length, and traveled in a more-or-less straight line through the center of the city. It did not lead directly from the Sanctuary of Bel, but was set sightly off axis to the monumental entrance to the temenos. It is highly likely that there was an open public space in front of the sanctuary, which—like the famous Oval Piazza in Gerasa in the Decapolis—would have smoothed the transition between the architectural features of the sanctuary and the main street.[159]

The streets of Palmyra were lined with tall columns, a number of which had consoles (Fig. 12). On these consoles, the elite of Palmyra was displayed, and we have to imagine that public Palmyra was once crammed with statues, just as the funerary sphere was stacked with images of deceased Palmyrenes and their living family members (Figs. 13–15).[160] While the creation and display of statues was well known from across the Roman world, the practice was also widely used in the East, both in the Hellenistic period and after, where

Figure 12 Colonnaded stretch of the main street in Palmyra with statue consoles (Rubina Raja).

sculptural representations expressed power and rulership. There were strong and long-established traditions across Mesopotamia, Persia, and Parthia in which the rulers and elite displayed themselves in different media—not least in the rock-cut relief art known from that region.[161] In Palmyra, although the statues would of course not have been erected in one go, they would undoubtedly have impacted the city's urban landscape, and it is possible to identify several locations other than the main street in which images of Palmyrenes or their gods would have been established. Busts would have been placed on architraves and on temples, for example, where they would have hovered over visitors. The agora space was likewise lined with columns carrying consoles upon which statues were displayed, and statues would also have been displayed at ground level. Through this extremely rich iconographic environment, the architecture of Palmyra mirrored the city's living environment.

Palmyra's water infrastructure was undoubtedly essential for the city's survival, so a lot of effort would clearly have been put into its maintenance and expansion. While the local springs, first and foremost the Efqa Spring, were used to provide the city with water for a range of purposes, potable drinking water was in fact brought in from outside the city through an extensive

Figure 13 Roman period limestone statue replaced in modern times on a console on the main street in Palmyra (Rubina Raja).

system of aqueducts that were maintained over the centuries and which have hitherto been relatively little explored.[162]

Other Buildings—Public and Private

The civic buildings and complexes in Palmyra included the Transverse Colonnade (which was a separate entity to the Grand Colonnade or main street), the Agora, the theater, and bath buildings. Together with the monumental arch, also known as the Triumphal Arch, and the Tetrapylon, these constitute the known monuments of Palmyra (Plate 5). The Transverse Colonnade was a stretch of shops along both sides of a monumental street in the northwest of the city, close to the Sanctuary of Allat. This stretch was about 230 m (755 ft) in length, and 35 m (115 ft) in width. The shops were lined by columns in the front which were erected over the course of a century, although it appears that this project may never have been completed. The street space that was left open provided a wide, uncovered space that was 22 m (72 ft) in width. At one end of the street, a monumental triple arch opened up to an oval piazza, while at the other end, the street led to the northern

Figure 14 Limestone portrait of Palmyrene man. The sculpture imitates bronze sculptural technique, 100 CE. Ny Carlsberg Glyptotek, Copenhagen, IN 1093 (Photo: Ny Carlsberg Glyptotek, Copenhagen / Anders Sune Berg).

necropolis of the city. Despite the relative breadth of the street, it should not be assumed that this was a location into which caravans with animals were allowed; rather, this space should be seen as the central market space to which merchants brought both local and imported produce for trade, and for which they used a means of transportation other than camels.

The Agora and the theater were situated behind the main street. The complex encompassing the Agora also held a basilica, which was never finished, and a building dubbed the "curia," in which the imperial cult was celebrated. This kind of building complex is not unknown in the East;[163] in Gerasa in the Decapolis, for example, a basilica was located with its long side toward a large open square and its short side opening on to a street on the other side of the council house, the so-called North Theater.[164] The agora was a closed square surrounded by porticoes, and the main entrance to this was not located on the main street, but on the so-called wadi street. The columns

Figure 15 Male head from an honorific statue, 230–250 CE. Ny Carlsberg Glyptotek, Copenhagen, IN 1121 (Photo: Ny Carlsberg Glyptotek, Copenhagen/ Anders Sune Berg).

had consoles, many of which carried statues and dedicatory inscriptions telling us about Palmyra's elite and their involvement in the caravan trade; these were the individuals who had often organized the caravan trade and its protection, and now they were honored in the public spaces of Palmyra. The agora was constructed around the end of the first century CE. It was also adjacent to the Agora, in a corner in which the city council building was located. The construction of the Agora and its wider complex took place during the reigns of Trajan and Hadrian, in the period between the late first and second centuries CE, a period that saw Palmyra flourish.

Until the second century CE, the only paved road within Palmyra was the wadi road, the road south of the monumental city center onto which the Agora and Sanctuary of Nabu opened. This would have been the main focus of the city before the Great Colonnade was laid out. The construction of this street, which appears to have been conceived of as a holistic project, changed

Figure 16 Theatrical mask in stucco, late second/early third century CE. Found in a domestic setting in Palmyra. Ny Carlsberg Glyptotek, Copenhagen, IN 3718 (Photo: Ny Carlsberg Glyptotek, Copenhagen/Anders Sune Berg).

the cityscape immensely. It seems likely that the street was constructed with the intention of extending the city to the north and thus laying out a grid in that direction. Gawlikowski is most likely correct to suggest that this project was spurred on by Hadrian's visit to the city in 129 CE; however, the oldest inscription dates to 158 CE. The Great Colonnade was extended up to the Sanctuary of Bel, and because of the city's original layout, and the differing orientation of the older monuments, it was necessary to bend the new street in two different places, resulting in a 90-degree-bend at the oldest end of the street, and then a bend of almost 300 degrees at the Triumphal Arch. The Tetrapylon, with its sixteen columns made of red Egyptian granite, stood on the central stretch of the Grand Colonnade, while at the other end stood the Monumental Arch, close to the Sanctuary of Bel. This triumphal archway was constructed in the third century to commemorate the reign of Odaenathus, husband of Zenobia, and his son, after their victory over the Persians in

260 CE, events that are considered in more detail in Chapter 4. According to inscriptions, statues of Odaenathus, his son, Zenobia, and a high-ranking official named Worod were all placed on the arch. The entire stretch of road from the Tetrapylon to the Monumental Arch should, according to Gawlikowski, be understood as a royal monument.[165] The combination of the colonnades, the arch with its sculptural program, the Tetrapylon with its imported granite, a bath building that featured four granite columns in front of it, facing the street, and the vicinity of the Monumental Arch to the Sanctuary of Bel together underline the importance of the project and the attempts made in the third century to establish the royal house of Palmyra through the public, built environment of the city.

Relatively little is known about the private houses of Palmyra from the Roman period, since archeological research within the city has primarily focused on the public and funerary monuments.[166] During the Roman period, however, several houses would have lined the central streets of the city, and we know that Roman-period houses were located elsewhere in the city, in the so-called Hellenistic Quarter.[167] A limited number of houses have been explored (Fig. 16), and in recent years, a set of Late Antique houses have been partly excavated.

Roman Palmyra—Island or Node?

While the architecture of Palmyra undoubtedly drew inspiration from Graeco-Roman models, as seen most clearly in the Temples of Bel and Baalshamin, the theater, the agora, and the bath building, it is also true that most complexes were adapted to local customs. The Temple of Bel, for example, was entered from the long side, a feature that was very un-Roman indeed. It was also embellished with niches for the display of cult images at each short end of the temple, thus providing the temple with two focal points in another obvious contrast to traditional Greek or Roman temples. This blend of cultural influences is also true of other sanctuaries in Palmyra, which lent themselves equally to Graeco-Roman trends and to local and Near Eastern traditions. The stacking of statues into consoles inserted into columns and pilasters across both public and religious spaces is, however, a phenomenon unique to Palmyra. It clearly demonstrates that the Palmyrenes did not simply copy cultural trends from elsewhere, but they considered how to absorb and adapt such traditions, ensuring that they could be integrated into more than one sociocultural sphere.[168] As Andrade has noted: "Of the Syrian settlements that provide substantial epigraphic and material evidence, Palmyra perhaps exhibits the most definitively 'indigenous,' 'native,' or 'local' continuities."[169] I believe that we can now remove Andrade's cautious "perhaps" from this sentence and instead say with confidence that in Palmyra, it is indeed possible to trace a strong local continuity throughout the Roman period. Whether this continuity can be traced simply because we have extensive evidence or because such evidence points to a phenomenon that was indeed unique for the region is impossible to say. Nonetheless, what we can say about Palmyra and its society is that the people of Palmyra were well aware of the various cultural spheres in which they moved, and they actively used elements from each.

3

Family Networks

The World of the Dead

The funerary sphere from Palmyra provides us with unique insights into the world of the dead and therefore the wider values and identities of Palmyrene society. In Antiquity, numerous tall, square funerary towers were constructed around Palmyra and these buildings must have dominated the landscape surrounding the city, just as they still do today (Plate 6).[1] In addition to the several hundred tombs that are visible in the city's landscape, a high number of tombs were also located underground, taking the number of known graves to above 500.[2] These grave monuments, which were for the most part constructed in the Roman period before Palmyra was sacked in 272 CE, were lavishly decorated with the portraits of deceased Palmyrenes, some of whom were represented together with still living family members. Over time, these often monumental graves turned into family galleries, and they could display several hundred such funerary portraits.[3] This evidence from the funerary sphere enables us to study local Palmyrene society and aspects of its development under the Romans in a way that would simply not be possible using the evidence from the public and religious spheres alone.

The monumental tower tombs were featured prominently in the paintings, tapestries, and drawings done by many of the European artists who visited Palmyra from the seventeenth century onward. In van Essen's panorama painting of Palmyra from 1695, for example, some of the tower tombs are visible in the background, and they provide a prominent backdrop to the monuments and colonnaded city streets of his image. Borra, who came to the site together with Dawkins and Woods in 1751, also did some drawings that included tombs. These drawings were not to scale, however, and often depicted monuments with proportions that clearly differ from reality. Another of the early visitors to the city was the Frenchman Louis-Francois Cassas, who was something of a polymath; this painter, sculptor, architect, archeologist, and antiquary visited Palmyra from May to June 1785. He described his encounter with the city as one that awoke spiritual emotions

Pearl of the Desert. Rubina Raja, Oxford University Press. © Oxford University Press 2022.
DOI: 10.1093/oso/9780190852221.003.0003

within him.[4] Cassas made a string of detailed drawings of various vistas of the city, as well as many of its monuments.[5] His drawings are often artistic to the point that monuments were changed and portraits and sculptures appear with a far more classical Graeco-Roman expression than they had in reality; however, his works vividly reveal the impact that Palmyra's funerary monuments and sculptural decorations made on some of the first European visitors.[6] Early visitors to the site were usually overwhelmed by the lavishness of the monuments that they found scattered across both city and cemeteries. Most of the sculptural finds came from the grave monuments, since these had to some extent been spared by a long-term and ongoing problem of looting and demolition, an activity described by many visitors to the site. Among these was the Danish traveler Johannes Elith Østrup who was writing in the 1890s and whose writing is explored further in Chapter 6.[7] It is largely as a result of these early paintings, drawings, and descriptions that the tower tombs have received such attention, but they in fact represent only part of the elite funerary sphere of Palmyra. These artworks certainly provide a vivid image of how the ruin landscape of Palmyra looked, but they do not represent the ruins in an accurate manner; rather, they mirrored the artistic taste of their time and of their creators, who often took liberties and produced classisized art rather than portraying Palmyrene sculpture as it actually looked.

Palmyra's necropoleis were located around its city center (Fig. 17). The so-called Valley of the Tombs is also known as the western necropolis, and is located along the road that leads toward Emesa, modern-day Homs. The northern necropolis line the road toward the River Euphrates. The southeastern necropolis lies in the direction of Hit, while the southwestern necropolis is situated along the road to Damascus. The location of some tombs that were included by Schnädelbach in his recent survey suggests that there was probably also a necropolis on what must have been an eastern road leading directly toward the Euphrates.[8] The graves were all oriented with their facades toward the ancient streets, and this makes it possible today to trace the layout of the paths that ran between the tombs and connected them.[9] After the sack of Palmyra, the Camp of Diocletian was constructed on the outskirts of Palmyra's urban center. Several of the tomb monuments from the surrounding area were reused to construct the wall surrounding the camp, with some even directly integrated into the walls of the military camp.[10]

We cannot determine the date of the earliest necropoleis in Palmyra with any certainty. There is evidence of burials from the Hellenistic period, with

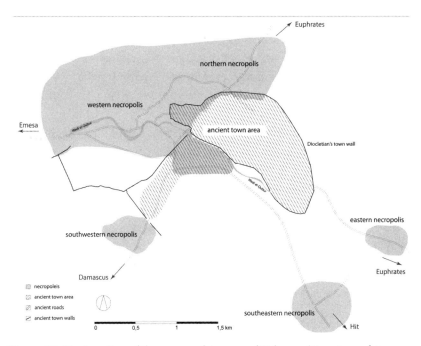

Figure 17 The location of the necropoleis around Palmyra (Courtesy of Agnes Henning)

the earliest dated tomb in Palmyra being from the second century BCE; this is a hypogeum, or underground tomb, with a mud-brick superstructure that was found behind the temple in the Sanctuary of Baalshamin.[11] It is only in the late first century BCE that we can begin to trace funerary ritual occurring in a more organized way, although this might also be a reflection on the nature of the archeological research so far undertaken in Palmyra.[12] Once the construction and use of necropoleis became established, it seems that activity took place equally across all necropolis areas, and all necropoleis held all types of grave monuments, with no chronological or typological division.

Grave Monuments and Burial Practices

Grave landscapes and vast cemeteries are known from across the ancient world, with well-known examples contemporaneous with the Palmyrene burials located outside the cities of Rome, Ostia, Hierapolis, and Tyre. In these cases, streets lined with grave monuments that led into cities were the rule rather than the exception. What makes Palmyra quite so exceptional, however, is that so many of these funerary monuments still exist.[13] In Palmyra, there were three main types of monumental grave: the tower tombs, the hypogea, and the so-called temple or house tombs.[14] The first tower tombs appear to have been constructed as early as the first century BCE, and this tomb style continued to be built into the first half of the second century CE[15] before being phased out and replaced by the later temple tombs.[16] These buildings constitute prominent landmarks in the central urban landscape of Palmyra, mirroring the cityscape in which Palmyrenes moved through their everyday lives, and ensuring that the graves of their ancestors remained in full sight.[17] Such prominent funerary monuments would have reminded both locals and visitors to the city of the rich local heritage that underpinned Palmyrene society.

As with the archeological and written evidence for lived Palmyrene society examined in Chapter 2, much of the evidence for how Palmyrenes treated their dead comes from the burials of the elite, although there is some evidence that freedmen might also on occasion have been interred in these monumental tombs, with seven inscriptions from funerary monuments referring to freedmen.[18] However, it seems that these individuals were not "ordinary" but rather freedmen of some social standing.[19] It is unknown what happened to slaves after their death; we may assume that they were buried with the families who owned them, in line with what we know of their treatment in other regions in Antiquity. Even so, we should not assume that they received funerary portraits, and very few such monuments exist for individuals who fell outside the category of the Palmyrene elite.

The ordinary people of Palmyra would have been buried under much simpler conditions than the social elite, probably being interred in pit or shaft graves and without lavish grave goods. Some evidence to support this idea comes from a cemetery on the northeast outskirts of the city, which was built over in modern times.[20] Small grave stelae were set up for some of these graves, which suggests that the graves were marked in at least some cases.[21] Although Palmyra has a high number of monumental graves, the lower-status shaft or pit burials are difficult to locate and are often identified only by accident. For this reason, little attention has been paid to these graves; no systematic work has yet been carried out, and there is therefore no comprehensive overview of them available to us.[22] There is likewise very little evidence for the burial of infants and children. We know from funerary portraits that children could be buried in the elite graves.[23] However, portraits of children make up a relatively small number of funerary portraits. Burials of some infants and small children have been found during excavations of some hypogea. These indicate that small children could be buried directly under the floors of the graves, in pits or in vases,[24] a custom also known from other parts of the Roman world.[25]

Inhumation was the predominant burial practice in Palmyra up until the third century CE, and cremation appears to have been extremely rare.[26] There is some evidence of mummification, but according to Henning, this burial form seems to have been reserved only for certain groups who were of very high status.[27] In all grave types, and later in sarcophagi, which could hold several burials, bodies were inhumed having been wrapped in textiles. The material used to wrap bodies varied widely, ranging from basic woolens to richly decorated textiles, including imported Chinese silk.[28] After the deposition of the body, the burial niches would be closed with a mix of rubble stones and mortar, after which loculus reliefs with portraits of the deceased were added.

More than 1,300 funerary inscriptions have been recorded from the graves.[29] These inscriptions, which range from basic funerary inscriptions giving the name of the deceased, to foundation texts and cession inscriptions, clearly demonstrate that sepulchers were intended for family use and were usually founded by Palmyrene family fathers to commemorate the deceased.[30] A number of terms were used for such tombs, among them "houses of eternity" and *nefesh*, which translates as "breath," "soul," or "person" in Semitic languages.[31]

Grave goods have been attested from Palmyra, but finds have been sporadic, not least because most graves appear to have been disturbed or even looted in the post-Antique period. However, a Japanese archeological mission was able to produce an important publication of in-situ grave goods that offers an insight into the kind of funerary offerings included in Palmyrene burials. Finds included a wide range of jewelry such as beads, alongside worked bone objects; metal and bronze objects; ceramic vessels such as incense burners; a wide range of different glass items; lamps and shells; and plaster and stucco items.[32] These finds—alongside the study of the textiles used to wrap the bodies, which were often high-quality imports—do not just offer insights into the kinds of goods that were included in graves, but they also reveal clear examples of the wealth of the Palmyrene elite.[33]

Tower Tombs

The tower tombs of Palmyra, approximately 180 of which are still extant, were constructed from local limestone. They measured between 5 and 13 m (16 and 43 ft) in width on each side.[34] While the earliest tower tombs had only one or two stories, over time, the height of the tower tomb types increased, with more stories and more elaborate decorations being added, both internally and externally. A study of the most completely preserved monuments shows that some tower tombs were between 20 and 28 m (66 and 92 ft) in height and could have up to seven stories.[35] Fourteen tower tombs can be precisely dated through inscriptions.[36] The earliest examples of these tombs were built using a fairly soft limestone, but by the first century CE, new quarries had opened outside Palmyra offering hard limestone, and after that this limestone type was used as a building material for graves.[37] The harder limestone was less prone to weathering.[38] Wood does not seem to have played a role in the construction of these tombs.[39]

The tombs themselves stood on short plinths known as socles and had a central entrance that could be accessed via a staircase. Sometimes tombs located on slopes also featured grave chambers below ground.[40] The tower tombs also held built-in sarcophagi-style niches, as well as later sarcophagi.[41] However, when sarcophagi are found in tower tombs, they are always located on the ground floor, presumably because they were too heavy and difficult to transport to the tomb's upper levels.[42]

The architectural development of the tombs has been studied in detail by Henning, who demonstrates that the continuous development of building

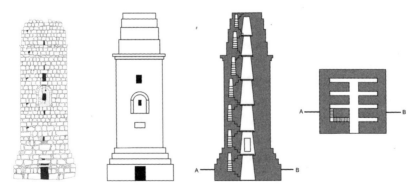

Figure 18 Elevation of Tower Tomb no. 71 and schematic view, section, and ground plan of a tower tomb (Courtesy of Agnes Henning).

Figure 19 Tomb of Elahbel, main chamber (Rubina Raja).

techniques, the location of staircases, and foundation constructions led to the ongoing increase in the size of tombs.[43] The largest tower tomb could in fact have held more than 300 burials, although we do not know whether this tomb—or other graves like it—were ever filled to their maximum capacity.[44] Not a single roof from any tower tomb has survived, and so we cannot say what form they would usually have taken.[45] Since no architectural elements have survived from the tombs to suggest that roofs were pyramidal, it seems most reasonable to assume that they were flat, which was the preferred roof-type seen in other buildings in Palmyra. Based on this assumption, Henning

argues that rituals could have taken place on the roofs of the graves.[46] This
is a likely conclusion, but given how little we know about grave rituals in
Palmyra, it should nonetheless be treated with significant caution.

Tombs could be decorated both inside and outside. Founder reliefs could
be inserted into large niches at the fronts of tombs, while architectural
decorations also embellished the towers on the outside. The earliest tower
tombs displayed funerary reliefs, the so-called loculus reliefs, on the exterior of their socles. These reliefs later developed to become the most commonly used form to commemorate the dead in Palmyra and were employed
throughout the Roman period, although they were moved from outside to
the interior of the grave monument. The reasons for this shift remain uncertain: perhaps being under shelter gave these reliefs better protection and
made them less prone to weathering so that they lasted longer, or perhaps
greater privacy was desired for the graves as they became increasingly monumentalized. It could even be a combination of both.

As tower tombs became increasingly monumentalized over time—a
point that would, in itself, have given them increasing prominence in the
Palmyrene landscape—more attention was also paid to the decoration
on the interior of these graves. They were embellished with architectural
decorations of various kinds, with stucco decorations on walls and ceilings,
and with wall paintings that have today largely disappeared. It is clear that
significant emphasis was paid to the interior of the tombs, and while much of
what we see today consists of white limestone portraits and stripped interiors,
the graves should be imagined as they once were—colorful spaces commemorating deceased family members. These tombs held the remains of families
over generations, with individuals usually commemorated through the display of so-called loculus reliefs: rectangular limestone slabs with carved high
reliefs that depicted the deceased either alone or sometimes with one or more
family members.

The Hypogea

The monumental hypogea, underground grave complexes, were introduced
in the second half of the first century CE and remained in use until around the
middle of the third century CE .[47] At one time, there were at least 170 of these
hypogea.[48] Since these complexes have collapsed over time or were gradually
covered by sand, they have been subject to significantly less looting than the

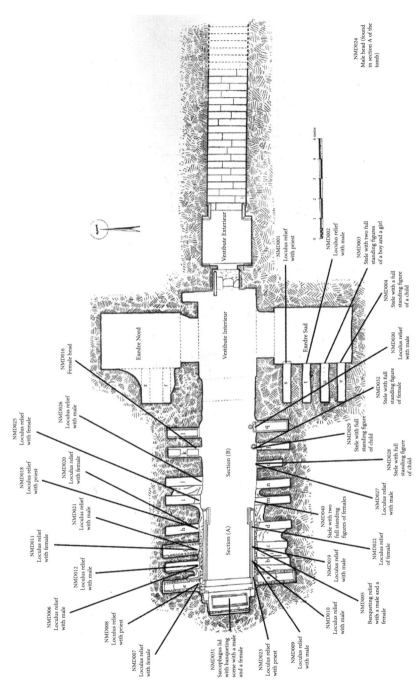

Figure 20 Hypogeum of Taai. All portraits still in-situ are marked (Rubina Raja and Palmyra Portrait Project). Plan adapted after Abdul-Hak, S. 1952.

NMD024
Male head (found in section A of the tomb)

NMD002
Loculus relief with male

NMD003
Stele with two full standing figures of a boy and a girl

NMD004
Stele with a full standing figure of a child

NMD001
Loculus relief with priest

NMD030
Loculus relief with male

NMD032
Stele with full standing figure of female

NMD029
Stele with full standing figure of child

NMD028
Stele with full standing figure of child

NMD040
Stele with two full standing figures of females

NMD027
Loculus relief with male

NMD022
Loculus relief of female

NMD019
Loculus relief with male

NMD005
Banqueting relief with a male and a female

NMD010
Loculus relief with male

NMD009
Loculus relief with male

NMD023
Loculus relief with priest

NMD031
Sarcophagus lid with banqueting scene with a male and a female

NMD007
Loculus relief with female

NMD008
Loculus relief with priest

NMD012
Loculus relief with male

NMD006
Loculus relief with male

NMD011
Loculus relief with female

NMD021
Loculus relief with male

NMD020
Loculus relief with female

NMD018
Loculus relief with priest

NMD025
Loculus relief with female

NMD026
Loculus relief with male

NMD016
Female head

Exedre Nord

Exedre Sud

Vestibute Interieur

Vestibute Exterieur

Section (A)

Section (B)

0 1 2 3 4 6 metre

tower tombs. These underground sepulchers were often large complexes cut directly into the bedrock under the sands of the desert landscape so that they could be extended gradually over time. Cutting the hypogea was difficult, due to the nature of the limestone, and so they were carved not only into the flat plains around Palmyra but also into the western and northwestern slopes of the surrounding hills. In many ways, the latter graves were more akin to burial caves, as they were not situated completely beneath the ground; nonetheless they followed the same plans as the hypogea.[49] The hypogea were found not only alongside roads but also a greater distance from Palmyra, which might reflect a difficulty in finding rock that was sufficiently stable for the hypogea to be cut safely.

The oldest known hypogeum from Palmyra was located behind the temple of Baalshamin and was a semi-subterranean tomb. It had a long corridor from which the burial niches branched off.[50] The oldest inscriptions relating to hypogea date to 81 CE and 87 CE, respectively, although we know that earlier hypogea existed,[51] while the youngest inscriptions date to either 232 or 242 CE.[52]

It is unknown how the hypogea might have been marked in Antiquity to ensure that they could clearly be seen by the inhabitants of Palmyra; but certainly they would not have attracted the same attention as the monumental tower tombs that hovered above the cityscape. The work undertaken by the Japanese mission at tomb F, a hypogeum in the southeastern necropolis, indicates that a colonnaded structure might have stood above the entrance to the stairs that led down into the tomb.[53] However, it is remarkable that out of so many known hypogea, there is so little evidence of structures above the ground that were connected to these monuments. Perhaps the hypogea, which came into use a little later than the tower tombs, simply better reflect Palmyrene social structure, in which family stood at the center and looked inward, closed around itself.

A rock-cut staircase or dromos would lead down to the entrance door of the underground graves. This opened up to a central aisle, at the end of which a founder relief or a central burial niche would often be located. The central niche would frequently contain reliefs depicting a banqueting scene, or it might be arranged as a dining space with reliefs on three sides.[54] Banqueting scenes might also be located on the side walls, in niches, or in the side aisles of the grave.[55] Sometimes a cession text would be located on the front of the grave, placed above the door on the lintel. However, the hypogea do not seem to have had elaborate facades. Located along the central aisle, which could be

10 to 20 m (33 to 67 ft) long, were burial niches and exedras, while several side aisles could be cut into the rock. In the vast majority of sepulchers, one aisle would branch on either each side of the central aisle, effectively creating an inverted T-shape for the grave.[56] In some hypogea, further aisles were evidently cut over time, indicating that these were flexible spaces that could be extended according to need.[57] These underground tombs clearly held certain advantages over tower tombs, being protected from weathering as well as open to adaptation over time, but it also makes them complex to understand as they were dynamic and changeable spaces. We also know that parts of these underground graves could, on occasion be sold off to other families, which involved taking out already existing burials and setting up new burial niches.[58]

Much like the tower tombs, the hypogea could be richly decorated with architectural ornamentation, stuccoed elements, and wall paintings produced in vivid colors (Plate 7).[59] The wall paintings that have survived up to the present day, although not abundant, reveal that tombs featured mythological scenes from Graeco-Roman mythology rather than from the Palmyrene religious sphere—Nikes and Eagles, for example—as well as portraits, sometimes with added names. These appear to have formed an important part of what was apparently a rich element of the funerary decoration, but they are now virtually lost to us. As mentioned in Chapter 2, in the tomb of Hairan, images of the honorific statues of both Hairan and his wife were painted onto the side walls of the niche where the couple had presumably been interred. These painted representations provide an important insight into the importance of honorific statues in Palmyra, including for women, a point we return to below.[60] It is in this hypogea that many of the grave goods mentioned earlier were found. Some of these funerary objects were found together with the burials; others were buried in small pits in the ground, perhaps indicating ritual activity that might have occurred after the burial. Some hypogea also have wells that are located close to the entrance and that might also have had some kind of ritual function.[61]

Temple or House Tombs

The third main type of grave monument to be found in Palmyra was the so-called house or temple tomb. These monuments were so named because they often had facades that were reminiscent of temple architecture, but they

Figure 21 Temple Tomb no. 86, reconstructed elevation of the facade (Rubina Raja).

could also be two to three stories in height and featuring a peristyle court-yard, leading to their designation as house tombs (Figs. 21–22).[62] These grave monuments were introduced in the first half of the second century CE, just as the tower tombs began to fall out of favor, and they continued to be built right into the third century CE.[63] Dates recorded on foundation inscriptions on certain tombs cover a span of time between 143 and 253 CE.[64] In contrast to the tower tombs, some house or temple tombs had a central location in Palmyra's cityscape, with the so-called Funerary Temple, for example, located directly on the main street.[65] Around seventy of these tombs have been recorded, making this the smallest category of the three main types of elite graves identified. Today, many of these graves are so heavily fragmented that they resemble little more than heaps of rubble in the landscape, a conse-quence both of structural collapse and of pillaging.

Palmyra's temple tombs stood on podiums and had facades with pilaster columns, entablatures, and pseudo-pediments that were placed in front of the otherwise flat roofs of the graves.[66] They lined the streets of the necrop-olis and would have been notable monuments in the necropolis landscape, due both to their height and their central courtyard. This courtyard opened to the upper stories as well, and some tombs were not roofed, allowing light

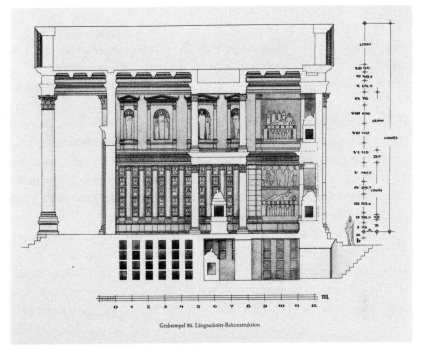

Grabtempel 86. Längsschnitt-Rekonstruktion

Figure 22 Section and reconstruction of the inner design of Temple Tomb no. 86 (Public domain, Universitätsbibliothek Heidelberg/Wiegand, T. 1932, Palmyra—Ergebnisse der Expeditionen von 1902 und 1917 (Tafeln)/plate 41).

to stream into the building.[67] Within the tombs, burial niches were located along the inside of the walls, and sarcophagi were often placed in niches. The house or temple tombs were the most stylistically elaborate and refined of the three main types of grave monuments in Palmyra. The facades of tombs seem to have varied significantly, and must have provided the families who owned the tombs with a possibility to show off different styles and types of ornamentation, to adapt the monument to their private taste, and to exhibit their wealth to wider society. In this, they offer a contrast with what we know of both the hypogea and the simpler facades of tower tombs. They also demonstrate what appears to have been a wider focus on the incorporation of Hellenistic and Roman architectural traits into Palmyrene buildings, thus emulating contemporary monuments known from Alexandria or Rome.[68] Nonetheless, the same burial customs were followed here as elsewhere in the city: inhumation burials in loculus niches (horizontal burial niches), and later on, in sarcophagi.

The Meaning of the Graves

The various grave types were mixed in the necropoleis around Palmyra. This suggests that these houses of the dead must have been every bit as dynamic and open to change as Palmyra's living social center. However, the grave complexes, which at the most recent count number more than 500, give very different insights into Palmyrene society than the evidence from the city's public and religious spheres.[69] The monumental tombs described above were reserved for Palmyra's elite, and many of these buildings were in use for several centuries. Reference to these tombs in the local Palmyrene Aramaic dialect as "houses of eternity" occurs from as early as the late first century BCE (Fig. 23).[70] Other terminology included "eternal monument" or "in eternity," which could be used to refer to specific parts of the monuments.[71] These inscriptions do not necessarily reflect a belief in an afterlife but rather should be understood pragmatically; these monuments signified both the importance of the families inhumed there and the legacy that they bequeathed to following generations. The tombs should thus be seen as expressions of social

Figure 23 Lintel over the entrance of the hypogeum of 'Atenatan, with an inscription (After Ingholt 1935, pl. XXIV, 2).

status and wealth, and they underline the ways that elite families in Palmyra were able to hold on to their power and influence for centuries.[72] There is in fact no evidence from either the funerary or religious sphere to show that Palmyrenes believed in an afterlife.[73] The emphasis given to elaborate burials seems therefore to have focused on commemorating the deceased, providing a way of expressing grief and sorrow at a family member's death at the same time as providing a timely reminder of the importance and high social status of those who still lived.[74]

The term *nefesh*, discussed earlier in relation to tombs, was also used to refer specifically to funerary portraits. The term means breath, or soul, or spirit of the deceased, and it was a well-known commemoration form from the Near East.[75] Thus just as the *baetyls*—the stone stelae that were a widespread phenomenon in the region—were termed the "house of the god," so the nefesh can be interpreted as "house of the soul."[76] It is a term that is widespread from funerary contexts both within Palmyra itself and more generally across the wider region, including in Petra and Palestine.[77] In the Roman period, the meaning of the term seems to have widened, and nefesh could be applied to a simple grave stele as well as to a monumental tomb. In Palmyra, a bilingual inscription refers to one of the tower tombs as both a nefesh and στήλη (stele).[78] Perhaps then, nefesh, when used alongside the Greek term stele, was meant to signify that the tombs contained the "souls" of an entire family. In this case, it is likely that nefesh was simply used as an alternative wording to the customary Aramaic *QBR'*, or tomb.[79] While it remains unclear whether the term nefesh held any wider religious significance or referred to beliefs in an afterlife in Roman-period Palmyra, the use of this term alongside the Greek stele does seem to suggest that it carried a more pragmatic meaning.

Funerary Portraits

Alongside the construction of the first tower tombs in Palmyra came the introduction of the funerary portrait tradition. This practice of carving images of the deceased and the person's wider family in relief on a stone slab, often accompanied by a short text inscribed next to the portrait, continued up until the sack of Palmyra in 272 CE. These relief portraits are known as loculus reliefs, and as recent research has shown, they make up the largest corpus of funerary portraits produced in any one place in the Roman world. More than

4,000 of these carvings are still extant, and they have been studied in depth by the Palmyra Portrait Project.[80]

An examination of Palmyra's loculus reliefs provides unique insight into both the continuity and changes in tradition that occurred during the Roman period and sheds light on previously unknown elements of Palmyrene society. Studied on a smaller scale, these reliefs make it possible to trace otherwise hidden trends, such as changes in clothing and fashions, gender balance in grave portrayals, the social role of women and children, the nature of Palmyrene priesthoods, and fluctuating traditions of workshops.[81] However, a broader chronological overview of the portraits, with an eye to the flow and fluctuations of the production process, makes it possible to speculate on events and developments that would have impacted Palmyrene society at all levels.[82]

So far, a total of 2,050 relief slabs have been collected from graves, featuring an incredible 3,002 portraits of individuals (Figs. 24–26), as well as twenty wall-paintings. Of these, there are 1,654 male portraits, 238 of which portray Palmyrene priests. The remaining 1,416 depict Palmyrene men, dressed typically in Graeco-Roman-style garb or Parthian-inspired banqueting dress. Of the rest, 1,025 of the portraits show women and 230 portray children. In addition to these, there are 139 portraits that are too badly preserved for us to determine the gender, as well as 671 heads and fragments of figures that likely come from funerary contexts.

Alongside these portraits, a total of 1,360 Palmyrene funerary inscriptions have been collected. For almost the whole three centuries in which these portraits were produced, the inscriptions of the funerary sphere were almost exclusively written in the local language (Fig. 27). This is in clear contrast to the extreme bilingualism found on publicly displayed monuments and further indicates that the funerary sphere had a decided focus on local society. These Palmyrene Aramaic funerary inscriptions are also for the most part pragmatic; they record the name of the deceased, together with the individual's genealogy over several generations. In contrast, some thirty-nine Greek inscriptions occur across thirty-six objects—in certain cases limited to just a single word—while a mere five funerary inscriptions were written in Latin; it is noteworthy that all of these relate either to non-Palmyrenes or else to individuals linked with the Roman army (Fig. 28).[83] None of these Latin inscriptions come with a Palmyrene counterpart, but they can all be dated on stylistic grounds to the second half of the second century CE. The Greek inscriptions show a little more variation (Fig. 29). Five items simply have Greek words such as "eternity," which are found inscribed onto images of

Figure 24 Loculus relief depicting a male (Nurbel), 181 CE. Metropolitan Museum of Art, New York, 02.29.4, Purchase, 1902 (Courtesy of the Metropolitan Museum of Art).

keys that are held by the deceased, while thirteen comprise bilingual Greek/ Palmyrene Aramaic inscriptions on funerary reliefs.[84] All of these seem to commemorate Palmyrenes, except for one, which explicitly states that the deceased was a settler from the colony Berytus. Nine inscriptions recorded from eight objects are written only in Greek, but they all record Palmyrene names. Like their Latin counterparts, these almost all stem from the second half of the second century CE, except for two that are slightly earlier and two that are a little later.[85] The sporadic use of Greek and in particular Latin, together with their almost exclusive confinement to the second half of the second century CE, suggests that these inscriptions either reflect a trend that was at that time in fashion, or else in the case of Latin, belong to non-Palmyrenes. From a linguistic perspective, however, it is fair to say that the funerary sphere remained very firmly Palmyrene for a period of almost three centuries.

The limestone loculus portraits were carved in deep relief on rectangular slabs (Figs. 24–29). They depicted the entire upper body of the deceased person as a bust relief, often accompanied by other members of the family and frequently with an inscription that not only named the deceased but also listed the family genealogy, sometimes going as far back as five generations.[86] These portraits were therefore more than just portraits; the body, often shown down to the navel area, functioned as a space that could be used for the display of further attributes. The loculus slabs were usually set up inside Palmyrene graves, where they were used to close off the burial niches in the graves,[87] although in the early period they also occasionally appeared outside graves.[88] In the late first century CE, large limestone sarcophagi also became a popular elite funerary monument in monumental graves (Fig. 30).[89] The lids of these could display numerous family members, but they invariably show a reclining family

Figure 25 Loculus relief depicting a female, the so-called Beauty of Palmyra. Ny Carlsberg Glyptotek, Copenhagen, IN 2795 (Photo: Ny Carlsberg Glyptotek, Copenhagen/Anders Sune Berg).

father, the *pater familias,* flanked by his seated wife and surrounded by standing children and other family members. Over 600 such sarcophagi existed in Palmyra, which is an extremely high number.[90] While fifty graves in Palmyra still hold in-situ portraits, the vast majority of extant Palmyrene funerary portraiture comes from unknown contexts, having been dispersed into collections across the world since the late nineteenth century.[91] Nonetheless, these portraits are absolutely crucial to our understanding of ancient Palmyra. They are an extraordinary source of evidence not just for the funerary sphere in Palmyra but also for elsewhere in the region and the wider Roman world, and they provide unique insights into the ways families, and particularly the Palmyrene elite, celebrated and mourned their dead.

Portraits and the Funerary Sphere

The portraiture of Palmyra is traditionally divided into two categories, public and funerary portraits, although as noted in Chapter 2, relatively little of the

Figure 26 Loculus relief depicting two males and a child. Ny Carlsberg Glyptotek, Copenhagen, IN 1027 (Photo: Ny Carlsberg Glyptotek, Copenhagen/ Anders Sune Berg).

Figure 27　Palmyrene Aramaic inscription on a loculus relief. Ny Carlsberg Glyptotek, Copenhagen, IN 1052 (Photo: Ny Carlsberg Glyptotek, Copenhagen/ Anders Sune Berg).

public statuary has survived, in contrast to the large number of extant funerary reliefs.

By far the most common form of funerary portrait was the locally produced limestone bust relief, which was carved onto a square or rectangular loculus slab and was commonly used to cover a burial niche within a tomb. The loculi were arranged like shelves, and several hundred could be found within one tomb, effectively forming a vast portrait gallery that represented generations of Palmyrenes from the same family. Over the course of the first century CE, these loculus busts appear to have gradually replaced an earlier form of commemorative decoration known from Palmyra, namely, the free-standing funerary stelae with rounded tops that depicted full-length figures in relief in a manner more akin to Hellenistic models.[92] However, the stele-motif can also be identified on loculus slabs from the first centuries CE, which represent the full, albeit smaller-than-life-size figures of both

Figure 28 Loculus relief with Latin inscription. Musée du Louvre, Paris, AO 14924 (Rubina Raja and Palmyra Portrait Project, Ingholt Archive at Ny Carlsberg Glyptotek, PS 798).

adults and children (Fig. 31).[93] Loculus slabs, in contrast, depict what we might often understand as the "bust," including head—often with elaborate headgear in the case of the women—neck and shoulders, arms, and hands. However, in these reliefs, the individual represented often carries attributes in the hands, or else uses the hands to make gestures. As such, these images are far more than mere busts, and so a more reasonable term for them might be "half-figures."

The immediate models for loculus reliefs are thought to be the reliefs of freedmen that were produced in their hundreds in Rome, particularly in the Augustan period.[94] However, it seems somewhat unlikely that Palmyra's elite would be keen to invest in representations of themselves in the shape of Roman freedmen, so perhaps other comparisons need to be sought to better understand the cultural context around the development of the Palmyrene portrait habit. Indeed, a more likely source of inspiration for the loculus

Figure 29 Loculus relief with bilingual inscription. Musée du Louvre, Paris, AO1556 (Rubina Raja and Palmyra Portrait Project, Ingholt Archive at Ny Carlsberg Glyptotek, PS 1010).

reliefs might have been the tradition of honorific statues, which had existed since the Hellenistic period in the East. These statues typically represented an individual wearing the Greek-style chiton and himation, often holding a book scroll.[95] The Palmyrene loculus reliefs might therefore best be interpreted as "excerpts" or "citations" of full-sized honorific statues that had been transferred into the funerary sphere in a slightly adapted model but that had retained the attention given to pose, dress, and even attributes.[96] The depictions of Palmyrene men found in this context are relatively conservative,[97] although in contrast to the public statuary, in which the male representations sometimes wear togas, the prevailing dress codes revealed in funerary portraiture were the Greek style (see Fig. 26), or else Parthian or Persian attire (see Fig. 32). Togas are rare in funerary representations.[98] Representations of Palmyrene women, in contrast, were quite different. These clearly adhere to local styles of dress, headgear, and jewelry types, and

Figure 30 Sarcophagus from the hypogeum of Malku, 220–240 CE. National Museum of Damascus, Damascus, 10.941 (Rubina Raja and Palmyra Portrait Project, Ingholt Archive at Ny Carlsberg Glyptotek, PS 1094).

through these detailed reliefs, we can even trace the way in which styles and fashions changed over time.

The early grave-stelae markers and the stelae loculus slabs appear to have drawn on Hellenistic motifs, which indicates that a portrait tradition might already have been established in Palmyra in this period.[99] Regardless of whether the Palmyrene loculus portraits drew on earlier regional models, they were very distinctive and appear to have deliberately made use of styles that were different to those found in Roman imperial and provincial models. As such, they were recognizably Palmyrene. This is important, given that this funerary sculpture was never intended to be circulated outside of Palmyra, but was rather produced exclusively for the numerous tombs surrounding the city and thus created for an audience of family, not foreigners. This is one factor that is commonly overlooked when discussing Palmyrene funerary portraiture, but it must be remembered that these portraits were not official

Figure 31 Stele depicting a standing male (Sha'del), 172 CE. Metropolitan Museum of Art, New York, 02.29.6, Purchase, 1902 (Courtesy of Metropolitan Museum of Art).

portraits, but rather had a specific purpose: the commemoration of the dead by the private, familial circle.[100]

One such example that clearly, if poignantly, shows the trajectory between public and funerary sculpture is that of the wall paintings in the Hypogeum of Hairan (Plate 8). This was excavated by Harald Ingholt and partly published in 1932, with a particular emphasis given to the paintings.[101] Hairan's tomb held close-to-life-size wall paintings that represented honorific statues of both the deceased and his wife. These were painted on walls that flanked the central burial niches in one of the side *exedras* (recesses) in the grave. According to Ingholt's excavation diary, there were other painted elements in natural colors here, including an eagle, a male portrait in a medallion, Nikes, and floral motifs. Nonetheless, the central motifs were the two painted honorific statues, which faced each other from opposing walls.[102] To the right, on the sidewall of the exedra, a woman is painted. She stands 1.65 m (5.41 ft) high (including the base of the statue), and is 0.48 m (1.6 ft) wide. She is dressed in a green tunic with a red *clavus*, and a yellow himation is also painted, while her black hair is pulled back, with a row of curls visible across her forehead. Her himation is fastened with a brooch over her left shoulder, from which two keys are suspended—a brooch type only used by women in Palmyra.[103] A yellow veil is pulled over her hair, and she is wearing black closed shoes. The woman stands on a square tall base with a profile, a clear indication that this painting is not intended to be a representation of a person in the flesh, but is rather a painted representation of a sculpture in the round.

This is also true of the painting of the man, found on the left short side exedra wall, which stands 1.45 m (4.8 ft) in height including the base of the statue, and 0.45 m (1.5 ft) wide. An inscription added above his head identifies this individual as Ḥairan, son of Taimarsou. He has brown curly hair and wears a yellow tunic with a black clavus running over his right shoulder and down the front of his garb. He wears a yellow himation of the "arm-sling" type, with red bands along the edges and thicker finishing stripes on the lower left side, as well as tassels. Like his wife, he wears black shoes. The painting features red and green vine motifs, above which part of a pediment or architrave has been added, giving the impression that the statue is located in front of a building, or else in a niche either within or outside a building. These two wall paintings are thus clearly representations, not of the two individuals themselves, but of their honorific statues, which were set up in a public space to commemorate their importance to Palmyrene society, most likely as benefactors for some cause now unknown.[104] These two paintings provide important evidence of the sculptural habit in public Palmyra, but also show that Palmyrene craftsmen made clear choices about which styles to apply in different contexts. While the funerary limestone portraits in the grave would certainly have been executed in line with local funerary traditions, the paintings of the statues were deliberately done in a style that followed Roman imperial trends, both in hair and dress fashion. There was nothing provincial in Palmyra about stylistic choice. Rather there was an evident, high level of consciousness about exactly which styles should be employed in a given context, and why.

The positioning of loculus reliefs within the tombs was carefully adapted to meet the specific burial circumstances of Palmyra, where bodies were laid on shelves wrapped in textiles. The development of the loculus slab motifs, with their more-than-bust-shaped representations, can therefore be considered as a truly Palmyrene creation, which likely developed around the turn of the first millennium and spread out from Palmyra to other cities across the region.[105] Reliefs were not only used to cover burial niches, but could be placed in a range of locations within a tomb. They were used as decorations on walls, lintels, and coffers in the ceilings, and might be added to gables both inside and on the exterior of a tomb. When featured on walls and ceilings, they were often painted or made in stucco, showing that these motifs could be executed in material other than limestone. In these cases, it can be seen that the portraiture was not connected with a specific burial, but was instead used to signify the importance of the family, including the individual who founded the tomb and other family members. Sometimes these busts were accompanied by inscriptions, but more often than not these have not survived, making it an impossible task to connect each portrait with the name of the individual they were meant to represent.

Another type of relief used as funerary commemoration was the banqueting relief (Fig. 32), which depicted dining scenes, most often featuring reclining men and their family members or servants.[106] These scenes were not representations of funerary banquets but instead showed the deceased when still alive.[107] In the later first century CE, the first limestone sarcophagi begin to appear in tombs. These lavish monuments could depict more than ten family members dispersed across the lid and the box of the sarcophagus itself. The lids typically featured banqueting scenes, which would often show the male head of the family reclining on a kline, or couch, with his wife seated at the end of the kline and children standing behind. The box, meanwhile, was sometimes used for depictions of other individuals within the family. In both of these types of portraiture—the banqueting scenes and the sarcophagi—the men regularly appear wearing Parthian-inspired clothing, a fashion that features extensively in funerary portraiture.[108] Men would wear tunics that were sometimes decorated with pearl-like borders on the neckline or with broad bands of decorated textiles that could be attached to the front or along the finishing of the garment, to the arms, or at the bottom. These tunics were worn together with baggy, loose, and decorated trousers, and soft leather boots.

Representations of Palmyra's priestly class form another core category identified across funerary monuments. There are about 500 representations of priests in the funerary corpus (see Fig. 6).[109] In these reliefs, the priests are depicted wearing local and Parthian-inspired clothing, often including a decorated tunic with a cloak on top, which was fastened with a brooch on the shoulder,[110] and a cylindrical hat with a flat top, incorrectly termed a modius

Figure 32 Banquet relief, 180–240 CE. Musée du Louvre, Paris, AO2000 (Rubina Raja and Palmyra Portrait Project, Ingholt Archive at Ny Carlsberg Glyptotek, PS 73).

in scholarship until recently.[111] Often they hold a pitcher and bowl in their hands, a reference to the importance of the sacrificial activity that they led. On sarcophagi, numerous priests might be represented together, a reminder that due to the high social status awarded to priests in ancient Palmyra, and the need for elite families to retain this authority and influence, priesthoods were probably passed down or extended within families. It should not be assumed that Palmyrene priests performed their office constantly but rather that they served at certain points in time, and this seems to be indicated by a number of portraits in which Palmyrene men are shown with their priestly hat placed next to them on a pedestal.[112] A study of these portrait depictions suggests that Palmyrene priests were represented in a very distinctive, local way. The flat-topped priestly hats appear to have been unique to Palmyra, for example, as priests from elsewhere in the Roman world were usually shown sporting conical hats, while the rest of the priestly garb, although plausibly inspired by Parthian fashions, was nonetheless different from the outfits worn by other male members of Palmyra's social elite on the numerous banqueting reliefs.

Finally, there is one last group of funerary representations that should be mentioned in this discussion, although relatively little is known about them—namely, the freestanding statues that were located inside tombs. There are few of these, but given that they do not form a fixed part of the grave architecture and so would have been easier to loot or destroy than many of the other items outlined here, it is perhaps unsurprising that such items have largely disappeared over the centuries. However, a few fragments of such sculptures have survived in some tombs, including in the temple tomb known as Qasr Abjad (Fig. 33).[113]

Family Ties and Self-Representation

Palmyra's funerary sphere is a vast and complex area, but as this brief survey has shown, there is evidence from the extant funerary monuments and different representation types that there was an overarching and almost exclusive focus given to the family, its social status, and its heritage. In some graves in which the relief portraits and other funerary representations have survived in context, attempts have been made to reconstruct family genealogies.[114] This work is difficult because only first names, and never family names, were used in funerary inscriptions. Nonetheless, these attempts help to shed light on the manner in which Palmyrenes transformed tombs into portrait galleries with subtle or obvious connections between close and extended family.[115] It is also noteworthy that the Palmyrenes elected to focus on family and lineage in their funerary inscription and not civic office or professions, once again underlining the emphasis given to family within the funerary sphere.[116]

While a close examination of the complete corpus of Palmyrene funerary portraits reveals that the different and individualized details found in many portraits have often been overlooked, this kind of holistic overview also makes it possible to examine them as the product of a 300-year time span and to establish a distribution pattern based on the portrait style and the date of the objects on which the portraits were depicted.[117] This pattern clearly shows that there was a rapid increase in the production of funerary portraits at around the time that the site as a whole was undergoing urban

Figure 33 Male statue from the Qasr-Abjad tomb (Rubina Raja and Palmyra Portrait Project, Ingholt Archive at Ny Carlsberg Glyptotek, PS 998).

development. This steep increase from the middle of the second century CE onward also indicates that the city was prospering and expanding in the relative peace afforded by the Pax Romana, although this was offset by a steep drop in production between 160 CE and 180 CE, when it is likely that many of the city's inhabitants died from the Antonine Plague, and those who were left did not have the resources to produce many portraits. The period between 180 CE and 240 CE shows a return to stability and even prosperity, but this was offset by a further steep drop in the production of funerary portraits around 240 CE, apparently linked to the political and military instability in the East around this time, a point that is examined in Chapter 4, with the Persians leading attacks in the area.[118] As a result of this political and military tension, it would appear that the Palmyrenes elected to channel their resources in other directions than that of the funerary sphere. This trend was further compounded by the sack of Palmyra in 272 CE under Aurelian, which broadly marks the end of funerary portrait production, even though some tombs remained in use in the years after the city was sacked. It is striking that sociopolitical and cultural developments known from this time can so clearly be traced in the funerary portraiture, a point that further emphasizes the extraordinary nature of this material as well as the importance of considering the entire corpus in a holistic way.

The funerary material from Palmyra is quite unique when compared to material from other places across the Roman world. It comprises a corpus of tombs and representations of the Palmyrene elite from almost three centuries; studying it provides not only detailed insights into the ways families constructed their graves and commemorated their dead but also sheds light on the development of fashions and social trends. Above all, what this corpus appears to reveal is that members of the elite in Palmyra were very well aware of the various spheres in which they moved—whether funerary, public, or religious—and they also understood how these different contexts influenced behavior and choices. The funerary sphere was thus very much family focused; it looked internally rather than orienting itself outward toward broader social expectations. And although the corpus is limited to a set of parameters such as sculptural developments and grave types, this funerary material also makes it possible to trace historical events, such as the regional strife of the third century, that would otherwise not be visible in Palmyrene material culture.

4

Making—and Breaking—Ties

Palmyra, Rome, and Parthia

Part of the fascination that Palmyra continues to inspire lies in the fact that the structure of this long-disappeared desert society is quite foreign to us, difficult to fathom and wreathed in layers of later myth and romanticism. It takes much imagination to draw together the bare bones of our scattered evidence from the desert sands, flesh them out with a fully formed image of society, and clothe them with a useful narrative about how Palmyra functioned at its zenith. The city's circumstances were very different from those of other cities in the Near East such as the heavily urbanized areas of the Decapolis and Tetrapolis or the coastal areas that were brought under Roman influence with Pompey's conquest of the East in the 60s BCE.[1] There is no doubt that Palmyrene society was extremely united, tightly knit, and—to a large extent—quite closed, even though the families must have constantly jostled one another as they competed for local social status and wealth. Yet conversely, much of this status and wealth could have been derived only by looking outward: Roman Palmyra's riches were based on trade, largely organized by the male elites, with contacts that extended far beyond the realms ever experienced by most Palmyrenes.[2] Developing and maintaining these trading interests outside of Palmyra must have demanded an extreme social and cultural consensus in local society managed by the local elite infrastructure, and crucially it also demanded a degree of "Fingerspitzengefühl"—a combination of tact, diplomacy, and intuitive flair—to dealing with the ruling empires of Rome and Parthia located either side of Palmyra.[3] This aspect has, however, received little attention in accounts of Palmyra's history, perhaps because it is simply assumed knowledge.

We often—and with good reason—end up situating Palmyra in the field of conflict between Rome and Parthia, just as Pliny did in his description of the city.[4] However, Palmyra was more than just a buffer zone or punching ball between two empires that were often in conflict with one other. Palmyrene society was rapidly able to adapt to changing circumstances, as already seen,

Pearl of the Desert. Rubina Raja, Oxford University Press. © Oxford University Press 2022.
DOI: 10.1093/oso/9780190852221.003.0004

for example, in the city's funerary sculpture and the public use of bilingualism. While Palmyra was indeed located geographically between Rome and Parthia, the city's population undoubtedly saw the world from its own perspective and it developed strong local traditions, perhaps in response to the city's isolated but often exposed location in a borderland.

On the one hand, the emphasis given to local culture is perhaps surprising; one might expect Palmyra, caught between two large empires, to be buffeted by whatever trends swept toward them over the desert from both Parthia and Rome. On the other hand, societies situated in what anthropologists have termed the "Middle Ground" have in fact been shown to have a greater resilience to outside influence, being able to develop and maintain strong identities as a way of staying adaptable in the face of opposing influences;[5] and this appears to have been the case in Palmyra. Certainly, as shown in previous chapters, there is clear evidence of both Roman and Parthian influence in Palmyra. The architecture of the city, especially monuments such as the Temple of Bel, the theater, the colonnaded streets, and the agora are all good examples of these influences and the particular ways they were fused and consolidated within a Palmyrene framework. So, too, are the clothing styles that we encounter in the city's vast iconographic corpus, as well as the several hundred Greek inscriptions and small handful of Latin inscriptions derived from the public sphere. Crucially, however, Palmyrene society was also able to deviate from, and to adapt these external influences to construct an exclusively local world.[6] This is shown most clearly in the evidence from the funerary and the religious spheres, where tomb architecture and decoration and the so-called banqueting tesserae clearly exemplify the Palmyrene ability to switch codes according to sociocultural context.

While recent archeological work in Palmyra has shown that some construction activities date back to as early as the third century BCE, the settlement's exact nature and the extent to which the city was already developed at this time remain unclear, with far more, and more focused, archeological fieldwork needed to gain a solid overview of the Hellenistic-period phases of the settlement.[7] A well from the second century BCE certainly indicates a more stable human presence at the site at this time,[8] as shown by Michael Sommer, but the evidence shows that it is only in the first century BCE that we start to see a real neighborhood with city traits emerging.[9] Parthian imitations of Western-type ceramics can be identified in Palmyra from as early as the mid-second century BCE, and these imports remain in the material evidence for some four centuries, with an active increase in the second century CE.[10] Sommer has, probably correctly, argued for a growing Parthian influence from 129 BCE onward, when Phraates II, the son of the Parthian ruler Mithradates I (r. 165–132 BCE), defeated the Seleucids under Anthiochus VII at the Battle of Ecbatana.[11] This increase in influence can to a degree be traced in the material evidence; but the evidence nonetheless remains slight, largely due to the relative lack of well-published excavations.

It is also unclear what kind of impact an increase in Parthian influence might have made on everyday life in Palmyra. No monumental remains from this period have yet been excavated in Palmyra, and so we cannot say whether the architecture of this period, for example, had a heavily Eastern influence. The city of Dura-Europos, located farther to the east along the Euphrates, might perhaps constitute the best comparison.[12] However, this settlement was also a garrison town, with a different population and sociocultural structure than that of Palmyra.[13] Cultural, religious, and social influences in Dura-Europos were drawn from a different tapestry of networks that would have included Greek veterans, merchants from the East, and from 129 BCE, a clear Parthian influence,[14] while Palmyra, in contrast, was subject to Rome from around the turn of the millennium. Although the situation in the borderlands between Rome and Parthia has been the subject of much scholarly discussion in the past two decades, with an overarching consensus being that a nuanced perspective is required, it remains the case that Dura-Europos and Palmyra should be seen as cities with different political situations and therefore different interests.[15]

Palmyra, Rome, and Parthia—Interrelations

While Palmyra undoubtedly retained its own local perspectives and traditions, its development cannot be considered in isolation but must instead be examined in the broader context of the city's relationships with Parthia and with the Romans, who exercised a strong presence in the Near East from the middle of the first century BCE until the beginning of the third century CE.[16] While it can be argued that Palmyrene society retained its own identity, Roman rule must surely have had some impact on the structure of civic life, with the city becoming increasingly influenced—and entangled—with the Roman imperial system and its provincial government in the first centuries CE. At the same time, the ever-present and often fluctuating tensions between Rome and Parthia would most assuredly also have been felt within Palmyrene society.

The period before the arrival of the Romans in the region is somewhat hazy in our knowledge. Before Pompey's conquest of the Near East, did Palmyra belong to what remained of the fading Seleucid Empire, or should it be understood better as an independent merchant state?[17] Neither model fully answers all questions. As Jean-Baptiste Yon first suggested, we might do best to think about Palmyra as "a client state without kings" in the period before new civic institutions began to develop. This argument is based on the finding that several leading families repeatedly appear in the inscriptional evidence from the city in the centuries following the introduction of Roman rule.[18] Yon's argument finds further support in the evidence for a high number of priests in Palmyra throughout the Roman period. Almost 500 representations of priests are known, the majority of which are from the funerary sphere, and the clear iconographic emphasis given to these individuals seemingly points to the connection between religious role and social status rather than to the importance of office of priesthood.[19] As noted in Chapter 3, the representations of priests on funerary reliefs suggest that the priesthood was as much a symbol of status as a religious office—and one that many Palmyrene male elites would hold at some point in time.

Roman influence in Palmyra increased over time as interest in the Near East intensified in both the Roman state and its emperors. The Pax Romana had brought stability to the region and provided a basis on which urban societies could develop, but the subsequent increase in wealth also intensified Roman interest. Under the emperor Augustus (r. 27 BCE–14 CE), relationships between Rome and Parthia can already be identified via inscriptions that also mention Palmyrenes. However, it was during the reign of Augustus's successor, Tiberius (r. 14–37 CE), that Roman attention to the Near East increased markedly. Tiberius appears to have had a far greater interest in the Empire's eastern provinces than did Augustus, and Tiberius's adopted son, Germanicus, spent time traveling in this region. Thus, when Antiochus III, the ruler of the kingdom of Commagene (today part of eastern Turkey), died in 17 CE, the country was absorbed into the Roman province of Syria. The kingdom of Cappadocia (also now a part of modern-day Turkey) followed in the same year. The Roman expansion in the East, and Roman interests in Palmyra, can be linked to Palmyra's rise to prominence as an important caravan city and nodal point for luxury trade between East and West.[20] In one fragmented Palmyrene inscription found during the demolition of a house in the old village of Palmyra, in the courtyard of the Sanctuary of Bel, for example, Germanicus is said to have sent an individual named Alexandros from Palmyra to Mesene near the Persian Gulf to visit a *rbz*, in all probability a local ruler, as well as to Sampsigeramus, the king of Emesa. This inscription might indicate that Germanicus was building on already existing Palmyrene trading links with these regions.[21]

One of Palmyra's few Latin inscriptions comes from the cella of the Temple of Bel. This is a dedication by one Minucius Rufus, the legatus of the legion *X Fretensis*, to Drusus, Tiberius Augustus, and Germanicus, IMPERATORIBUS.[22] Evidently, three statues were established somewhere in the sanctuary, an event that must have occurred in the small interval between Tiberius's accession in 14 CE and Germanicus's death in 19 CE, and the inscription thus provides one of our earliest pieces of evidence that Palmyra was firmly under Roman rule at this time. A milestone on a road leading from Palmyra to the Euphrates and dating from the reign of Vespasian (r. 69–79 CE) testifies that the region was integrated into the Roman road network.[23]

The first attestation to Palmyra's *demos*, or citizen body, dates from an inscription from 24 CE added to the base of a statue that honored an individual named Malku. According to this inscription, written in Greek, the statue had been dedicated to its subject by the demos of Palmyra.[24] A later inscription from Palmyra dating to 74 CE attests to the *boule*, or city council of Palmyra, as well as the demos, demonstrating that by this time Greek-named institutions had been firmly adopted by, and established in, Palmyrene civic society.[25] However, it is only from the rule of Hadrian (r. 117–138 CE) onward that we find more extensive evidence about the civic organization of the city. The Tax Tariff discussed in previous chapters, for example, informs us about various offices, such as those of *proedros* (president), *grammateus* (secretary), *archontes* (magistrates), and *syndikos* (advocate), in a clear indication that offices known from numerous other Roman cities in the Near East had also become established in Palmyrene society. In 131 CE, Hadrian visited the city as part of his grand tour of the Near East. While this has been seen by some as a particular honor for Palmyra, it should be remembered that Hadrian visited numerous other cities in the region in order to emphasize Roman domination and bolster local political support. Certainly it seems to have been effective; Palmyrenes were strong supporters of the Roman emperor at this point, and after his visit, the city was renamed *Hadrianè Tadmor* (*hdryn' tdmr*), most likely a title given to the city by Palmyra's leading body of citizens.[26] There has been discussion about whether the city was also granted status as a free city at this time, but it remains uncertain.[27]

From as early as the Trajanic period (98–117 CE), Palmyra was important to Roman military interests, both for its location and for its highly renowned archers, who served throughout the Roman army. However, only in the later decades of the second century CE was a Roman garrison encamped in Palmyra, most probably during the reign of Lucius Verus (r. 161–169) in connection with his Parthian campaign and the subsequent need for an increased Roman military presence in Syria and Mesopotamia.[28] We also have evidence from Dura-Europa that the *Cohors XX Palmyrenorum*, an auxiliary cohort of the army that was most likely instituted around 170 CE, was stationed in the city. Evidence shows that Palmyrenes continued to play a role within the Roman army until into the third century CE.[29]

Palmyra was a pivotal force in the trade network of the Roman Empire in the third century, well consolidated as a city with what might arguably be considered a monopoly on large parts of the East-West moving trade. It gave the city a special standing, and when the Antonines, an imperial family originating from Syrian elite, decided to build up support for the Syrian region in general, Palmyra became one of the leading cities. During the reign of Septimius Severus (r. 192–211), the province of Syria was divided into two separate entities, Syria Coele in the north, and Syria Phoenice in the south, with Palmyra belonging to the latter. In 212 CE, under either Septimius Severus or his sometime co-emperor Caracalla (r. 198–217), Palmyra became a *colonia*, a Roman colony, like many other cities in the Near East, and received *ius italicum*.[30] Most free Palmyrenes would by this time have received Roman citizenship. Becoming a colonia and receiving citizenship were honors granted by the Roman state that became relatively common in this period; extending such rights beyond the central Roman area was a useful political tool with which the emperor could influence his subjects, earning their loyalty and shoring up his power base. This was particularly important in border regions, which tended to have more political and military instability than the secure central regions.[31]

By the middle of the third century CE, Palmyra seems to have been fully integrated into the Roman imperial system, something reflected in the structure of the political institutions in the city.[32] Palmyra's elite began to demonstrate a clear commitment to the Roman emperor and became involved in the Roman imperial administration.[33] There is further evidence of new titles from this time, such as the Greek *strategos*, previously used only in the army, which came to signify the highest civil annual magistrates of the city, as well as *duumvir*, *aediles*, and *agoranomos*.[34] Indeed, the visit of Severus Alexander to Palmyra in 232 CE is known to us through an inscription that honors a duumvir of the city.[35] The inscription, however, dates to 242/243 CE and honors Julius Aurelius Zenobios.[36] Honorific inscriptions from the city center's public spaces, meanwhile, reflect an increasing emphasis on expressions of loyalty toward the Roman Empire and its ruler.[37] Yet as noted in previous chapters, for all that Palmyrenes consensually and fully integrated themselves into the Roman imperial civic system, they still retained their own local language for public and particularly funerary inscriptions, and they consciously held onto their own strong local identity.

It was also in this context that the city saw a period of unrest leading up to efforts to break from the Roman Empire and gain full freedom and control. As the political climate in the region became increasingly tense, it seems possible that Palmyra's close links with Rome, including a Palmyrene presence in the Roman army, could have affected the way the city traded with its neighbors to the east, although if this were the case, it is not especially visible in the evidence. Michael Sommer has collected the inscriptions that bear witness to the presence of trade caravans in Palmyra,[38] and his research suggests that the number of caravans peaked first in the first half of the second century CE, before tailing off and then peaking again in the late second century CE. These findings, however, are drawn from a limited dataset of only thirty-one inscriptions, and as such they do not offer a solid statistical base on which to found conclusions about fluctuations in Palmyrene trade. They could equally be seen as reflecting changes in epigraphical habits over time, trends that in part have been impacted by changing rulership in Palmyra and the gradual concentration of power in the hands of Odaenathus, Zenobia's husband, in the third century CE.[39] These events are discussed in more detail below, but we know that efforts to wrest power from Rome lasted for only a short while under Zenobia. Thereafter, the city was sacked in 272 CE by Emperor Aurelian's troops and it never regained its status as the pearl of the desert.

Palmyrenes Away from Palmyra

For many lower-ranked Palmyrenes, the city and its hinterlands would have been their world; other groups of people in the city were able to travel and to do so widely.[40] Those Palmyrenes who left the city tended to do so for two main reasons: for trade or because they were involved in the Roman military. In pursuit of these objectives, a Palmyrene presence has been identified in places as far-flung as Dura-Europos, the Arabian Gulf, Egypt, Rome, and Roman Britain (Fig. 34).[41] In all of these locations, Palmyrenes lived, worshipped, and traded. The historian Appian, writing in the second century CE, refers to Palmyrene trade in connection with Mark Antony's sack of Palmyra in 41 BCE—our earliest account of the city's commercial activities. Appian's account is not contemporary, and the accuracy of his descriptions has been

Figure 34 Funerary relief found in Roman Britain mentioning Regina, wife of a Palmyrene man (Arbeia Roman Fort & Museum, Tyne & Wear Archives & Museums/© Tyne & Wear Archives & Museums/Bridgeman).

questioned; nonetheless, it seems that his information on Palmyrene in-volvement in trade was correct to some extent.[42] Certainly, we can iden-tify imports in the material record from Palmyra in the first century CE. However, further evidence is needed for us to fully understand the nature of this trade.[43] Michael I. Rostovtzeff, writing in the 1930s, was correct to name Palmyra as an important caravan city in the East.[44] In the years since Rostovtzeff was working, research in this area, including evidence about the nature of Palmyrene trade toward the East, has grown hugely. A recent con-tribution by David Graf sums up the vast amounts of evidence in an elegant narrative about the complicated processes of Eastern trade routes in which the Palmyrenes were involved over centuries in the Roman period. The work by Eivind H. Seland and Katia Schörle has also given good insights into the evidence available to us about Palmyrenes abroad.[45]

Our evidence for a Palmyrene presence outside of Palmyra is fairly scattered, with most of the material available to us coming from the city of Dura-Europos, where Palmyrenes were present in significant numbers from the first century CE onward.[46] It is therefore not surprising that our earliest piece of evidence comes from this site, an inscription recording the dedi-cation of a temple to Yarhibol and Bel by Zabdibol of the tribe of Gadibol, and Malku of the tribe of the Kmr, in the year 33 BCE.[47] Palmyrene military units appear in Dura-Europos in the second century CE, and the auxiliary Cohors XX Palmyrenorum was garrisoned there between 208 and 256 CE. The most significant piece of evidence for the presence of Palmyrene troops is the wall painting in the pronaos of the so-called Temple of the Palmyrene Gods; this features the Roman tribune Julius Terentius performing a sacrifice, accompanied by a standard-bearer (Plate 9). The *tyches*, the protective gods, of both Dura-Europos and Palmyra, appear in the painting, and this mirrors their representation on a set of two well-known limestone reliefs from Dura-Europos (Plate 10).[48]

Palmyrene military units were also found elsewhere in the Roman world. We know, for example, that there was a strong presence of Palmyrene military units in the Balkan region, in an area that corresponds mostly to ancient Dacia. One such unit was the *Numerus Palmyrenorum sagittarorium* (Palmyrene archers).[49] Palmyrene soldiers also served in North Africa on the desert frontier, and this is evidenced by a gravestone that was set up in this area by a Palmyrene to commemorate his deceased wife.[50]

A fascinating piece of evidence to show long-distance travel for trade comes from the Dioscourides, the modern island of Socotra, in the northwestern

Indian Ocean. Here, in a vast cave alongside more than 200 other pieces of graffiti written in Brahmi, Bactrian, Greek, Axumite, and South Arabian scripts, a Palmyrene Aramaic inscription on a wooden tablet was found. This inscription, dated to 258 CE, tells us about the Palmyrene man Abgar, and can most likely be seen as a simple dedication made by Agbar on a journey through this area.[51] Evidence from a similarly exotic location comes in the form of an inscription in a sanctuary found outside the Hadramawt capital, Sabah, on the southern Arabian Peninsula. This text mentions two Palmyrenes dedicating to the local god together with the king of Hadramawt, two Indians, and two Chaldeans, and can most plausibly be interpreted as part of a Palmyrene embassy to the Hadramawt Kingdom.[52] These two inscriptions are quite unique in providing stand-alone evidence for travel, with most inscriptions about Palmyrenes located far from their home pertaining to the city's trade relationships.

Palmyrene traders were undoubtedly involved in a number of different trade routes since it was more lucrative to diversify economic interests and trade routes could be influenced by seasonal change (Fig. 35).[53] Inscriptions found within Palmyra attest to the city's connections with Babylon and Seleucia in the early part of the first century CE.[54] The majority of this evidence testifies

Figure 35 Sarcophagus fragment depicting a camel and a man with a ship in his left hand. Palmyra Museum, Palmyra, 1046/2249 (Courtesy of Jørgen Christian Meyer).

that the major trading cities of Vologesias and Spasinou Charax very quickly gained their status as the most important departure stations in the region for trade caravans returning to Palmyra.[55] Inscriptions also appear to point to the presence of a community of Palmyrene traders based in Vologesias, with a certain Palmyrene man named Soades being mentioned, together with his co-citizens within the city.[56] These individuals might have been based here in order to manage and develop trade in the Persian Gulf, and certainly this fits with possible—albeit disputed—evidence from the islands of Kharg and Tylos (Bahrain) that a Palmyrene acted as *satrap* (governor) here in 131 CE.[57]

A long-term Palmyrene presence is evidenced from Egypt, where an individual named Zabdallas dedicated a *propylon* together with "the merchants from Hadriane Palmyra" in an inscription that also mentions the "Palmyrene ship owners on the Red Sea."[58] Meanwhile an inscription from Denderah in Palmyrene Aramaic references a Palmyrene man and fellow traders.[59] These routes were secured by the Roman army, with forts located along the routes during the Trajanic period. The Palmyrene presence in Egypt was also augmented by individuals serving in the Roman army in this region—a military presence that should probably be understood in relation to trading interests in this area[60]—and dedications by these Palmyrenes, dating from 215/216 CE onward, can be found along the routes between Koptos on the Nile and the harbors of the Red Sea.[61] There is also evidence for the presence of various military units, with the body of evidence for a Palmyrene military presence in Egypt enlarging in recent decades.[62]

Elsewhere in the Near East, the site of the Beth She'arim (ancient Besara) necropolis in Palestine testifies to an important Palmyrene presence in the area, with some thirty-three inscriptions showing that several generations of Palmyrenes were interred in this cemetery. The necropolis contains at least thirty catacombs with numerous sarcophagi, epitaphs, and graffiti. Epitaphs within the tomb show that the deceased who were interred here had originated from a wide range of places, among them Babylon, Mesene, and South Arabia (Himyar). Palmyrenes, however, formed by far the largest non-local community recorded from within the tomb.[63]

Palmyrenes in Rome

The Palmyrene presence in Rome is of particular relevance to an account of Palmyra and its society, since it clearly testifies to the presence and integration of Palmyrenes into communities outside of their own. The evidence for a Palmyrene presence in Rome comes from the area around Trastevere (*regio XIV Transtiberim*, close to Monteverde and the Janiculum Hill) and points to the presence of a Palmyrene community involved in trade who lived and worshipped here.[64] The Roman poet Juvenal, working in the late first century CE, noted in his *Satires* (*Satyrae* 3.62–65), "Iam pridem Syrus in Tiberim defluxit Orontes et linguam et mores" (The Syrian Orontes has for a long time now been polluting the Tiber, bringing with it its language and customs),[65] in a reminder that Syrians and their cultural traditions in Rome were clearly a tangible and notable presence. A sanctuary from the end of the Hadrianic era dedicated to Bel and other Palmyrene divinities has been identified in the regio XIV Transtiberim, located on the site of the ancient Horti Caesarisi, which corresponds to the later Vigna Bonelli-Mangani, but no remains can be seen today. Remains of another sanctuary dedicated to the Syrian Gods, however, are still visible, and probably Palmyrene individuals would have worshipped there as well (Fig. 36).[66] Two dedicatory inscriptions stem from the temple dedicated to the Palmyrene deities, with a dedication in Latin to Bel and a dedication in Greek to Malakbel.[67] The Latin inscription, which seems to have been the primary inscription, also includes a reference to the Roman emperor.[68] The temple was constructed in an area in which finds attesting to the worship of other Eastern divinities have also been identified (Fig. 37).[69] These finds include another altar, dedicated to Ares Patroos—the Palmyrene Arsu, who also had a temple in Palmyra—and featured a Greek inscription.[70] The altar was also dedicated to Hadrian and dates to April 134 CE.[71] Another bilingual fragmentary inscription stems from the base of a slab on which traces of a relief can also be identified. The inscription allows for the reconstruction of part of the apparent dedication by the Palmyrenes Maqqai and Soa'du to the deities Dii Patrii, Bel, and Yarhibol.[72] The associated relief, depicting several deities, is dated to the end of the second century or the beginning of the third century CE.

Another temple in this area was dedicated to the goddess Syria-Atargatis— probably the first Syrian divinity to be introduced to the capital, in the Neronian era[73]—and the temple remained in use right into the third century CE.[74] Evidence of a sun cult has also been identified in the regio XIV Transtiberim, as indicated through two Latin inscriptions.[75] These texts were inscribed on two votive altars now generally accepted as originating from around Villa Bonelli-Mangani, in line with the suggestion first put forward by Rodolfo A. Lanciani, and they constitute important evidence for a Palmyrene

Figure 36 Remains of the sanctuary of the Syrian Gods in Rome (Courtesy of Michael Blömer).

presence in the area.[76] One altar, usually dated to the end of the first/early second century CE, is dedicated "to Sol Sanctissimus-Malachbel by Tiberius Claudius Felix, his wife Claudia Helpis, his son Tiberius Claudius Alypus, Calbienses de cohorte tertia" (Fig. 38). On the front of the altar, above the Latin inscription, is depicted a radiate bust of the sun god above an eagle with spread wings. On the altar's left side, there is a representation of another sun god in Eastern dress, seated in a quadriga drawn by four winged griffins. Behind the chariot, a standing Victory is shown in the act of crowning the

Figure 37   Marble fragment of a relief with a woman's head with a *calathos* and veil. Musei Capitolini, Rome, MC 2970/S (Archivio Fotografico dei Musei Capitolini. © Roma, Sovrintendenza Capitolina ai Beni Culturali).

young god, and in her left hand she holds a palm branch. This scene is similar to that found on an altar from the Sanctuary of Baalshamin in Palmyra.[77] On the lower part of the altar, there is a dedication by a named Palmyrene and "the Palmyrenes" to Malakbel, and to the Palmyrene gods, while the right side of the altar features a bust of Saturn. Finally, a cypress tree, its top branches tied with a ribbon, and the bust of a child carrying a lamb across his shoulders, are both represented on the back of the altar. Both inscriptions mention one donor explicitly by name: Tiberius Claudius Felix, a Roman citizen and a *libertus* or imperial official, who might have been of Palmyrene origin although this is not explicitly stated.[78] The Latin term *Calbienses* identifies the donors as staff attached to the Horrea Galbana, the warehouses on the left bank of the Tiber bank.[79] In line with the suggestion first put forward by Franz Cumont, the reliefs on the altar are taken to convey solar theology.[80] According to this interpretation, they depict the rising sun (the young god on the chariot), the midday sun (the god with his radiant halo, while the eagle symbolizes the heavenly vault), and the sun at night (typified by Saturn, in line with a widespread astrological doctrine that originated in Babylon). The

Figure 38 Altar for Sol, Malakbel, and Palmyrene Gods. Musei Capitolini, Rome, MC 107/S (Archivio Fotografico dei Musei Capitolini. © Roma, Sovrintendenza Capitolina ai Beni Culturali).

final representation, which is also perhaps the most discussed, might refer to the *dies natalis Invicti*, 25 December.[81] The altar can be identified as a prime example of the transmission and interpretation of the local Palmyrene religion into a firmly rooted Roman imperial context.

The possibility of material as pointing to the presence of a Hadad-Jupiter Heliopolitanus cult in Rome remains open to discussion, but it has been suggested that this material might in fact belong to a Late Antique villa that hosted a private sanctuary of Osiris.[82] Meanwhile, a votive *aedicula* to the gods Aglibol and Malakbel, dedicated by one Ioulios Aurelios Heliodoros, son of Antiocos, Adrianos Palmirenos, at his own expense, and for his health and that of his children, in the month of Sebat of the year 547 of the Seleucid era (that is, in February 236 CE), is the latest of the Palmyrene dedications identified in the Roman material (Fig. 39).[83] The Palmyrene name of the donor, Iarhai, appears in the Aramaic inscription and is accompanied by his entire genealogy.[84] Aglibol is here depicted in military dress, with cuirass,

Figure 39 Aedicula for Aglibol and Malakbel. Musei Capitolini, Rome, MC 1206/S (Archivio Fotografico dei Musei Capitolini. © Roma, Sovrintendenza Capitolina ai Beni Culturali).

chlamys, and spear, together with a radiate nimbus and the lunar crescent behind his head, while Malakbel instead wears Palmyrene Parthian-inspired dress comprising trousers, a short tunic, and a cloak. The two divinities are envisaged shaking hands in front of a tree.

Other evidence for the presence of Palmyrenes in Rome is connected to the funerary sphere. An extant epitaph of the Palmyrene equus singularis from the Flavian period (69–96 CE) reads *eques sin(gularis) Aug(usti) P. Aelius Annius Palmyre(nus) d.d. Fortunae s.* This epitaph features a relief that, although very fragmented, is engraved with a seated goddess represented frontally, who has been interpreted as Fortuna Redux.[85] Two additional funerary inscriptions from Rome with potential connections to Palmyrenes have also been identified. The first is an inscription dedicated to "Tiberio Claudio Onesimo *ostiario imperatoris Caesaris* . . . by his son Tiberius Claudius Onesimus, by his daughter Claudia Palmyris, and by Iulia Feicula *contubernalis suo*"; it seems most likely that this was a family of imperial *liberti* from the Julio-Claudian house, but it is not absolutely certain that Palmyris refers here to a person of Palmyrene origin.[86] The second such inscription, found on the Via Appia, was dedicated to "d. m. Habibi Annubathi f. Palmurenus" by his brother and heir. A Palmyrene version of this text appears alongside the Latin, with the inscription generally being attributed to the third century CE.[87]

The monumental Palmyrene sanctuary dedicated to Bel and other Palmyrene deities outside Rome's Porta Portese appears to have declined after the conquest of Palmyra. When the emperor Aurelian, who was responsible for Palmyra's sacking, had a new city wall constructed, this sanctuary was not included in the inner city. Instead, the newly constructed Sol Invictus Temple, which was built in region VII and dedicated sometime prior to 274 CE, was used as a location to house the trophies brought back from Palmyra by Aurelian's troops.[88] This marked the end of a continuous Palmyrene presence in Rome that had begun in the first century CE and increased in the centuries following as trading relations also intensified.[89]

A Local Society in a Global World

It remains a challenge to pull together our evidence about Palmyrenes and Palmyrene society, both within the city and elsewhere, into one coherent narrative. While Palmyra might not have been special in the sense that it was unusual for its time, we nonetheless have to acknowledge that the evidence provided by the city and its society certainly is extraordinary. It offers unique insights into the ability of the Palmyrene people to adapt to volatile situations—often involving political and military instability, changing borders, and differing trade patterns—while continuing to preserve local and unique cultures and traditions, even in the face of Greek influences and an increased Roman presence.[90] Our evidence suggests that Palmyrene society could adapt and absorb global influences as needed, but that the people carefully chose which elements they wanted and needed in local society, as well as in their communications and in their relationships with the rest of the world. They were not a society that was easily influenced, but rather one that chose its own way of navigating the world. This seems to have been one of the utmost strengths of the Palmyrenes, at least up to the time of Zenobia, and one that still deserves to be studied in more detail. From the mid-third century CE onward, however, the ties that Palmyra had managed to build up with the world around it began to break down and weaken.

Making and Breaking Ties with Rome and Parthia

But now the conqueror's brighter hour has passed,
And fair Zenobia's star goes down at last.
The Roman comes,—his legions file around
Doomed Tadmor's walls, to deafening trumpets' sound.
Aurelian bids the desert princess yield,
But hark! her answer—clashing sword and shield!
Girt by her chiefs, her proud plumed head she rears,
Defies the foe, and each faint spirit cheers;
Her milk-white courser prances round the wall,
Her gestures, looks, and words inspiring all.
Through opened gates her troops are sallying now,
Still in their front appears that dauntless brow;
Where'er her silver wand is seen to wave,
There rush the boldest, and there fall the brave,
And when borne back by Rome's immense array,
She fights retreating, pauses still to slay.

(Nicholas Mitchell, *Ruins of Many Lands*, 1849)

Nicholas Mitchell's poem about Palmyra, quoted only in part here, was written in the nineteenth century and should be read within the context of that time. Nonetheless, his words paint a picturesque image of Palmyra and its queen Zenobia in the heat of the Roman attack on the city in 272 CE. Had it not been for Zenobia and her conflict with the Romans, the city might not have gained the hold on the world's imagination that it still exercises today.

If we analyze production patterns for Palmyra's famous funerary portraits, discussed in Chapter 3, with the notion that urban production cycles and the manufacture of local elite goods provide indications of a city's wealth linked to political and economic stability, the third century was certainly a flourishing period until around 240 CE, at which time there was a marked decrease in portrait production.[91] This decline in production seems likely to be linked to the neo-Persian/Sassanian invasion of Dura-Europos in 239 CE, followed by Hatra the year after. This regional instability, although initially focused much further east, seems almost certain to have impacted Palmyra's trade and military organization and is likely to have also influenced other facets of Palmyrene society and economy. Resources would have been increasingly concentrated on military campaigns and the need to provide increased protection for the caravan trade, while the unrest in the region could well have led to reduced spending on luxury goods and on the embellishment of private and funerary dwellings, with resources channeled elsewhere. Despite these changes, Palmyra remains clearly visible in the archeological and written sources as a strong society that was struggling to gain, retain, and expand power in the region, until these ambitions came to an abrupt end with the city's sack in 272 CE.[92]

By the third century, Palmyra was in many ways an integrated part of the Roman world, and this is reflected not just in the city's material culture but also in its inscriptions and the way in which public life was structured. Palmyra was a pivotal force in the Roman Empire's trade network, and in many ways the city exercised what was virtually a monopoly on trade moving between East and West. But then the third century came crashing in with increased and renewed influences from the East, and the sociopolitical circumstances in the region began to shift. Against this backdrop, we can trace the rise to power of Odaenathus, the short-lived establishment of a royal house—Odaenathus was the first sole ruler of Palmyra and his son was the last[93]—and the city's final fall in the second half of the century. Palmyrene society was traditionally based on a tribal structure, and there is nothing to show that Palmyra was home to a royal house before this time.

The concentration of power in the hands of Odaenathus and subsequently Zenobia in the 260s and early 270s, and the later secession from Rome, therefore, needs to be examined within the context of a wider regional instability.[94] Hartmann has suggested that the Palmyrene rulers did not initially intend to break away from Rome; rather, they were simply trying to protect their own interests at a time when a weakened Roman imperial presence did not support Palmyrene intentions.[95] However, Palmyra should not be viewed as a client kingdom either, despite the fact that this concept had been widespread across the region in earlier times. Palmyra in some ways remained special due to its remote location in the Syrian Desert and its position as one of the region's foremost trading stations, replete with special forces to protect the caravans that allowed for the rapid mobilization of troops.

Parthia and Its Influences on Palmyra

The region around the River Euphrates had for a long time formed a geographical border between Rome and Parthia, and from the second century onward, there was an intensification of the Roman presence in the region. This was increased still further under the Severan dynasty in the context of ongoing unrest in Armenia, Cappadocia, and other regions fairly close to Palmyra.[96] But it was from the regions beyond Palmyra to the east that the political moves of the first half of the third century were to come. This led to an increase in tensions in the region, evidenced by the construction of new fortifications in the river valleys of the middle Euphrates and Khaber rivers during the early part of the century, as well as an enlargement of the garrison stationed at Dura-Europos and an intensification in the presence of Roman soldiers at Palmyra.[97]

In the year 224 CE, the Sassanian ruler Ardashir I (r. 224–240/42), defeated the king of Parthia, Artaban IV (r. 213–224), in battle near Hormozdgan (Fig. 40).[98] This victory fundamentally changed the geopolitical reality along the frontier of the Roman Empire; the Sassanid dynasty, based in Persia, had effectively cemented their position as a new political and military power in the region and as a new opponent in this often fraught political arena. Ardashir's defeat of the Parthians broke a relatively long and undisturbed peace in the region of Palmyra that had lasted since the early Roman period. For a Palmyrene living in 224 CE, therefore, the events of the years that followed and the insecurity they brought would have been unprecedented. Ardashir I's

Plate 1 *Queen Zenobia's Last Look upon Palmyra*, painting by Herbert
G. Schmalz, 1988. Art Gallery of South Australia, Adelaide, South Australia
Government Grant, 0.86 (Artepics/Alamy Stock Photo).

Plate 2 View of Palmyra with the oasis in the background (Courtesy of Jørgen Christian Meyer).

Plate 3 The Temple of Bel with a view of the main entrance (Rubina Raja).

Plate 4 Drawing of the Temple of Baalshamin from the 1920s by Charles Christensen (Rubina Raja and Palmyra Portrait Project, courtesy of Mary Ebba Underdown).

Plate 5 The so-called Monumental Arch in Palmyra (Rubina Raja).

Plate 6 Tower tombs in the landscape (Rubina Raja).

Plate 7 Tomb of the Three Brothers, central chamber (Courtesy of Claude Vibert-Guigue).

Plate 8. 1-3. Watercolor paintings from the Hypogeum of Hairan by Charles Christensen (Rubina Raja and the Palmyra Portrait Project, courtesy of Mary Ebba Underdown).

Plate 8. 1-3. Continued

Plate 9 Wall painting from the Temple of the Palmyrene Gods in Dura-Europos. Yale University Art Gallery, New Haven, 1931.386 (Courtesy of Yale University Art Gallery).

Plate 10 Cult relief of Fortune (Gad) of Palmyra, Dura-Europos. Yale University Art Gallery, New Haven, 1938.5313 (Courtesy of Yale University Art Gallery).

Plate 11 Mosaic of Odaenathus as Bellerophon fighting the Chimaera (Michał Gawlikowski, courtesy of the Polish Mission to Palmyra).

Plate 12 Mosaic of Herodianus hunting tigers (Michał Gawlikowski, courtesy of the Polish Mission to Palmyra).

Plate 13 *Queen Zenobia Addressing Her Soldiers*, oil painting by Giovanni Battista Tiepolo. National Gallery of Art, Washington, DC, Samuel H. Kress Collection, 1961.9.42 (Courtesy National Gallery of Art, Washington).

Plate 14 *James Dawkins and Robert Wood Discovering the Ruins of Palmyra*, painting by Gavin Hamilton, 1758. National Galleries of Scotland, Edinburgh, NG2666 (Gavin Hamilton, *James Dawkins and Robert Wood Discovering the Ruins of Palmyra*, National Galleries of Scotland. Purchased with support by the National Lottery through the Heritage Lottery Fund and with the assistance of the Art Fund 1997).

Plate 15 The Mariinsky Orchestra performing in the Roman theater of Palmyra, 2016 (By L-BBE, CC BY 3.0, https://commons. wikimedia.org/w/index.php?curid=60824623).

Figure 40 Tetradrachm of Ardashir I, third century CE. Yale University Art Gallery, New Haven, 2001.87.14366 (Public domain, Yale University Art Gallery).

armies occupied the Characene in southern Mesopotamia and restricted trade in the Persian Gulf. Spasinou Charax, Forat, and Vologesias, all important *emporia* for the Palmyrenes, were shut down.[99] Thereafter, Ardashir I moved against Rome and attacked Roman Mesopotamia, destabilizing the whole region. These shifting political circumstances, together with the uncertainty that they engendered, would have been felt right along the trade routes that went through Palmyra, influencing in particular the regions that neighbored Palmyra and through which trade goods had to pass to reach the city.[100]

Ardashir's policy of aggressive expansionism was continued by his successor, his son Shapur I (r. 239/40–272). In 239 CE, he invaded the city of Dura-Europos and rapidly followed this by occupying all of the Palmyrene trading stations along the River Euphrates from Dura-Europos up to the island of Anatha.[101] According to Persian sources, in the year 244 CE, Shapur defeated the Roman emperor, Gordian III (r. 238–244), in battle at the site of Misiche on the Euphrates, and the emperor died from his injuries soon after—although this account is not confirmed by Roman sources. However, Roman control over Syria was no longer secure, leaving Palmyrene society exposed to the wider instability in the region. The situation worsened as nomadic tribes in the region began to increase their control over the desert. Trade networks were dangerously weakened, and Palmyra plunged into military, political, and economic crisis.[102] It is telling that there are very few caravan inscriptions stemming from the period between 212 and 273 CE.[103] However, one such inscription, an honorific text to Septimius Vorodes from 264 CE, tells us that he brought back caravans at his own expense, which was something that he was honored for doing.[104]

It was in this context of political turmoil, beginning with the Sassanid invasion of Dura-Europos, that Septimius Odaenathus was named "exarchos of the Palmyrenes" in Greek, or "head of Tadmōr" (rš' dy tdmwr) in Palmyrene Aramaic.[105] His appointment to this new position is recorded in three inscriptions.[106] With the institution of this new title, a new Palmyrene dynasty was forged, and it is likely that Odaenathus also claimed control of Palmyra's army.[107] Certainly, we know from written sources that Odaenathus invested in upgrading Palmyra's military with a heavily armored cavalry and in this way was able to reclaim some control and security in the region.[108] In roughly 250 CE, Odaenathus and his son Ḥairān became members of the Roman senate—the very first Palmyrene members to be so elected.[109] Increasingly close ties were knitted with Rome, and the emperor must have been aware that Palmyra was at this time a crucial political and military stronghold in a region that seemed to be gradually slipping from Roman control.

Odaenathus would almost certainly have belonged to an elite Palmyrene family. He might have been a caravan leader and officer of the Palmyrene militia.[110] His marriage to Zenobia, while his most famous, was in fact his second;[111] Septimius Ḥairān, a son from his first marriage, was his heir,[112] and the son received several honorific titles in Palmyra, some of which were awarded jointly with his father.[113] Zenobia, whose full name is recorded as Septimia Zenobia Bat-Zabbai, was the daughter of one Antiochus.[114] After her marriage to Odaenathus, she gave birth to their first son at some point between 258 and 260. The child was named Lucius Iulius Aurelius Septimius Vaballathus Athenodorus, but he is better known to history as Vaballat or Vaballathus.[115]

The Roman emperor Valerian appointed Odaenathus to the position of consul in 257/258 CE (Plates 11 and 12).[116] The exact meaning of the title remains open to discussion, but as Hartmann states, it is most likely that Valerian appointed Odaenathus consul suffectus in absentia and governor of Syria Phoenice.[117] In 259 CE, Valerian planned for a great offensive against the Sassanids in northern Mesopotamia and for this he must have needed Palmyrene support.[118] The Battle of Edessa, however, which occurred in June 260, ended in disarray for the Romans. Valerian was captured and never set free (Fig. 41). Gallienus (r. 260–268 CE), who had up to this time ruled over the western part of the Roman Empire, now became emperor over the East as well, but faced with unrest in the western provinces, he never traveled to Rome's eastern frontier. Shortly after Valerian's defeat at Edessa and with no substantial Roman presence in the region, Shapur invaded Syria, Cilicia, and Cappadocia.[119] Fulvius Macrianus, a military tribune under Valerian and usurper to the imperial throne, was, with the support of Odaenathus, able to stand up to the Persians and force them to retreat but his seizure of imperial power in the East also triggered a Roman civil war. By the following year, Fulvius Macrianus was dead and Odaenathus was the most powerful commander in the Roman Near East.[120]

In 261 CE, Odaenathus received the title *corrector totius Orientis* (surviving only in Palmyrene: *mtqnn' dy mdnḥ' klh*), governor of the entire East, from Gallienus.[121] It is unclear whether this title came with real power, but either way, the very act of being granted such a title indicated that Odaenathus was second only to the Roman emperor. On this basis, Odaenathus expanded his power, and in the spring of 262 CE, he launched a campaign against

Figure 41 Relief of Shapur I's victory over Valerian after the Battle of Edessa in 260 CE. Rockcut relief at Naqsh-e Rostam (Rubina Raja).

the Persians, which finally resulted in his crossing the River Euphrates and taking control of Mesopotamia.[122] Gallienus celebrated this victory with a triumph in Rome in the second half of 263.[123] In the aftermath of this battle, Odaenathus—perhaps in response to the Roman triumph—bestowed the Persian title "king of kings" on himself and his son Ḥairān at the Orontes near Antioch, although notably he never claimed the Roman title of Augustus (Fig. 42).[124]

Odaenathus restored peace to the Roman Near East, and he was an admired leader in the region.[125] Palmyra's internal structure was quick to adapt to the introduction of a royal power to the city, very much in keeping with eastern Persian tradition, and Palmyra was promoted by Rome to the status of *metrocolonia*, making it the most important city in the province.[126] In many ways, the social changes that can be identified here are much in line with other developments seen within Palmyrene society: the basis of power remained with the city's elite, but it was now cleverly merged with expressions of loyalty toward the Roman Empire as well, in a clear example of the city's ability to adapt to shifting social and political changes while still retaining core elements of tradition.

Breaking Ties—the Rise of Zenobia

In the winter of 267 CE or 268 CE, while in the city of Emesa, Odaenathus was assassinated, with most sources suggesting that Gallienus was behind

Figure 42 Inscription mentioning Odaenathus as "king of kings", *IGLS* 120 (Jean-Baptiste Yon).

his death.[127] Odaenathus's second campaign against the Sassanids had been derailed by the Gothic invasion of Asia Minor in spring 267 CE; Odaenathus had promptly marched with his troops toward Heraclea Pontica but had arrived in the area too late and is then presumed to have headed to Emesa.[128] It seems not improbable that Gallienus, watching these events from far to the west, was growing concerned that Odaenathus was becoming too powerful and that he might make a bid for imperial power. Odaenathus's assassination, however, did not lead to Palmyra's fall, although it seems likely that this was Gallienus's hope.[129] Instead, Septimia Zenobia, known in her native tongue of Palmyrene Aramaic as Bat-Zabbai, entered the scene.

Zenobia's initial aim appears to have been to secure rule in Syria for her son, Vaballatus, who was at this time under age, but she was also able to secure continued Palmyrene rule in the province of Syria.[130] At first, Vaballathus and Zenobia officially recognized the authority of the Roman emperor; but before long, it appears that Zenobia used her position in Palmyra to act as sole ruler of a vast region. In doing so, she also became the first female ruler of an exclusively male-dominated society.

We in fact know very little about Zenobia as a historical figure. Our sources are few and scattered and, with the exception of a handful of inscriptions and a small amount of coinage, they are also not contemporary.[131] We have no portraits of Zenobia outside of coinage, despite the fact that we know they must have existed, while our main literary text for her reign is the *Historia Augusta*, which is neither contemporary nor especially reliable, instead containing a mass of doubtful and often contradictory information.[132] A separate, albeit late, literary account was produced by the Greek historian Zosimus in around 500 CE; but this also appears to draw on unreliable source material.[133] Finally, reference is made to Zenobia in certain later Jewish, Christian, and Arab sources.[134]

Based on what we can surmise about Zenobia, it seems clear that she expanded Palmyrene power in the East significantly between 268 CE and 272 CE, and she was able to consolidate the concept of a royal family in Palmyra to a far greater degree than her husband had done.[135] Initially, she appears to have operated in line with the wider political agenda of the Roman Empire; later, however, she pursued her own agenda, and took measures deemed unacceptable by Aurelian, resulting in his campaigns against the Palmyrenes in 272 CE (Fig. 43). The little contemporary evidence that we have for Zenobia, such as inscriptions made during her lifetime, offers a fascinating insight into her dramatic expansion of Palmyrene territory as well as the changes that she initiated for communicating both local and regional authority within a relatively short time span.

One such inscription that can be clearly dated to Zenobia's reign comes from a milestone, erected between 268 and 270 CE. The text is inscribed in both Greek and Palmyrene Aramaic, and the text can be read as follows:

> (in Greek)
> . . . [for] the safety
> of Septimia Zenobia, most
> illustrious queen (*basilissēs*), mother
> of the king (*mētros tou basileōs*) . . .

> (in Palmyrene Aramaic)
> For the life and victory of Septimius
> Wahballath Athenodoros, illustrious king
> of kings (mlk mlk') and *epanorthotēs*
> of all the East ('pnrṭ' dy mdnḥ' klh),

Figure 43 Inscription mentioning Zenobia as "*clarissima* and pious queen," *IGLS* 57 (Jean-Baptiste Yon).

son of Septimius Odainath, king of kings,
and for the life of Septimia Bathzabbai,
illustrious queen (mlkt'), mother of the king of kings
('mh dy mlk mlk'), daughter of Antiochus
(bt 'ntywkws), mile 14.[136]

In these early inscriptions, it is notable that while the originally Persian title king of kings, also employed by Odaenathus, was used, no titles here could challenge the authority of the Roman emperor. This was to change, however. By early 272 CE at the latest, new titles for both Zenobia and her son were introduced. Milestones from Arabia and Syria Palestina have been found, inscribed with Latin texts that read variously:

> For *imperator* Caesar L. Iulius Aurelius Septimius Vaballathus
> Athenodorus, Persicus Maximus, Arabicus Maximus, Adiabenicus
>   Maximus,
> pious, lucky, unconquered Augustus.[137]

and

> For . . . unconquered Augustus (*Sebastos*), and Septimia Zenobia Augusta
>   (*Sebastē*), mother of [our] eternal [lord] *imperator* Vaballathus
>   Athenodorus.[138]

In these later inscriptions, Zenobia and her son are titled, respectively, Augustus and Augusta—the highest imperial title that could be bestowed or claimed for oneself. The introduction of these titles would have been an obvious provocation to Aurelian. The dramatic shift in the official titles held by Vaballathus and his mother between 268/270 and 272 CE is clearly indicative that Zenobia, in this period, had made a grab for power in the region. There was no return for the Palmyrenes now. They had to stand up to the Romans.

Another key contemporary source from Zenobia's reign is coinage, with the image struck on coins offering a clear insight into how Zenobia wished to represent herself (Fig. 44). It is interesting to note that the very first coins from Palmyra were only minted in the late third century CE. This suggests that until this point in time, the city, despite being the most important trade *emporium* in the region, might not have been monetized to any great extent, and so coinage struck elsewhere had been sufficient for its

(a)   (b)

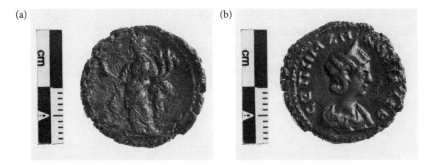

Figure 44 Coin featuring Queen Zenobia. National Museum of Denmark, Copenhagen, KP 2237.1 (Courtesy of the National Museum of Denmark. Photo: Rasmus Holst Nielsen).

needs.[139] By the second half of the third century, however, the situation had changed; coinage of a greater significance than small local change was now needed for the Palmyrenes to pay their troops, and so it became necessary for the city to issue its own money. Coinage, as a mass medium of its time, also proved a convenient tool of propaganda, providing a vehicle through which portraits, symbols, and legends of various rulers could be widely circulated across a territory. Between 270 and 272 CE, Palmyrene coins were struck outside Palmyra, in Antioch and Alexandria. These were meant for wide circulation and bear no resemblance to the small local coinage found in Palmyra.[140] The majority of these coins depict Vaballathus, but in issues from early 272 CE, Zenobia is represented wearing a stephane (a type of diadem or crown).[141] Coins from Anthiochia bear Latin legends in which Zenobia is entitled S(eptimia) Zenobia Aug(usta), while Greek versions of these titles appear on coins from Alexandria. These coins depict Zenobia in the visual tradition of other female leaders, in particular that of Cleopatra, from whom Zenobia drew inspiration, as well as the Empress Salonina, wife of Gallienus, which indicates that Zenobia wished to be perceived as an imperial woman and an empress. However, a slightly different portrait can be seen on some coins from Alexandria, in which Zenobia is depicted with a straight, pointed nose and large ears; such an image seems to stand in the tradition of the Ptolemaic portraits.[142] It was customary for local rulers to represent the ruling Roman emperor on one side of the coin and themselves on the other, but on later coinage, Zenobia appears to have dropped Aurelian's portrait, another fact that would have provoked the emperor.

Aurelian moved against the Palmyrenes in 272 CE, leaving Zenobia with little option but to make a last bid for imperial power. In the spring of 272 CE, she honored her son as *imperator*, a title that gave him equal status with the Roman emperor. He was now called "Imperator Caesar Lucius Iulius Aurelius Septimius Vaballathus Athenodorus Persicus maximus Arabicus maximus Adiabenicus maximus pius felix invictus Augustus."[143] Despite these ambitious claims, however, Zenobia's troops were defeated twice in battle by Aurelian, first near Antioch and then at Emesa. In the wake of these defeats, Zenobia's troops retreated to Palmyra, but Aurelian followed and captured Zenobia on the Euphrates.[144] Contrary to the drama outlined in later sources, Palmyra appears to have been handed over in relative peace under the Palmyrene Roman senator Septimius Ḥaddūdan in August 272 CE. There is little evidence of intensive destruction in the city from this time, but a Roman garrison was now stationed there.[145] Nonetheless, the event is referred to as a sack, since the Roman army took the city and it surrendered only thereafter.

We do not know what happened to Zenobia after the siege of Palmyra, and sources are divided on the matter. Recent scholarship, however, seems to agree that both Zenobia and Vaballathus were brought to trial in Emesa and then taken to Rome in several stages by Aurelian after he had secured the eastern border.[146] Several sources describe Aurelian's later triumph in Rome in the later summer of 274 CE, at which Zenobia, together with the defeated Gallic usurper Tetricus, was purportedly displayed.[147] On this occasion, we are told, she wore so much jewelry and so many heavy golden chains that she could not carry the weight herself.[148] Thereafter, Aurelian reportedly gifted Zenobia with a villa in Concae, near Hadrian's villa in Tivoli, and later she married a Roman senator.[149] The truth of these accounts will never be known, but it is these sources, and the romance of a female ruler of the East who tried but failed to take on the might of Rome, yet who won forgiveness from the emperor and was taken to Rome to live happily ever after, that inspired history's later fascination with Zenobia. The creation of her myth began soon after the fall of Palmyra.[150]

Zenobia's capture was not, however, the end of the story. It is often assumed that when Zenobia fell, Palmyra must have fallen too and that the city was destroyed by the Romans in 272 CE. However, this does not seem to have happened. While the evidence, archeological and epigraphic, suggests that the city was no longer benefiting from the caravan trade at this time and had therefore lost its major source of income, Palmyra still existed as a presence in the region, which at this time lay under the control of Aurelius Marcellinus. He had been given responsibility for the Eastern provinces by Aurelian, in 272 CE, before the emperor returned westward.[151] Yet despite Zenobia's defeat and its aftermath, the Palmyrenes tried once again to rebel against the Romans. In late 272/early 273, the governor of Palmyra, Septimius Apsaeus, launched a new plan of attack and attempted to convince Marcellinus to rebel against Aurelian.[152] This plan did not work: Marcellinus instead had Apsaeus and his partners murdered. If we can believe the sources, the Palmyrenes responded to this by proclaiming the father of Zenobia as augustus.[153] Aurelian crushed this second rebellion rapidly; Roman troops that had been stationed in the Balkans easily recaptured Palmyra in the summer of 273 CE, purportedly plundering the city in the process, and while Zenobia's father was spared, the other Palmyrene rebels were executed.[154] According to one source, the *Legio I Illyricorum* were stationed in Palmyra from this time, and Palmyra's bid to make itself into a regional power was over.[155] Within the span of a generation, Palmyra had been reduced from a city that had dominated the Near East to an insignificant provincial town on the frontier of the Roman Empire (Fig. 45).[156]

Figure 45 Antoninianus of Aurelian, third century CE. Yale University Art Gallery, New Haven, 2001.87.17024 (Courtesy of Yale University Art Gallery).

5

Changing Ties

Palmyra After Rome

After Aurelian's second sacking of Palmyra in 273 CE, the city entered a dramatically different phase in its history, although it remained under Roman domination until the Arab invasion of 634 CE. The city went from being a focal point of trade and politics in the Near East to a small military garrison town located on the frontier of the struggling Roman Empire. The executions of many of Palmyra's male elite, who had been involved in the city's second planned uprising, would have had a huge impact on the function and makeup of Palmyrene society, while the loss of the caravan trade effectively stripped the city of its wealth. As a result of these changes, many historians, perhaps most famous among them Edward Gibbon, have argued that the city was abandoned. In his monumental work, *The History of the Decline and Fall of the Roman Empire*, Gibbon states that from the end of the third century onward, Palmyra, "the seat of commerce, of arts, and of Zenobia, gradually sank into an obscure town, a trifling fortress, and at length a miserable village."[1]

We now know this not to be true, and occupation of the city did continue. The last few decades of research have improved our understanding of Palmyra in the period between Late Antiquity and the medieval period, and there is no doubt that still more evidence is waiting to be discovered. The first truly synthetic work on post-Roman Palmyra was produced by Slawomir Kowalski, and this was built on by the larger-scale and more archeologically focused research of Denis Genequand and Emanuele Intagliata.[2] Kowalski's article from 1997 constitutes the first systematic attempt at providing an account of Palmyra in the years after the sack of 273 CE,[3] and it was followed soon after by Genequand's immensely important work on the early Islamic period in the hinterland of Palmyra. Intagliata's work on Palmyra after 273 CE is likewise a welcome contribution to the field and it currently constitutes the most thorough overview of the work undertaken on these periods. Usefully, Intagliata's book also includes an overview of the ancient literary sources connected to these periods, whose descriptions of a city devastated after the

Pearl of the Desert. Rubina Raja, Oxford University Press. © Oxford University Press 2022.
DOI: 10.1093/oso/9780190852221.003.0005

Roman sack have for a long time heavily influenced scholarship of the period. Together with recent work by Annie Sartre-Fauriat on the earliest European travelers to Palmyra, we are finally able to begin forming a more nuanced and holistic overview of the evidence available to us.[4]

While the archeological, epigraphic, and literary evidence from post-Roman Palmyra certainly differs in amount and quality when compared to the material available to us from the Late Antique period, it is now clear that Palmyra and its hinterland continued to function and to interact with various other cities in the area, long beyond Aurelian's last sack of the city, and up to the collapse of the Umayyad dynasty in around 750 CE, in the aftermath of the devastating earthquake of 749 CE. Thereafter, activity in the city appears to have declined markedly until around the ninth century, although a presence at the site has continued up to modern times. But while this broad sketch of constant occupation of Palmyra has significantly altered the way the city should be viewed, understanding the overall nature of the developments remains complicated, and this must almost certainly be explored against the wider context of events across the region.

From Zenobia to the Umayyads

Two Late Antique sources, often said to be quite unreliable, inform us about Aurelian's destruction of Palmyra during its second sacking; both Zosimus (*Hist. Nov.* 1.61–62) and the *Historia Augusta Vita Aureliani* (31.5–9) report that Roman soldiers caused significant damage.[5] While recent research has documented some damage from the city center that appears to be connected to the sack,[6] however, there is no evidence in the archeological record that the city was completely destroyed.[7] We do know that the city contracted significantly in size; the area to the south of Wādī al-Qubūr, the so-called Hellenistic quarter of the city, was abandoned.[8] Some building projects were also discontinued, with unfinished architectural elements found in the quarries surrounding the city.[9] Evidence for continuous activity in the period following the sack is sparse, and we know almost nothing about the public organization of the city from this time.[10] While Palmyra retained its status as a Roman colony,[11] it is virtually impossible to trace building activity or the large-scale production of inscriptions and sculptures in the material evidence, nor is there a single funerary portrait stemming from the period after the sack.

Despite this, we should not assume that Palmyrene society ceased to exist entirely. Some tombs continued to be used, indicating that a degree of social activity remained, and religious dedications were also made. Two inscriptions exist, for example, honoring the *symposiarch* Septimius Ḥaddūdan, one from 272 CE, and one from 273 CE, after the second sack.[12] Inscriptions also record renovations in the area of the Great Colonnade and one includes the title of a *logistos*.[13] These inscriptions give us valuable evidence that Palmyrene Aramaic remained in use to some extent as a public civic language. The sanctuaries of Baalshamin and Allat/Athene also appear to have still been in use around 300 CE,[14] with a dedication to Zeus the Highest found at the Sanctuary of Baalshamin, dating from 302 CE. This inscription was dedicated by the *princeps* Avitus, who might have been a military person connected to the garrison that was stationed in the city after the sack.[15] Even mosaics continued to garner interest. In the first half of the fourth century CE, the famous Bellerophon mosaic, located in a private banqueting hall in the northwest quarter of Palmyra, was augmented with panels featuring pairs of open hands; these are presumed to be connected with the cult of the Anonymous God and echo iconography also known from altars in Palmyra.[16]

Nonetheless, the second sack of Palmyra had firmly shown that the city was no longer a center of power in the region, while the Palmyrene elite had been forced to once again pledge their loyalty to Rome.[17] The nature of the city also began to change due to Aurelian's establishment of a permanent military garrison. After Zenobia's failed uprising in 272 CE, some 600 archers were stationed in the city, although the *Historia Augusta* tells us—perhaps erroneously—that this garrison was massacred during the second uprising of 273.[18] A large compound dating to the third quarter of the third century CE has been identified to the southwest of the city, at the entrance to the Valley of the Tombs, and it is possible that this was the home of the 272 CE garrison.

Under Diocletian (r. 284–305), although the city continued to lose commercial importance, it became one of the emperor's new fortification initiatives along the Strata Diocletiana, the fortified road that ran along the eastern border of the Roman Empire.[19] As mentioned above, the *Legio I Illyricorum* was stationed in Palmyra,[20] and around the turn of the fourth century, a military camp was built in the westernmost part of the city, known as the Camp of Diocletian.[21] Many of the materials used to construct this camp were sourced from existing buildings in the city, leading to an intense process of spoliation. The governor of Syria Phoenice, Sossianus Hierocles, also ordered the construction of a camp in the eastern parts of the town, together with a bath complex, which was built into an already existing house adjacent to the main colonnaded street. As we know from other places, soldiers might have been stationed in a camp while also living in the city itself, and the construction of the Late Antique bathhouse in the city, together with the relatively small size of the Diocletianic compound, suggests that this might have been the case in Palmyra.[22]

Concurrent with the building of the camps was the construction of new fortification walls in Palmyra. While these have, on occasion, been attributed to the period of Zenobia's rule,[23] this later date is partially confirmed by a Latin inscription that mentions the fort constructed by Sossianus Hierocles between 292 and 303 CE, as well as by written sources that report Diocletian's activities along the eastern frontier.[24] The new city walls had ninety-eight towers, including twenty-three U-shaped towers; nine tombs were incorporated into the ramparts.[25] Importantly, these Late Antique walls enclosed only the core of the city around the main colonnaded street, the agora, and the residential area north of the main street. This reconfiguration significantly reduced Palmyra's early cityscape.[26]

Not until the fifth century, under the rule of Justinian (r. 527–565 CE), do we once again find references to a military presence in Palmyra. Chronicles written by the Byzantine historians Malalas, Procopius, and Theophanes all contain accounts of soldiers moving to Palmyra together with the *dux* of Emesa.[27] The Legio I Illyricorum must have moved out of Palmyra by this point, because the new garrison was based at least partially in the Camp of Diocletian, which was renovated for the occasion.[28] Thereafter, however, there are no references within the literary sources testifying to the presence of a garrison in Palmyra, and this also seems to have been the case even at the time of the Arab invasion in 634 CE. This event was reported by Ibn A'tham al-Kūfī, an Arab historian writing between the late eighth and early ninth centuries CE, who stated that "the Romans came out and approached Khālid b. al-Walīd like fierce lions," but it is notable that in his account, he never refers to them as soldiers.[29]

Palmyra, then, appears to have undergone an abrupt transformation from the late third century onward, morphing from metropolis to military garrison, and this change can also be identified in the urban layout of the city. There was a considerable drop in building activity, but at the same time, the urban space of Palmyra became increasingly chaotic, cluttered with different types of buildings that reused Roman period structures and their materials in an intense process of spoliation, encroaching on the layout of the Roman streets. Palmyra's main street, the Great Colonnade, continued to serve as the key thoroughfare of the city, with restoration work taking place in the fourth century, and the street's paving apparently being maintained into the seventh century.[30] Shops from along the Great Colonnade have been identified in the archeological record, and retail activity in this area appears to have continued, at least to an extent, into the Umayyad period.[31] The so-called suburban market in the northern quarter of Palmyra was also renovated after the third century, with its western half being used for housing and workshops; its eastern half was transformed into a cemetery from which wooden coffins have been excavated.[32] The sanctuaries of Palmyra were also repurposed, as new faiths began to be practiced in the city. The Sanctuaries of Nabu and Baalshamin were reused for habitation and production[33] while the Temple of Bel was converted into a church, possibly from as early as the fifth century. We know very little about the Late Antique phases of the theater or the agora, although there is evidence that the annex on the agora was transformed into workshops,[34] nor do we have much knowledge of the amphitheater, as this has never been excavated. This scattered knowledge is a reflection of the early periods of clearance of these complexes, which took place from the beginning of the French Mandate in 1923 onward.

Palmyra is known to have held at least eight churches, all constructed in Late Antiquity, within its city walls. This is in fact a relatively low number when compared to other places in the Near East,[35] and especially when one considers that Palmyra had been an episcopal see since before the Council of Nicaea, which was attended by Marinus, the city's bishop.[36] There is also some evidence that Christians had destroyed pagan monuments in the late fourth century. The Sanctuary of Allat, as well as the cult statue of Athena, both suffered injury,[37] while the mosaics in the Bellerophon Hall linked to the pagan worship of the Anonymous God were covered over by mortar, possibly in a deliberate act of vandalism.[38]

Four of the city's churches were located in the northwest of the city.[39] One had an atrium, some fifty meters in length, that opened onto the Great Colonnade;[40] the three others, all basilicas, were accessed from a street perpendicular to the main road.[41] Palmyra's other churches, consisting of three smaller chapels and the church within what had once been the Temple of Bel and which was dedicated to the Virgin Mary, were also situated in the vicinity of the Great Colonnade.[42] There is no doubt that these buildings were important symbols of the Christian religion within Palmyra. However, in some ways they also once again reflect a continuity of local tradition within the city; members of the elite directed their resources toward the building of churches as part of the same tradition of *euergetism* that had once led wealthy donors to finance pagan monuments. The Christian religion also influenced the urban landscape in other ways. Whereas funerary monuments had for the most part traditionally been constructed away from the cityscape, as outlined in Chapter 3, with the coming of Christianity came the establishment of Christian burial places in the city center. A cemetery has been excavated in the northwest quarter of the city, located between two of the churches,[43] and a seventh- to eighth-century cemetery in the suburban market has also been investigated.[44] The largest Late Antique and early Islamic graveyard is situated outside the city walls in the area of the museum, and some seventy-eight graves from this site have been excavated.[45]

After the sack of Palmyra in 273 CE, the Romans endeavored to secure allegiances with some of the nomadic tribes from the wider region, among them the Tanukhids (fourth century CE), the Salihids (fifth century), and the Jafnids (sixth century). There is substantial evidence in the sources for a Jafnid presence in and around Palmyra; six inscriptions mention the Jafnid *phylarchs*, one of which was found at Qasr al-Hayr al-Gharbi, a site located eighty kilometers to the southwest of Palmyra.[46] The Byzantine Greek scholar Procopius, meanwhile, reports that a conflict broke out in the first half of the sixth century between the Jafnids and the philo-Persians over who controlled the territories to the south of Palmyra.[47] A Syriac codex, which may have come from a monastery close to Palmyra, refers to one King Abokarib (MLK' 'BWKRYB), the brother of al-Ḥārith b. Jabala, while a study of our Arab sources, Ḥamza al-Hiṣfahānī (Tā'rīkh 121) and Abū al-Fidā' (Taqwīm al-Buldān, 128–130), suggests that al-Ayham b. Jabala b. al-Ḥārith ruled Palmyra in the early seventh century.[48]

Islamic Palmyra

The region of Syria was under Sassanian control between 613 and 628 CE and thereafter under Byzantine control, but in neither case can we identify any traces in the archeological evidence from Palmyra.[49] In 634 CE, however, Palmyra was conquered by the Muslim general Khālid b. al-Walīd, in an event that has been recorded—albeit in apparently unreliable fashion—in a somewhat later work by al-Wāqidī (c. 747–823 CE).[50] Khālid b. al-Walīd's troops came to Syria either from Iraq or through the site of Dūmat al-Jandal,

located in modern-day Saudi Arabia.[51] Palmyra is described in our sources
as a well-protected settlement that was not easy to take. This suggests both
that Palmyrene society was well organized and that either the city's population was quite sizable at this time, or that the conquering army was relatively
small.[52] While the city itself is said to have been fortified, the same sources
also report that Palmyra in fact surrendered without any use of force, a statement that finds support in the archeological evidence. Thereafter, Palmyra
was incorporated into the province (Jund) of Homs.[53]

Two other important events connected to Palmyra in the early Islamic
period can be found in literary accounts of the period. In 684 CE, conflict
broke out between the Umayyad caliph, ʿAbd al-Malik b. Marwān, and
ʿAbd Allāh b. al-Zubayr, who, with the support of al-Ḍaḥḥāk b. Qays, tried
to seize power. Abū Mikhnaf, cited by al-Ṭabarī (839–923 CE), records that
during this conflict, the Umayyad caliph retreated to Tadmor. There, he
was able to gain the support of the Tadmorians, and as a result, elected to
fight al-Ḍaḥḥāk b. Qays. The battle was held at Marj Rāhiṭ, near Damascus,
and al-Malik b. Marwān proved victorious.[54] In the aftermath of this battle,
however, further unrest developed between the Qays, who supported b. al-
Zubayr, and the Yemenites, who supported the Umayyads, with members of
the Kalb tribe in Palmyra belonging to this latter group. The ongoing hostilities between the two groups led to several massacres, including the deaths
of tribe members in Tadmor.[55] While there is a paucity of archeological evidence from this period in Palmyra, and so very little that might shed further
light on our literary sources, it is interesting to note that two metal hoards
dating to this period have been found in the city; their burial is indicative of
ongoing unrest, leading to people attempting to preserve their wealth and
valuables by hiding them until the situation was calmer. The first of these,
found in the Camp of Diocletian, contained six pieces of jewelry and twenty-
seven gold coins, the latest of which dates to the mid-seventh century.[56] The
second hoard, meanwhile, was found in the northwest quarter by the road
known as Church Street. This comprised two coin assemblages that together
contained over 700 issues, with the latest being Islamic-Sassanian dirhams
minted between 683 and 695 CE.[57]

The second event known from our sources to involve Tadmor is connected
to the conflict that broke out in 745 CE, between Thābit b. Nuʿaym, the
governor of Palestine, and his followers, against the last Umayyad caliph,
Marwān II. Al-Ṭabarī reports that Palmyra surrendered by treaty, but that
the caliph had ordered the razing of the city walls.[58] Yāqūt, in contrast, notes

that the city was taken by force, and its inhabitants massacred.[59] Again, it is not possible to use the archeological material available to confirm or deny either of these scenarios. However, we can say that up to now, no destruction layers have been found, and the city walls also seem to have been intact after this period.[60]

Very few buildings from the Islamic period exist, but both a mosque and a *suq*, or open market, have been identified. The mosque was installed within an already existing building that was slightly modified to reorient its south wall in the direction of Mecca.[61] The suq, meanwhile, was a much larger construction. Built between the late seventh and early eighth centuries, this market was located in the area around the Roman Tetrapylon and it included at least forty-seven shops situated along the middle of the carriageway.[62] It is broadly comparable to suqs found in other early Islamic locations, among them Jerash, Resafa, Anjar, and Amman.[63] While archeological evidence from the city is relatively limited and the urban space ostensibly chaotic, with buildings being reused and spoliated, early Islamic Palmyra up to the end of the Umayyad dynasty in fact seems to have been home to a largely prosperous society in common with many other cities of the period. The construction of the large suq and the mosque, together with the establishment of new private houses and centers of production, all point to a city with a considerable population.[64]

Nonetheless, Palmyrene society appears to have gone into a decline in the years after 750 CE and following the collapse of the Umayyad dynasty, even while there is evidence to suggest that the city center remained partly occupied into the ninth century CE.[65] Thereafter, the settlement retracted in on itself, and was contained within the Sanctuary of Bel. Here, it developed to fill the 200 x 200 m (656 x 656 ft) precinct in its entirety, while the Temple of Bel was converted into a fortress (Fig. 46). This was the nucleus of Palmyra as the first Western travelers found it in the seventeenth century, and this is how the settlement stayed until excavation and reconstruction work began on the temple around 1930, some years after the institution of the French Mandate in Syria (Fig. 47).[66]

Palmyra Rediscovered

Some Arabic sources mention Palmyra and Zenobia in the ninth century and onward. The *Historia Augusta*, however, remained known to the

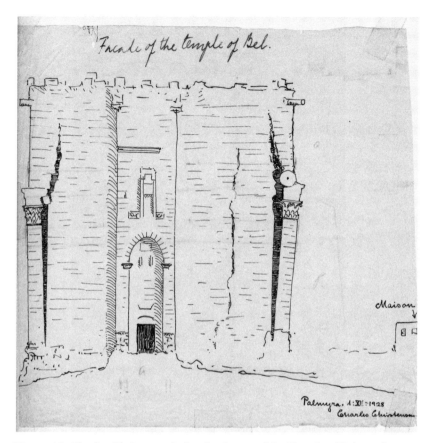

Figure 46 Charles Christensen's sketch of parts of the Temple of Bel as a fortress (Rubina Raja and Palmyra Portrait Project, courtesy of Mary Ebba Underdown).

educated classes from Late Antiquity forward, and Zenobia and Palmyra repeatedly appeared in writings. One well-known example from the medieval period sees Geoffrey Chaucer's moralizing monk citing Zenobia as a cautionary example of the folly of pride in the *Canterbury Tales*.[67] As noted in Chapter 1, it is with the travels of the Spanish Rabbi Benjamin de Tudela that Palmyra first reentered the European orbit.[68] Benjamin of Tudela traveled in the Holy Land and Mesopotamia between 1160 and 1173,[69] and while he might never have visited Palmyra, he certainly wrote about the site, claiming that a community of some 2,000 Jews lived in the settlement in 1172. By the sixteenth century, Syria had been absorbed into the expanding Ottoman Empire. However, it is only in the seventeenth century that we

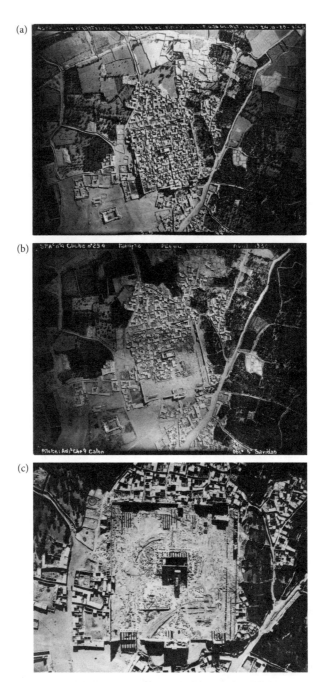

Figure 47 Aerial view of the Bel Temple a) before (1929), b) during, and c) after the restoration (1934) (Courtesy of Rolf Stucky, Private Collection, Switzerland).

have the first testimonies about the city from European travelers. Visitors to the region include the Italian Pietro della Valle (1616), the Frenchman Jean-Baptiste Tavernier (1630), and the Jesuit Manuel Godinho (1663), all of whom were reported to have been close to Palmyra on their travels, but none of whom actually appear to have entered the city, only viewing its ruins from afar.[70] It was around this time, in the seventeenth century, that the figure of Zenobia began to appear in operatic works, and this trend was only to continue throughout the eighteenth and nineteenth centuries (Plate 13; Figs. 48–49).[71]

The first attempt to reach Palmyra by a Western expedition was made by a group of British merchants in 1678. As outlined in Chapter 1, this failed when the group was held hostage by local Bedouins.[72] The same group, however, returned in 1691, at which point it also included the Reverend William Halifax and the Dutch painter Gerard Hofstede van Essen; the latter painted the earliest known panorama of Palmyra, which today hangs in Amsterdam (Fig. 50).[73] Halifax wrote descriptions of Palmyra and copied some inscriptions, but the expedition stayed for only four days because the site was considered unsafe.[74] Nonetheless, it was a success, and when the visitors disseminated their results, including the grand view of the site painted by van Essen, there was a European-wide surge in interest in Palmyra. Some of the visitors to Palmyra in the early eighteenth century included Giraud and Sautet, in 1706, as well as the doctor Claude Tourtechot, also known later as Granger, in 1735.[75]

In March 1751, James Dawkins and Robert Wood reached Palmyra, traveling together with the Italian architect and painter Giovanni Battista Borra (Plate 14). Together, they produced the first large-scale account of the site's monuments, featuring fifty-seven sketches by Borra. The work was by no means comprehensive, nor were Borra's drawings entirely accurate, as the artist employed artistic license and adapted the monuments slightly in line with Graeco-Roman ideals. Nonetheless, the volume took Europe by storm, and it was to prove hugely influential on the architectural and artistic worlds. In 1754, the abbot Jean-Jacques Barthélemy was the first to decode the Palmyrene Aramaic dialect, which provided a revolution among scholars of linguistics,[76] and in 1785, Louis-Francois Cassas visited Palmyra and produced a series of sketches and drawings, although these were even more heavily classicized than those of Borra.[77] By the nineteenth century, Palmyra, much like other Late Antique cities of the region, was receiving a steady stream of foreign visitors. Included among them were Johann Ludwig

Figure 48 Zenobia in Chains, marble sculpture by Harriet Goodhue Hosmer, 2007.26. The Huntington Library, Art Collections, and Botanical Gardens, San Marino, California. Purchased with the Virginia Steele Scott Acquisition fund for American Art (Photo: Fredrik Nilsen. Courtesy of the Huntington Art Collections, San Marino, California).

Burckhardt, the individual responsible for the rediscovery of Petra, as well as William John Bankes in 1816, Charles Irby and James Mangles in 1818, and Léon de Laborde in 1827. In 1813, Lady Hester Stanhope, a famously flamboyant individual, entered Palmyra dressed to look like Zenobia.[78] She was, to the best of our knowledge, the first Western female traveler to reach the site. Many others must also have traveled to the ruins of Palmyra, but up

ATRIO
Cp. Aureliano in Palmira

Figure 49 Theatrical set designed by Paolo Landriani for the opera *Aureliano in Palmira*, which premiered in Milan in 1813 (Public domain, via Wikimedia Commons).

to now no comprehensive list of nineteenth-century Western travelers to the city has yet been compiled.

By this time, there was also a movement toward treating the inscriptions and monuments of Palmyra in a more systematic fashion despite the fact that no archeological excavation had yet been carried out at the site. The works of Melchior de Vogüé and William Henry Waddington in 1861 and Vogüé and Edmond Duthoit in 1863 constitute the first attempts to produce systematic studies on the Palmyrene material, focusing on the inscriptions from the site and the monuments to which they were connected.[79] In the later nineteenth century, there was a surge of interest in the antique art from Palmyra, and it is in this period that the earliest collections of Palmyrene material in Europe were established.[80] The interest went hand in hand with a general growing interest in collecting antiquities from the Greek and Roman cultural spheres; the expeditions headed by Europeans who made their way

Figure 50 *View of Palmyra*, painting by Gerald Hofstede van Essen's, 1693, Allard Pierson Museum, Amsterdam, 000.049 (Allard Pierson, University of Amsterdam).

to the Near East reported on the sites of the region, which held lavish ruins influenced by Graeco-Roman traditions, and wrote accounts about the ancient art found there, which soon came to fascinate collectors. It was also around this time, in 1881, that the Tax Tariff was discovered by the Russian Prince S. S. Abamelek-Lazarev and acquired for the Hermitage Museum in St. Petersburg, although keen interest was also expressed by Danish brewer and antiquarian Carl Jacobsen.[81]

Only at the very end of the nineteenth century did archeological work in the area become possible, an event facilitated by the visit of German emperor and king of Prussia, Wilhelm II (1888–1918), in autumn 1898.[82] The first large-scale archeological work in Palmyra was carried out under the supervision of German archeologist Theodor Wiegand while Syria was still under Ottoman rule. Wiegand headed the "German-Turkish Command," the Denkmalschutzkommando, which was responsible for archeological work carried out at sites across Palestine and Syria, although the best known of these sites were undoubtedly Baalbek and Palmyra.[83] With the outbreak of the First World War and the dissolution of the Ottoman Empire came the institution of the French Mandate in Syria. Under its authority, archeological work occurred in Palmyra from the early 1920s, most notably by the Danish archeologist Harald Ingholt, whose work on the funerary sculptures from Palmyra was truly pioneering.[84] The Second World War once again brought a halt to archeological work at the site, but it resumed soon after the armistice, initially led by a Swiss team under the direction of Paul Collard and thereafter by the Polish Mission in the later 1950s.[85] In more recent years, several international teams have worked in Palmyra, and archeological work at the site was ongoing until 2011, when civil war broke out in Syria.

6

Cutting Ties

Palmyra in a Warzone

The fertility of the soil is reflected in the ancient ruins of Palmyra by the Palmyrene fellahins' (peasant) planless messing around in the soil, which usually is motivated by the hope of finding wealth, (a hope) which in fact never disappoints, despite the fact that the value of the objects is other than the fellahins expect. These haphazardly dug sculptures are usually treated with the utmost vandalistic behaviour. In earlier times, the faces of the sculptures were demolished by religious fanatics, now the heads are cut off out of commercial concerns. All export of antiquities is illegal, and an entire statue or relief is not easy to hide or to transport; a decapitated head, on the other hand, is a simple thing to make disappear and sell for a few francs to a travelling Englishman. This is the reason for the demolished torsos, which one sees lying around on the southwestern edges of the ruin-city.[1]

This description of the destruction of antiquities in Palmyra could well have been written today if we were to substitute the use of the term *fellahins* for modern treasure hunters. It stems, however, from an account written by the Danish scholar Johannes Elith Østrup (1867–1938), who traveled from Egypt to Copenhagen on horseback in the 1890s, and who described his travels, including his visit to Palmyra, in two publications.[2] In later years, Østrup went on to become professor of Islamic Culture at the University of Copenhagen, the first such professorship of its kind in Denmark. At the time of his visit, however, Østrup was twenty-four, and had just defended his higher doctoral degree. He traveled to the Near East to study various Arabic dialects and regional cultures, arriving in Egypt in 1891 before traveling via Syria and Asia Minor back to Denmark in a journey that would take two years.

Pearl of the Desert. Rubina Raja, Oxford University Press. © Oxford University Press 2022.
DOI: 10.1093/oso/9780190852221.003.0006

During or shortly after his journey, Østrup wrote the account cited at the beginning of the chapter, published in his 1894 monograph, which clearly outlines the situation in Palmyra at the time of his visit. Here, he identifies two underlying causes behind the destruction of cultural heritage, both of which remain prevalent today. First, he references the pillaging and trade of Palmyra's archeological remains in order to sell items to the art market (which in Østrup's time largely consisted of wealthy Europeans); and second, he describes the deliberate, religiously motivated destruction of antiquities, an action that can often also be ascribed to underlying political motives. Østrup is more outspoken still in his second account of his travels; here, he also condemns the way in which the antiquities are treated and writes about the lack of protection offered to cultural heritage by Palmyra's Ottoman rulers.[3] Yet despite this condemnation of locals, Ottomans, and Europeans alike, Østrup himself purchased objects from Palmyra, which he brought with him back to Copenhagen.[4] The contradiction between his poignant analysis of the situation in nineteenth-century Palmyra in the 1890s and his own actions reflects the core of the problem when dealing with issues of trade in antiquities. It is easy, and an obvious standpoint to take, to condemn the destruction, looting, and export of items of cultural heritage, as well as to point the finger of blame at those involved in these activities. But this did not prevent Østrup from desiring such items for himself, an action that could be justified with the suggestion that he was better able to take care of such items than "others" could.[5] These arguments—and the juxtapositions, complexities, and contrition inherent within them—continue to drive the antiquities market to this day.[6] It is clear that the poorer and more unstable a region, the more vulnerable and endangered its cultural heritage is likely to be, since the protection of such items demands both resources and education. But the topic is by no means an easy one, overlapping as it does with broader historical, political, religious, and cultural developments, and sensitive issues such as who has ownership of objects, and if and how antiquities should be repatriated, have often left deep scars on the relationships between regions and national states.[7]

Cultural Heritage—Who Owns the Past?

Even before the Syrian civil war broke out in 2011, it is clear that Palmyra, like so many other sites of historical importance, had been damaged by centuries of illegal excavations and the looting of unexplored archeological areas. Palmyra comprises a vast, open archeological area that has never been protected by fences or, in modern times, by digital surveillance. As is evidenced by Østrup's writings, many travelers chose to export cultural heritage objects, despite the fact that it was not always legal to do so. Thus the earliest collections of Palmyrene objects in European museums were first built up in the late nineteenth century. These include the now world-renowned collections held at the Musée du Louvre in Paris, and the Ny Carlsberg Glyptotek in Copenhagen. But Palmyrene objects are also found in numerous other collections across the world, with funerary sculpture from the site being particularly common. These reliefs were fairly easy to obtain and—according to our early sources—they were inexpensive.

Carl Jacobsen, who is largely responsible for the Palmyrene collection that is today housed in the Ny Carlsberg Glyptotek, was immensely interested in Palmyra's funerary portraits, which he saw as providing an important body of comparative material that can sit alongside his already existing collection of portraits from the Greek and Roman period. He was able to acquire objects through the Danish consul Julius Løytved in Beirut, who acted as his agent in Syria.[8] Jacobsen even considered undertaking excavations in Palmyra, as his correspondence with Løytved shows, and he was, for a brief time, interested in acquiring the recently discovered Tax Tariff.[9]

Jacobsen, in choosing to purchase an extensive collection of cultural heritage items, was acting very much in line with the standards of his time. While today we may look on collecting antiquities with different eyes, it is perhaps unfair to project our views onto practices that took place well over a century ago. The conventions on cultural heritage, drawn up in the wake of the Second World War, provided some degree of regulation as to how and if items in museums could—or should—be repatriated. Nonetheless, ongoing disputes such as the controversy over the Elgin Marbles provide a clear reminder that even with international regulations in place, there is no consensus on the matter, with cultural and national identities feeding into a complex and often emotionally laden debate.[10] While numerous international rules may exist, and have been ratified by many countries, these remain difficult to enforce, especially in times of conflict.[11]

A separate issue to that of looting is the problem of deliberate destruction, whatever the motivation behind it. In Palmyra this can be said to include the impact of the earliest archeological excavations in the region, with Roman-period monuments being consciously stripped of any evidence of later reuse in what was a common practice at the time. As noted earlier, we know that over time, the Sanctuary of Bel gradually developed into a village. However, in the period of the French Mandate, Henri Seyrig was appointed head of the antiquities service in the region, and he initiated a number of projects that entailed the removal—and inevitably, destruction—of all post-Roman phases from the site. One of the large-scale projects that he instigated was to clear the sanctuary perimeter of all phases later than the Roman-period temple and temenos. As a result, hundreds of locals were displaced from their home to areas outside the ancient site and the necropoleis. Seyrig was well aware that his projects would lead to the loss of important cultural heritage from later periods. His aim, nonetheless, was to reconstruct the temple and its surroundings to their glory days of the Roman period, and he was driven by both a love for antiquity and the need to appeal to the growing numbers of tourists who flocked to the region in search of evidence for Western (in this case, Roman) influence in the Orient.[12]

Today, Seyrig's approach would of course be considered insensitive, both from a cultural heritage perspective in terms of the damage done to the post-Roman phrases of the site and also to the local societies who lived within these cultural remains, and who were forcibly displaced to a new-built village. Seyrig oversaw a similarly large-scale project in Baalbek, in Lebanon, where the remains of a Byzantine-period basilica and later Umayyad palace were stripped away from the earlier Roman-period Sanctuary of Jupiter Heliopolitanus. But such practices were by no means unique to Seyrig. They were—and indeed still are—widespread in archeological excavations where the need to present ruins to the public, and conservation issues, often take precedence over the preservation of all chronological phases, which often can be difficult to present in coherent ways or extremely expensive to preserve in an adequate manner.

Another author who offers insight into the archeological practices of the late nineteenth and early twentieth century is the author Agatha Christie. She was married to the archeologist Max Mallowan, who worked extensively in Syria, and in her *Come, Tell Me How You Live: An Archaeological Memoir*, she vividly describes how the excavation team headed by her husband dug through, and left unrecorded, millennia of cultural heritage in order to get to the prehistoric phases that interested Mallowan.[13] While not exactly firsthand documentation for events in Palmyra, Christie's account aligns closely with photographic documentation from excavations in this period.

In sum, the destruction, looting, and export of cultural heritage, both past and present, as well as the histories and practices behind excavations and museum collections, inevitably exert an influence on discussions about the future protection of cultural heritage. This is particularly true in zones where cultural heritage is threatened. There is no easy fix or solution and no direct path to reconciliation or common understanding. Nonetheless, the more we try to understand the past and the processes that have taken place, the more informed will become the basis on which we make future decisions.

Conflict in Syria

Palmyra was inscribed on UNESCO's list of World Heritage sites in 1980— a list that today comprises some 1,121 sites across the globe, of which 869 are categorized as cultural heritage sites[14]—and in the years before 2011, it was the most visited archeological site in Syria. Tourism in Syria flourished in the decade before the civil war, with people taking advantage of what seemed to be a growing stability in the region to visit the country, experience its culture, and visit the famed sites of Antiquity. Both cultural and religious tourism expanded, with tourists arriving not only from Europe but also from other Arab states. The economy and the local infrastructure developed, and Damascus became known as a regional metropolis, where tourists could visit historical neighborhoods and archeological ruins but also stay in comfort. Tourists heading to Palmyra typically left from Damascus, Homs, or Deir-az-Zor to see the ancient ruins. The city is by no means easy to navigate, meaning most tourists would not stray too far from the central streets and monuments of the city, but some would have visited Palmyra's celebrated tombs as well as the medieval fortress located near to the city on one of the surrounding hills. Many tourists would have visited Palmyra on an organized one-day trip, but others would have taken several days to explore the vast site, perhaps taking advantage of the newer hotels constructed in the oasis or electing to stay in the historic Hotel Zenobia, which was constructed in the 1930s.[15] For many of these foreign visitors, the site was imbued with a sense of romance, haunted by the life and legends of its queen, Zenobia; for others, a visit to Palmyra was an opportunity to walk in the footsteps of the first travelers to the site and to see the ruins that had inspired them to produce such emotionally charged descriptions.[16]

In 2011, however, in the wake of the Arab Spring, conflict broke out in Syria, and since then the country, its people, and its rich cultural heritage have all suffered hugely.[17] The civil war in Syria has turned into one of the most devastating humanitarian crises of recent times. Several hundred thousand people have lost their lives, while millions have been displaced. At a time of humanitarian crisis, concerns about cultural heritage should not take center stage. Nonetheless, the country's archeological remains have been exposed to severe damage—the result of armed violence, deliberate targeting, and looting—and provide a timely reminder that in a time of conflict, tangible cultural heritage can often be made into a target. Despite the international conventions in place, it has been impossible for either Syrians or the international community at large to prevent damage to their cultural heritage. Moreover, the civil war has led to huge setbacks within the country, and it would be naïve to believe that it will ever recover entirely from the losses incurred during this almost decade-long armed conflict.[18]

While there has been a failure to implement many international conventions successfully, several national and international groups have established initiatives to document and record all instances of the loss of cultural heritage in Syria by collecting and disseminating knowledge about destructions, looted materials, and earlier archival materials.[19] Such a task has been made virtually impossible, however, due to the current state of affairs in the region. Some damage to material remains has been on a relatively small scale, albeit still detrimental to the country's cultural heritage; in other cases, the damage caused has been both huge and irreversible. It is also difficult to assess the extent of the problem because while some of the cultural heritage destroyed occurred to monuments or sites that were well known and documented, in other cases, the damage was made to sites or objects that had not yet been discovered or investigated. This is an important distinction since it brings to the forefront the complications faced when attempts are made to assess the scale of the damage in Syria.[20] Some of the destruction will thus stay hidden, or at least the extent of it will remain unknown. If and when peace returns to the region, it will be a crucial assignment to coordinate and collect as much information as we can about the state of the damage done, both in Palmyra itself and across Syria more widely.

In 2013, some thirty-three years after being inscribed on the UNESCO World Heritage list, Palmyra's name was included on a new, and much shorter list—World Heritage in Danger. Here, the city is named alongside just fifty-one other locations.[21] Such an action was deemed necessary as the escalating conflict in Syria was leading to destruction at a scale previously unseen in the region. These fears were confirmed in January 2017, when UNESCO received information about the destruction of Palmyra's Triumphal Arch and damage to the Roman theater. On this occasion, the then-general director of UNESCO, Irina Bokova (2009–2017), publicly condemned the destruction that had been done by ISIS in Palmyra since 2015.[22] Bokova had by this time already founded the Unite4Heritage initiative,[23] one of a number of initiatives spearheaded by UNESCO under her directorship to protect cultural heritage within zones of armed conflict. Yet despite best efforts, these have not been very active in recent years, hampered by lack of funding and limited access to the region, as well as by a lack of the political will needed to keep pushing such projects forward.[24]

From Palmyra to Tadmor

For Syrians, Palmyra, which is still known today in Arabic as Tadmor, is not only associated with cultural heritage and tourist wealth but also with the country's oppressive political regime. The site was renowned for a prison that allegedly held numerous prisoners at the time that civil conflict broke out in 2011.[25] While concern about the destruction of archeological remains was— with good reason—very high, little international attention has so far been paid to the fact that Tadmor was home to the country's most brutal prison before its destruction in 2015. The Tadmor prison had begun life as a military barrack, constructed in the 1930s to house forces in the area during the period of the French Mandate.[26] After Syria gained its independence, the buildings were transformed into a military prison, and then, from the late 1970s onward, they served as a jail for political prisoners. During the 1980s, when use of the prison was allegedly at its peak, it is estimated that several thousand were incarcerated, tortured, and often killed there—horrendous conditions that were laid bare in a 2002 report by Amnesty International.[27] In 1980, an assassination attempt, purportedly linked to the Muslim Brotherhood, was made against President Hafez al-Assad. On the day following this attempt, a wholesale massacre took place within the prison. Sixty soldiers were dispatched to Tadmor by al-Assad's brother, and any prisoner presumed to have links with the Muslim Brotherhood was summarily executed. There are no precise figures as to how many people died that day; most reports start at 500–600 individuals, but it could have been as many as 2,400.[28]

When Bashar al-Assad succeeded his father to the presidency in 2001, he closed down the prison in Tadmor. It was a clear political statement that in taking office, he also hoped to begin a new political era in Syria. This didn't last: with the outbreak of conflict in 2011, the prison was reopened and again used to house political prisoners before the city was taken by ISIS in May 2015. It remains unclear what exactly happened at this point, but certainly photographs were circulated worldwide by the media showing the prison emptied of its captives. While it is unlikely that capturing the prison was the primary aim of ISIS, it was nonetheless an act that garnered significant international attention. A more likely reason behind ISIS's seizure of Tadmor in 2015 is that the site was—just as it had been in Antiquity—a nodal point in the Syrian Desert between East and West, and a center of infrastructural importance in the region. In the aftermath of the prison's destruction, there has been some debate as to whether it can ever be desirable to simply erase a legacy of history in this way.[29] However, former prisoners once kept in Tadmor have suggested that the destruction of the prison was one way of wiping out memories of the political and humanitarian injustices that have taken place there over the decades.

ISIS wrought massive devastation in Tadmor in the weeks after they claimed the city, events that have been covered in depth by the international media (Fig. 51). Images cataloguing the destruction of the Temples of Bel and Baalshamin, as well as the Triumphal Arch and several of the city's prominent tower tombs, have circulated worldwide (Fig. 52).[30] It is worthy of note, however, that some of the first monuments to be attacked by ISIS units were in fact connected to the early Islamic past.[31] These included the grave shrines of Muhammad ibn ʿAli, a descendant of the prophet Muhammad, which was located north of the city, and that of the Muslim holy man Nizra Abou Baha ed-Din, whose shrine was located in the oasis itself and dated from the seventeenth century.[32] While ISIS has been accused of specifically targeting Roman period monuments to obliterate the region's pagan past, it is clear that this is not the whole truth. The group has also destroyed monuments from later periods, including those belonging to the Islamic period, from not only Palmyra but also elsewhere in Syria and across their strongholds in the wider Near East. The destruction by ISIS of these Islamic period monuments clearly underlines the tensions between religious groups that have long played a role in struggles in this region.

In August 2015, Khaled al-Asaad, the director of both the archeological site of Palmyra and its museum, was publicly beheaded by ISIS, and his body

Figure 51 The explosion of the temple of Baalshamin in 2015 (CPA Media Pte Ltd/Alamy Stock Photo).

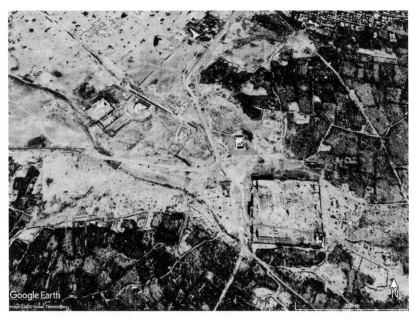

Figure 52 Aerial view of parts of Palmyra with the visible destructions to various buildings in the city (Google Earth Image 2020, Maxar Technologies).

hung from a column on Palmyra's ancient main street.[33] He had insisted on protecting the site and the objects in the Palmyra Museum and had paid the ultimate price for his dedication. ISIS transformed Palmyra's ancient theater into a backdrop for the killings of their numerous enemies and turned the ancient ruins of the dead city into the scene of a living nightmare for Palmyra's people.[34] The past was used to stage real-time atrocities and to emphasize cultural differences between East and West, as well as hostilities between different political and religious groups in the region.

Reclaiming Palmyra—The Work Ahead

By 2016, attempts were being made by Syrian troops, backed by airstrikes from their Russian allies, to reclaim Palmyra. The city was recaptured in March of that year, and on 5 May 2016, Palmyra's Roman theater was filled with the strains of classical music as St. Petersburg's Mariinsky Orchestra performed a concert, conducted by the Russian Valery Gergiev (Plate 15). This event, entitled *A Prayer for Palmyra*, was attended by the heads of many of Syria's different religious and ethnic communities, as well as representatives of Syrian and Russian troops, Russian officials, heritage professionals, and even ten key ambassadors to UNESCO.[35] During the event, the president of Russia, Vladimir Putin, gave a speech via video-link, in which he claimed that the orchestra's performance gave "hope for Palmyra's revival as the heritage of the whole community" as well as "hope that our contemporary civilization will be relieved from this horrible disease, international terrorism."

The concert was very much a hyper-politicized event and one carefully designed by the Syrian and Russian regimes to cement their allegiance with backing from the cultural heritage community, among them the ambassadors from UNESCO and other cultural heritage personalities, and against the backdrop of a world-famous cultural heritage city. The staging of the concert in Palmyra offers a clear reminder that cultural heritage remains, as it has always been, an effective tool for political propaganda. Once again, Palmyra stood caught between East and West in the great play of international politics—a situation not unlike that of the third century CE, when Parthia and Rome faced off across the Syrian Desert, with Palmyra in the middle.[36] A few months after the concert, in December 2016, Palmyra once again fell to ISIS, before being reclaimed by Syrian troops with the help of their Russian allies in March 2017 after several earlier attempts to regain control of the area.[37]

Since this time, Palmyra has remained under Syrian governmental control, and some foreign archeological missions who have previously worked in Palmyra have returned to the site in the hope that they can help to rebuild the destroyed museums and provide an inventory of objects left after the devastation.[38] There is absolutely no doubt that throughout the years of political turmoil in Palmyra, antiquities continued to be exported illegally from the city. Although these objects occasionally surface in the catalogues of international auction houses, this route has largely been blocked to those wishing to sell antiquities, as auction houses are aware that almost all objects from Syria result from illegal excavations and exports. The vast majority of artifacts therefore circulate on the black market, and no amount of monitoring can hope to provide a full overview of the objects that end up in private collections or even in some museums.

As the conflict in Syria has continued, several projects have been initiated that are designed to monitor the destruction, looting, and trafficking of cultural heritage in addition to a number of policy papers that have also been published.[39] New programs have been designed that allow monuments from Palmyra and elsewhere to be reconstructed in virtual reality or in digital format.[40] The #NEWPALMYRA project, for example, has focused on creating readily accessible digital models of Palmyra's damaged monuments,[41] allowing "visitors" to the site to navigate through virtual environments to visit the city's now-lost artifacts.[42] Meanwhile, a London project set up in 2016 after the destruction of Palmyra's Triumphal Arch has created a scaled 3D-model of the monument from marble, gaining significant media attention in the process.[43] Other projects have focused instead on disseminating Palmyra's cultural heritage through online exhibitions, such as that organized by the Getty Institute in 2017 under the title *The Legacy of Ancient Palmyra*,[44] or through important archival work.[45] Examples of the latter type of work include a Swiss-based project that uses the archives of the archeologist Paul Collart to create a digital restoration of the destroyed Baalshamin Temple and a Danish project to digitize the archive of Harald Ingholt.[46] Alongside these projects can be listed the work of not-for-profit organizations such as Syrianforheritage[47] and the Syrian Heritage Archive Project, which aim to make documentation about Syria's cultural heritage available to both scholars and the wider public in the hope that it can facilitate later reconstruction in the country.[48] Several international academic conferences and exhibitions have also taken Palmyra and its important cultural heritage as their main theme.[49] Yet while there is no doubt that these initiatives make it possible to disseminate knowledge about Palmyra, Syria, and the wider loss of our cultural heritage, we cannot ignore the fact that the damage done to this ancient city is irreversible. Support is now desperately needed to assess the level of destruction for conservation and preservation projects and for future reconstruction work. These are our most crucial tasks, if peace can be restored to the region.

In the case of Palmyra, the damage done to the site is so extensive that archeologists must unfortunately accept the possibility that they might never return to the sites where they once worked. This provides those archeologists who can work in Palmyra with a large responsibility, namely, to document all new finds as they come out of the ground. This has immense implications with regard to the kinds of resources that can be put toward excavation and documentation, but it is also an incredibly important responsibility, and it can only be carried out by the various archeological missions in charge. If we can learn anything from the damage that has been done to Syrian cultural heritage—and more broadly, to the cultural heritage that belongs to us all—it is that documentation and publication of finds are vital and deserving of the highest priority.

This book has not set out to be a comprehensive account of Palmyrene history. Rather, the intention was to provide broad overviews as well as to offer more detailed insights into some aspects of Palmyrene archeology and history across a long durée perspective. It also attempts to reflect the current state of our knowledge of Palmyra's archeology and history, with the knowledge presented here allowing us to peer beneath the legends that still enshroud the city to get a glimpse of the reality underneath. However, this volume has also inevitably touched on broader contemporary issues as a result of the Syrian civil war and the latent threat this poses to cultural heritage; such issues are now an inextricable part of Palmyra's history and demand our attention.

Today, we stand at a crossroads. It would be naïve to wish that political power-holders around the globe could reconcile their differences and that the protection of cultural heritage might become a priority in a world that faces many pressing challenges. What we can do, however, is focus on our own practices, and the impact these might make. Palmyra remains a pearl of the desert, and we must hope that one day we can revisit this site with new research agendas that will shed more light on this fascinating place and the people who once dwelt there. In doing so, we could not only open up new perspectives on the ancient world, but also on the world in which we live today. If study of the past can tell us anything, it is that we do not know what the future will hold. Nonetheless, we must aim at optimizing how we work with the material and evidence we have at our disposal, and take what responsibility we can in the here and now.

Postludium

Palmyra—A Tie in an Ever-Changing Network

The aim of this book was to provide an overview of the archeology and history of Palmyra in the light of scholarship that has been conducted both on and off the site since the late nineteenth century. The book also provided a survey of the site's earliest visitors before archeological work was carried out in a systematic way, and it explored the treatment of the site in the midst of the ongoing conflict in Syria. While I do not claim to have exhaustively covered all topics, it is my hope that the book can be used as a point of departure for further specialist reading, references to which can be found here in the notes and bibliography. Parts of this book have provided new insights into the material collected within the framework of the Palmyra Portrait Project, which I established in 2012, and the impact that this corpus has had on our understanding of Roman Palmyra and its society as a place situated between Rome and Parthia.[1] While this material cannot provide answers to all questions, it does underline the importance of baseline projects for changing the way in which we can approach the study of the past and for drawing out nuances that could not otherwise be identified in our usually scattered epigraphic, written, and archeological evidence.

While much scholarship has focused on Palmyra's situation as a site caught between East and West and as a city which was never entirely its own place, this book has instead focused on drawing out our evidence for a strong but often overlooked local Palmyrene identity. This was deeply rooted in the city's family-oriented and tribal-based society, which endured throughout the Roman period and which can be most clearly identified in the continuation of the city's local funerary portrait tradition. While Palmyrenes understood how to position themselves and their society in their interactions with other people and across a wide range of spheres, they only did so in ways that allowed them to keep local traditions alive among themselves. The city of Palmyra does not seem to have been an inclusive place, and certainly there is little in the evidence pointing to large-scale integration of foreigners

Pearl of the Desert. Rubina Raja, Oxford University Press. © Oxford University Press 2022.
DOI: 10.1093/oso/9780190852221.003.0007

or to a Palmyrene adoption of anything other than broad fashion trends. But it is also clear that when Palmyrenes themselves traveled abroad, they were quick to assimilate into new societies, despite continuing to use their native tongue alongside other languages and to make use of distinctively Palmyrene imagery.

One of my intentions with this book was to make it clear that Palmyra's development cannot be viewed solely along a linear evolutionary perspective set within the wider historical framework of the rise and fall of the Roman Empire. The book opened with a citation from Pliny that firmly identified Palmyra as a city caught between Rome and Parthia. Too often, however, only the influences from the West have been examined in history and archeology, and not those from the East. Perhaps most crucially, however, there is a need to remember Pliny's comment that Palmyra was a city "with a destiny of its own" between these two empires, and to examine Palmyra, its society, and the sources that relate to them on their own terms, set within an independent framework and from the perspective of Palmyrene society, albeit with an awareness of the wider surrounding world. The ethnic composition of Palmyra did not change with the coming of Roman domination or after the Umayyad conquest of the city. Tadmor existed long before it became Palmyra, and it has remained Tadmor ever since. In the future, then, we must hope that careful work, which considers ethnographic comparanda studies alongside our archeological and written sources, might shed further light on the ongoing resilience and ability of the Palmyrene people to adapt and to pursue their own destiny in a city that since Antiquity has formed part of a globalized world.

Notes

Acknowledgments

1. Andrade (2013), (2018).
2. Butcher (2003).
3. Dirven (1999).
4. Edwell (2008).
5. Gawlikowski (1970), (1987b).
6. Hartmann (2001).
7. Intagliata (2018).
8. Kaizer (2002).
9. Millar (1993).
10. Sartre (2001); Sartre-Fauriat and Sartre (2014), (2016).
11. Seland (2016).
12. Smith (2013).
13. Dupont-Sommer (1942); Sommer (2005), (2017a), (2017b).
14. Yon (2002), *IGLS* 17.1, (2013).
15. Palmyra Portrait Project, 'Bibliography'.

Chapter 1

1. Pliny, *NH* 5.88: *Palmyra urbs nobilis situ, divitiis soli et aquis amoensis, vasto undique ambitu harensis includit agros, ac velut terris exempta a rerum natura, privata sorte inter duo imperia summa Romanorum Parthorumque et prima in discordia semper utrimque cura.* Pliny's description of Palmyra's location stems from 77 CE and is taken from H. Rackman's translation from the Loeb series, Pliny, *NH* 5.88. Pliny the Elder (23 BCE–79 CE).
2. For example, the *Historia Augusta* is one source that gives information—but quite unreliably—about Palmyra and Zenobia. See Andrade (2018), (2019) for new contributions on Zenobia, and Sartre-Fauriat and Sartre (2014).
3. See Veyne (2015) for a recent account of the city's history. Contra: Sartre-Fauriat and Sartre (2016); Sartre (2016); Sartre-Fauriat (2019).
4. Hammad (2013).
5. UNESCO, "Site of Palmyra." Also see Raja (2016a).
6. On Pliny the Elder, see Gibson and Morello (2011) as well as Murphy (2004).
7. See Meyer (2017) for recent work on the Palmyrena, the hinterland of Palmyra.

8. See Shifman (2014) for an English translation of an earlier Russian work on the Tax Tariff. See also Shifman (2014) 55–56 for a discussion of the earlier tax law on which the edict of 137 CE was to a large extent based. This source is not as well known as the Tax Tariff of the Hadrianic period, but it tells us that a certain amount of legislation was, unsurprisingly, already in place. The Tax Tariff, which is today in the Hermitage Museum, was discovered by the Russian Prince S. S. Abamelek-Lazarev in 1881.

9. Shifman (2014) is the standard work on this important document about the socioeconomic history of Palmyra.

10. For a broader perspective on trade between the Roman Empire and other regions, see McLaughlin (2016).

11. Matthews (1984). Also see Gawlikowski (2013), (2014b).

12. See Meyer (2017) 17–27, in particular pp. 24–27 for an overview of wells and cisterns from the period between Roman and early Islamic times, and p. 26 for the problems concerning the chronology of cisterns and wells, which are difficult to date due to the nature of their construction.

13. See Meyer (2017) 24–25 for these springs and p. 41 for an example of a qanat (underground aqueduct) in the hinterland of Palmyra as well as Barański (1997) and Hammad (2010) 25–30 for a discussion of the Abu Fawares qanat that brought potable water into the city. See also Hammad (2010) 34–35 for details of the 11 km Abar al-Amy qanat, which also brought water to Palmyra.

14. Crouch (1975b) 151–186; Barański (1997). Furthermore Gawlikowski (1997b). Also see Hoffmann-Salz (2011) 402–405, (2015) 239–247, as well as Yon (2009).

15. Meyer (2017) 17. The work conducted between 2008 and 2011 by the Norwegian survey team has brought to light important knowledge about the territory of Tadmor in a longue durée perspective: Anfinset (2009); Anfinset and Hesse (2013). See also Schou (2014) and Meyer et al. (2016b) for a collection of articles, some of which relate to the nature of the territory and agriculture of Palmyra.

16. Meyer (2017) 17. The amount of rain could differ significantly from year to year: Seland (2016) 18.

17. Shifman (2014) lines 47–48 in the translation of the tariff, p. 119 on sheep from the territory brought in for shearing.

18. Seland (2016) 17 has rightly pointed out that the region of Palmyra is topographically diverse and features both mountains and ravines. It therefore does not fit the standard description of a steppe desert, even though this term is often used in the literature about the region of Palmyra.

19. Meyer (2017) 28–57.

20. Raja and Seland (2021); Schlumberger (1951) for the standard work on the art of the Palmyrene.

21. The area surveyed by the Syrian-Norwegian team was 30 km by 120 km (19 by 75 miles), and this did not cover the entire territory that once belonged to Palmyra: see Anfinset and Meyer (2010). The Tax Tariff gives information about taxation of water usage in the city itself (column 2, line 8), Shifman (2014) 116. For an important earlier comparative study on the complexities of desert landscapes and their developments in the Roman period (although not on the Palmyrene desert) see Barker (2002). Also

see Smith (2013) 71–74 on the territory of Palmyra. However, the work done by the Syrian-Norwegian team has significantly increased our knowledge about Palmyra's territory in the period since the publication of Smith's book.

22. Seland (2016) 15–17.

23. Seland (2016) 17.

24. See Rosen (2017) for a recent study on mobile pastoralism. Although focusing on the Negev, this work introduces important perspectives that are relevant for understanding Palmyrene society.

25. Edwell (2008), (2019).

26. Meyer and Seland (2016); Seland (2011), (2013), (2016); Schörle (2017).

27. See, for example, Raja (2016a), (2017c), (2017e), (2019b), (2020b). Also see Graf (2019).

28. Also see the accounts given by Sartre-Fauriat and Sartre (2008); Shifman (2014); Sommer (2017a); Intagliata (2018).

29. The debates surrounding the meaning of the Semitic, Greek, and Roman names of the site are extensive. Most suggestions revolve around Tadmor, which may be connected to the Semitic word for the date palm (*tamar*). This refers to the palm trees that surrounded the city. The Greek name of the city, ΠΑΛΜΥΡΑ, and Latin, Palmyra, are believed either to have been derived from the Semitic name Tadmor, or to be a direct translation of Tadmor into the Greek παλαμη. For further discussion on this, see O'Connor (1988) 235.

30. Sartre-Fauriat and Sartre (2016) 18–19.

31. Sommer (2017b) 14.

32. Sartre-Fauriat and Sartre (2016) 20; Seland (2019) 129.

33. Gawlikowski (forthcoming).

34. For the Cappadocian tablet, see Starcky (1952) 27–28. For the Mari documents see Michelini Tocci (1960) 94–95. One is a letter (ARM V, no. 23) from an individual named Tarin-Shakim to the king of Mari, Iasmah-Addu, in which Tarin-Shakim writes about nomads attacking Tadmor and the neighboring Nashalâ. The other document, by an unknown author, speaks about four Tadmorians who came from Qatna to Mari to see Iasmah-Addu: Dossin (1951) 19–21, esp. p. 20. See also Starcky and Gawlikowski (1985); Sommer (2005) 149–150.

35. Arbeitman (1988) 238, Mari archives (eighteenth century BCE and Egypt twelfth century BCE). Du Mesnil du Buisson (1966) 186–187 points to evidence that supports a date of origin for settlement at Tadmor in the last centuries of the third millennium BCE. Also, see Shifman (2014) 14–18 for a short account of the evidence from the second and first millennia BCE. For the archeological evidence, see Klengel (1972) 31; Haider (1987) 115; Scharrer (2002) 305. Also Sommer (2005) 149; Shifman (2014) 14–17 provides an excellent overview of the discussions surrounding the early sources on Tadmor.

36. 2 Chr 8:4.

37. 1 Kings 9:18. Also see Sommer (2017b) 24 for an overview of this discussion. For a contrary view see Veyne (2015) 54.

38. Sartre-Fauriat and Sartre (2016) 18; contra Veyne (2015) 54. Also Sommer (2017b) 24.

39. Shifman (2014) 15 also for further references.
40. However, also see Joannès (1997); Hesse (2016).
41. See Shifman (2014) 16 for this period.
42. Gawlikowski (2019) 79. Also absent in Cohen (2006).
43. See Graf (2019) 300 for the summary of sources: Polybius (5.79) writes about the Syrian general Zabdibēlos in charge of the "Arabs and neighboring tribes" under Antiochus III at Raphia in 217 BCE battling Ptolemy IV. The general Zabdibēlos bore a name similar to many at Palmyra, and according to Graf (referring to Milik (1972) 53) Zabdibēlos would have been used in Palmyra. An Aramaic text of Asoka in Afghanistan might mention a "tdmr," (Dupont-Sommer (1970)) but could equally refer to Timrid (Tmrd) on the Oxus: see Kaizer (2017b) 33–34.
44. Schmidt-Colinet and al-As'ad (2013). Also see Schmidt-Colinet (forthcoming) for an overview of the evidence connected to the Hellenistic period in Palmyra. Furthermore, see Graf (2018) 481–483 for a summary of the Hellenistic evidence.
45. For a comprehensive overview of the evidence see Schmidt-Colinet (forthcoming). See also Schmidt-Colinet and al-As'ad (2000); Schmidt-Colinet and Plattner (2001); Schmidt-Colinet and al-As'ad (2002); Schmidt-Colinet et al. (2008); Schmidt-Colinet and al-As'ad (2013).
46. Will (1983); Hammad (2010).
47. Schmidt-Colinet and al-As'ad (2000); Schmidt-Colinet and Plattner (2001); Schmidt-Colinet et al. (2008); Schmidt-Colinet and al-As'ad (2013). Schmidt-Colinet reports on remains that can be traced back as far as the third century BC. In particular Schmidt-Colinet and al-As'ad (2000) 79–169. Also see Schmidt-Colinet (forthcoming) for a complete overview of the evidence from Palmyra in the Hellenistic period, and Kaizer (2020) 24–26 for a succinct discussion of Hellenistic Palmyra.
48. Appian's passage on Palmyra, although discussed, does remind us that the site was known in the middle of the first century BCE and must have been monumentalized in some shape. See, for example, Cohen (2006). Also see Sartre (2001); Millar (1993). Jones (1937) still remains a standard work on the evidence (in particular written sources) of the cities in the Roman East and holds important overviews of the development of numerous places, including Palmyra (particularly 266–269). See, for example, several of the contributions in Blömer et al. (2015) for discussions of evidence—or lack thereof—at other sites in the region.
49. See Millar (1993) for cultural amnesia and Sartre (2005) for cultural continuity. See also Millar (1987a), (1987b). For a recent perspective on the evidence from the region in general, see the convincing argument by Andrade (2013), who tackles the problems with the approaches that have hitherto led to a dichotomy in the reading of the evidence.
50. Schmidt-Colinet (forthcoming).
51. See note 60. The area investigated by the Austrian-Syrian team was demolished in the late third century CE after the sack of the city; at this time the city had contracted and was enclosed by a new city wall, which left out almost half of the Roman-period city (Gawlikowski (2019) 79). This is discussed in more detail in Chapter 5.
52. See, for example, Clarke et al. (2016) for the evidence from Jebel Khalid.

53. Sartre (2005) 37–43 on the campaigns of Pompey in Syria. For a general history of the region in the Hellenistic and Roman periods, see Millar (1993); Sartre (2005); Butcher (2003). Despite some doubtful interpretations, Ball (2016) also tackles some of the evidence—in particular, architectural evidence. For a brief but insightful discussion of Palmyra's integration into the Roman Empire, see Kaizer (2020) 26–29.

54. Recent accounts of the urban development of the site include Burns (2017) 233–251; Smith (2013) 21–32; and Gawlikowski (2019). Other important publications on the site, its archeology, and its history include Butcher (2003); Millar (1993); and Sartre (2001). Also see Schlumberger (1935); van Berchem (1976); Frézouls (1976); Will (1983); and Hammad (2010) for accounts explaining the development of the city. For a recent contribution to the discussions about the cultural identity of Palmyra, see Andrade (2013) 171–210.

55. Schmidt-Colinet and Plattner (2001); Schmidt-Colinet (forthcoming).

56. Seyrig (1939) 322–323, Fig. 11, no. 28, (1940a); du Mesnil du Buisson (1966) 179–185, Figs. 5–6; Gawlikowski (1973) 53–66, esp. 54–56; Will (1992) 37–38; al-Maqdissi (2000); Bounni and al-Maqdissi (2001); Delplace and Dentzer-Feydy (2017) 73–74; Sommer (2017a) 61–62; Graf (2018) 483–489.

57. In 217 BCE a Palmyrene detachment fought for the Seleucid army at the battle of Raphia according to Polybius (Polyb. 5.79.8), also see Seyrig (1940b) 331; Gawlikowski (1973) 54; Fellmann (1976b) 214. Palmyrene proper names and a Palmyrene tribe are mentioned in connection with trade relations: see Fellmann (1970) 118–119, (1976b), 213–214; Milik (1972) 173; Gawlikowski (1973) 54; Will (1992) 34–35. See Seyrig (1939) 322–323, Fig. 11, no. 28, and Grainger (1990) 182 n. 52 for a potential mention of a Seleucid king Ephiphanes in Palmyra, c. 90/80 BCE.

58. Southern (2003); Seager (2002). Also see Rey-Coquais (1978) for a survey of the history of the region.

59. Appian, *Bell. Civ.* 5.9.38–39; Hekster and Kaizer (2004); Sommer (2017a) 76–81.

60. See van Wijlick (2021).

61. Perowne (1956), (2003) 77–79. Millar (1993) 27–42 for the time from the Battle of Actium in 31 BCE until the death of Herod the Great in 4 BCE.

62. See, for example, Gruen (2009) 11–28; Barrett (2008); Günther (2008).

63. See Sartre (2001), (2005) 88–92 for Herod the Great. In this book, I refer to the English translation of the French 2001 edition published in 2005.

64. Josephus, *AJ*; *BJ*; 15.331–341.

65. *PAT* 2636; *IGLS* 17.1.17–18: *gbl tdmry*; Παλμυρηνῶν ὁ δῆμος/ἡ πόλις. Smith (2013) 56–57.

66. Graf (2019) 295–318.

67. Henning (2013a), (2013b), (2019a); Amy and Seyrig (1936); Seyrig et al. (1968), (1975). Also see Gawlikowski (2019) 81.

68. Gawlikowski (2019).

69. Raja (2019f).

70. For general introductions to the history of Palmyra in this period, see Smith (2013); Edwell (2008), (2013); Sommer (2005).

71. Appian, *Bell. Civ.* V. 9, describes how Palmyra was sacked by Mark Antony and his troops in 41 BCE as a repercussion for the city's trade relations with the Parthians. Also, see Seyrig (1932a).
72. See, for example, Curtis (2017); Long (2017).
73. Hanson (2016), 769–770.
74. For summaries of discussions about population estimates (assumed to be between 40,000 and 60,000 with up to a quarter of a million living in the surrounding territory), see Savino (1999) 69–75; Kaizer (2002) 17–18. However, such estimations remain highly speculative.
75. Discussions about the nature of these groups are complex and have been undertaken elsewhere. They should not be looked upon merely as tribes—a term that carries many colonial implications—but perhaps rather as civic groups, such as the *phylai* known from other societies under Greek influence. For an outline of these discussions, see Kaizer (2002) 43–51; Smith (2013) 33–54.
76. Piersimoni (1995a), (1995b), which is unpublished but summarized in Kaizer (2002) 48–49.
77. Schlumberger (1971); contra Gawlikowski (1973). See also summary in Kaizer (2002) 48–49.
78. For a study of the representations of Palmyrene women and the sources connected to women in Palmyra, as well as further references, see Krag (2018). Also see Yon (2002) 165–196 and the contributions in Krag and Raja (2019b).
79. No female priests are known from Palmyra. The vast corpus of funerary sculpture depicts many Palmyrene male priests, but not a single female priestess, and we have to assume that women did not act as priestesses as also the epigraphic evidence does not indicate women in such roles. See Raja (2019d).
80. For an impressive volume including the most precise maps of Palmyra existing until now, see Schnädelbach (2010).
81. Gawlikowski (2019); Schlumberger (1935). For new excavations, which, though giving some Hellenistic evidence, are concerned mainly with the Roman period, see Schmidt-Colinet and al-As'ad (2013).
82. For a detailed overview of the development of Palmyra, see Hammad (2010). For an earlier contribution, see Schlumberger (1935). Also see Delplace and Dentzer-Feydy (2005); Barański (1995).
83. For many of these inscriptions and the interpretations of them, see Yon (2002), *IGLS* 17.1.
84. In the tetrapolis city of Apamea, in Syria, such consoles are found as well, although not to the extent that they appear in Palmyra.
85. For positions and professions in Palmyra, see Raja (2019k) and the contributions in Long and Sørensen (2017).
86. On the quarries of Palmyra, see Schmidt-Colinet (1995b), (2017).
87. Russell (2013).
88. Seyrig et al. (1975).
89. Bounni et al. (1992–2004); Collart and Vicari (1969); Gawlikowski (2019). For the standard work on Palmyrene religious life, see Kaizer (2002).

90. For the religious life of the city, see Kaizer (2002).
91. Raja (2017h), (2017i). For the sculptural representations of priests in Palmyra, see Raja (2019d). For the tesserae, see Raja (2015a), (2015d).
92. Raja (2015a), (2015d) as well as Will (1997); Kaizer (2002) 213–233; Gnoli (2016).
93. In Schnädelbach (2010) all known graves have been marked on maps and can be counted.
94. For the tower tombs, see Henning (2013a), (2013b), (2019a).
95. Gawlikowski (1970); Schmidt-Colinet (1992).
96. For a volume concerning families in Palmyra, see Krag and Raja (2019b).
97. Palmyra Portrait Project. Also see Krag and Raja (2019b); Krag et al. (2019); Raja (2018b), (2017e); Long and Sørensen (2017); Kropp and Raja (2016).
98. Raja (2019k).
99. Kropp and Raja (2014), (2015).
100. Raja (2017e) as well as Blömer and Raja (2019b).
101. Colledge (1976) 15–16. For the state of research on Palmyrene language, see the Wisconsin Palmyrene Aramaic Inscription Project. For general introductions to Aramaic, including Palmyrene Aramaic, see also Gzella (2011); Creason (2004).
102. Kaizer (2002) 28. Millar (1993) 470 states that "Palmyra . . . was the only publicly bilingual city in the Roman Near East." For a discussion of this citation and language issues in Palmyra in general, also see Kaizer (2017a) 87–94.
103. In general, for the inscriptions, see *PAT* and *IGLS*.
104. However, see a recent comprehensive summary of the debates about the Silk Road, about trade between the East and Syria, and about Palmyra's role in trade in the Roman period by Graf (2018).
105. Meyer and Seland (2016); Meyer et al. (2016). On the Palmyrene elite, see Yon (2002), (2019). For the dress codes of men in Palmyra, see Heyn and Raja (2019). Also see Raja and Seland (2021).
106. Seland (2017).
107. Schörle (2017); Seland (2015b), (2016).
108. For inscriptions relating to trade, see, for example, *PAT* nos. 1584, 1376, 0262, 0274, 0294. On Palmyrenes in the Gulf, see Will (1992) as well as Young (2001).
109. On Palmyrenes in Dura-Europos, see Dirven (1999).
110. Hannestad (1988) 160.
111. Colledge (1976), (1987), (1996). Also see Pliny, *NH* V.88 for this comment. Also see Raja (2019b) and Graf (2019).
112. Seyrig (1950b); Edwell (2019).
113. For introductions to the reception of Zenobia in history, see, for example, the exhibition catalogue Charles-Gaffiot et al. (2001); Sartre (2016).
114. Much literature has appeared on Zenobia in the last years. Most recently, Andrade (2018) published a monograph about Zenobia. The work by Sartre-Fauriat and Sartre (2014) is also recommended. In addition, see Yon (2002–2003) as well as the book in Danish by Hvidberg-Hansen (2002). See also Andrade (2019).
115. Hanson (2016); Hartmann (2008) 343–378, (2016). On Palmyra in the third century CE, see in general Hartmann (2001), (2016) as well as Smith (2013) 175–181.

116. For Palmyrene trade, see Seland (2015a), (2015b), (2016). For changes in trade routes, see Young (2001); Intagliata (2018). For the Indo-Roman trade in general, see the work by Gurukkal (2016).
117. For Late Antique and early Islamic Palmyra, see Gawlikowski (2009) as well as Intagliata (2018), (2019).
118. *HA* TT 30.27.
119. *HA* TT 30.15–16.
120. A recent study on human remains and in particular teeth from ancient Palmyra discusses the potential reasons for Zenobia's white teeth; see Yoshimura et al. (2016). However, the source describing her is in many ways unreliable, and the description of Zenobia—and her teeth—should not be trusted.
121. For an introduction to Zenobia, also see Andrade (2019).
122. For general introductions and an overview of aspects of Palmyrene archeology and history, see Veyne (2017); Smith (2013). For general overviews of the archeology and history of the Roman Near East, see the standard works by Millar (1993) and Sartre (2001) as well as the more recent book by Butcher (2003).
123. For a contribution on Palmyra's knowledge culture as reflected in the portrait habit of the city, see Raja (2017e).
124. See Intagliata (2018), (2019) for the Late Antique and early Islamic periods.
125. Adler (1907). Benjamin of Tudela visited the Near East between 1160 and 1173, though whether he visited Palmyra is disputed. See Sartre-Fauriat (2019). A concise and useful overview of the early travelers to Palmyra is given in the introduction to the English translation of the original Russian publication, Shifman (2014).
126. *The Ruins of Palmyra*, also found under the title *The ruins of Palmyra, otherwise Tedmor, in the desart* (Wood (1753)).
127. For the tower tombs, see Henning (2013a), (2013b). For an earlier publication, which also includes the underground tombs, the hypogea, see Gawlikowski (1970). Furthermore, see the following publications for the temple or house tombs: al-As'ad and Schmidt-Colinet (1985); Schmidt-Colinet (1987), (1992), (1997).
128. Raja (2018b) as well as "Palmyra and the collection in the Ny Carlsberg Glyptotek" in Raja (2019e) 11–59.
129. The number of museum and private collections registered in the Palmyra Portrait Project database come to a total of 188. This number does not include those collections that have come into existence since the civil war broke out in Syria, and where provenance of the objects cannot be verified with any certainty.
130. See Sartre-Fauriat (2019), also for further references.
131. A good place to begin is one of the newer general books on Palmyra: Andrade (2018) and Sommer (2017a), (2017b). For more archeologically focused research, the volumes in the series *Palmyrene Studies* give introductions to much of the recent work undertaken in Palmyra: Kropp and Raja (2016), Long and Sørensen (2017), Krag and Raja (2019b) as well as Raja (2019i); Nielsen and Raja (2019).
132. Palmyra Portrait Project.

Chapter 2

1. Schörle (forthcoming a).
2. Seland (2015b), (2016).
3. See Smith (2013) 33–40 for an overview of the strongest polarizations within these discussions, highlighting the opinions of Scharrer (2010) and Millar (1993), respectively. Scharrer is of the opinion that the Palmyrenes did not share an ethnic identity with the surrounding nomadic groups, contra Millar (1993), 319 and 331, as well as Millar (1987a). Also see Gawlikowski (1995a), (1995b), (1997b) 41–45.
4. Smith (2013) 33.
5. Anfinset and Meyer (2010); Meyer (2013), (2017); Hesse (2016); Meyer et al. (2016a), (2016b); Krzywinski and Krzywinski (2016).
6. Savino (1999) 69–75.
7. Seland (2010), (2011), (2013), (2015a), (2015b), (2016), (2017), (2019); Meyer and Seland (2016); Schörle (2017).
8. See Chapter 4. Dirven (1999).
9. Gawlikowski (2013), (2014b).
10. Shifman (2014) for the standard work on the tariff. Here also Shifman (2014) 93.
11. Shifman (2014) 85.
12. Shifman (2014) 85.
13. *PAT*; Cussini (2005), (2012), (2016a), (2016b); Saito (2005a), (2005b), (2005c); Raja and Steding (2021).
14. See Krag and Raja (2019a), (2019b) for a collection of articles focusing on Palmyrene families.
15. This situation is consistently reflected in the funerary sphere across the Roman period in Palmyra; see Chapter 3. The situation in the funerary sphere in many ways stands in contrast to much of the evidence from the public sphere, an interesting observation that again suggests that Palmyrene society could at once uphold local traditions while simultaneously integrating itself firmly into the Roman imperial world. The Palmyra Portrait Project, which since 2012 has collected all known funerary portraiture, has made this distinct situation extremely clear for the first time, revealing a consistent pattern across the three centuries in which the sculpture was produced. See, for example, Raja (2015c), (2019a), (2019d), (2019f).
16. Gawlikowski (1970); Henning (2013a and b); Sadurska and Bounni (1994).
17. Yon (1999a), (1999b), (2002), (2019); al-As'ad and Yon (2007); Heyn and Raja (2019).
18. Sadurska and Bounni (1994); Sadurska (1995); Gawlikowski (1996c).
19. The earliest of these reliefs was on the tower tomb of Kîtôt, dating to 40 CE: Henning (2013b) 312–313 with previous bibliography. Founder reliefs were also seen on the tower tombs of 'Ogeîlû, from 73 CE: Henning (2013b) 286 with previous bibliography; the tower tomb of Elahbel, 103 CE: Henning (2013b) 152–154 with previous bibliography; the tower tomb of Iamlikû: Henning (2013b) 192–195 with previous bibliography. Additionally, a founder relief that cannot be associated with a specific monument was found: Palmyra Museum, inv. no. A 3: Tanabe (1986) 42 pl. 416.

20. Dirven (1996), (1999), (2013); Smith (2013) chap. 6 on the Palmyrenes outside Palmyra; Schörle (forthcoming d).
21. Raja (forthcoming).
22. See Raja (2016d), (2017f), (2017g), (2017h), (2017i), (2018a), (2018b), (2019i) also for further references. Also see Graf (2019) drawing on research published by Raja. See Ingholt et al. (1955) for the tesserae.
23. Kaizer (2002) remains the standard work on the religious life of Palmyra. Now also see Raja (2019e) for a collection of contributions representing the status of our knowledge on Palmyrene religion.
24. Raja (2016d), (2017f), (2017h), (2019i).
25. Cussini (2005); Saito (2005b), (2005c); Heyn (2010), (2012); Cussini (2016a); Krag (2016), (2017a), (2017b), (2018), (2019); Krag and Raja (2016), (2017), (2018), (2019a); Henning (2019b); Yon (2002), (2002–2003), (2019); al-As'ad and Yon (2007).
26. For elite women and children, see Krag and Raja (2019b); Ringsborg (2017); Heyn (2019).
27. Yon (2002) 186–196.
28. There are currently 1,205 female representations in the Palmyra Portrait Project database. Yon (2002), (2019); Raja (2017c). Yon (2002–2003) mostly refers to inscriptions rather than surviving statues: See Yon (2002) 165–185 for elite women of Palmyra, and Yon (2002–2003) for women in the public sphere. For the position of women and their representation, see Krag (2018).
29. Krag (2018) is the standard work on the Palmyrene female funerary portraits.
30. Heyn (2012); Krag (2016), (2017b) (2018); Krag and Raja (2017), (2018), (2019b); Cussini (1995), (2005), (2012), (2016b); Yon (1999a), (2002–2003). Evidence from the last decades suggests that Palmyrene women could own property and had certain legal standing in some cases. However, we do not have any evidence that they held any sort of public offices, including priesthoods, throughout the entire Roman period.
31. Relief from the Temple of Allat: Palmyra Museum, inv. no. B 2310/8504: Krag (2018) 407, cat. 903; Gawlikowski (2017) 212. Relief from the Temple of Bel: Krag (2018) 407, cat. 904; Klaver (2019) 161, fig. 2.
32. Yon (2002–2003), (2019). Also see Cussini (2019); Henning (2019b); Klaver (2019); Sadurska (1991/1992).
33. Raja (2019e) cat. no. 136. Also see Vuolanto (2019); Kaizer (2019a) 82–84.
34. Cussini (1995), (2005), (2012), (2016b); Krag (2018) 124–128.
35. Raja (2017c).
36. Krag (2018) 34–35, 62, 117–120, cat. 301.
37. See, for example, objects in Ny Carlsberg Glyptotek's collection: Raja (2019e) cat. nos. 11, 47, 54 and 66.
38. Raja (2019e) cat. nos. 13 and 14.
39. For example, see Raja (2019e) cat. no. 67.
40. Kaizer (2002); Raja (2019a), (2019b), (2019f); Raja et al. (forthcoming a); Romanowska et al. (2021); Bobou et al. (2021).
41. Ingholt et al. (1955).
42. Smith (2013) 40; Kaizer (2002) 48–50.

43. Smith (2013) 40 and *PAT* 0296, 0297, 0299.
44. For founder reliefs in general, see Henning (2013b) 93–99. Thanks to the Palmyra Portrait Project database, we know of 1,364 funerary inscriptions associated with 1,083 objects (accessed 31.07.2020).
45. *PAT* 0168.
46. Translation from Smith (2013) 41.
47. Smith (2013) 42–43.
48. Kaizer (2002) 50.
49. See Kaizer (2002) 48–51 for an overview of these discussions. Most prominently Rostovtzeff (1935) 148 with a reference to Ingholt (1932a) 288, for the argument that these were the most important aristocratic families of the city. Contra Schlumberger (1971). For further important arguments, see Gawlikowski (1973); van Berchem (1976) 170–173 as well as Sartre (1996) 386.
50. See Chapter 2 for these sanctuaries.
51. See Smith (2013) 132–143 for a summary of the discussions.
52. Yon (2002) 66–72; Kaizer (2002) 43–51 and 60–66 as well as Smith (2013) 132–143.
53. Millar (1993); Sartre (1996), (2001); Sartre-Fauriat and Sartre (2016); Kaizer (2007). Bowersock (1990) 7 summarizes this discussion by concluding that Palmyra should not be considered a truly Greek city because it did not have a theater and gymnasium. In fact, construction of a theater, located by the main street, was started in Palmyra during the Severan period, but it was never finished. See Frézouls (1952) 87—91, (1959) 224.
54. Despite focusing on coinage, Kaizer (2007) gives a thorough overview of the discussions and views on the evidence from Palmyra.
55. Cohen (2006); Gawlikowski (2019) 79; Raja (2012) 137–190.
56. Sartre (1996); Sartre-Fauriat and Sartre (2016) 94–103; Millar (1993) 319–336 also rightly acknowledges that Palmyra was different from other urban locations in the region. See also Cohen (2006).
57. See, for example, Millar (1993) 320 for skepticism about the potential extent of Hellenistic phases.
58. Here, aspects of seasonal movements would also have played a large role, which is difficult to assess with any great certainty. See, for example, Rosen (2017). Although examining evidence from the Negev, this is a study that is methodologically relevant to Palmyra. See also Smith (2013) 33–54 for the evidence on Palmyra's tribes.
59. Seyrig (1932a), (1950b). Kaizer (2020) 26–29.
60. Andrade (2013).
61. Millar (1993) 470. The issues of the city's bilinguality has been treated intensively in recent decades by several scholars; among the most prominent are Millar (1993); Sartre (2001), (2005). See also Kaizer (2017a), (2017b).
62. See Chapter 3.
63. *PAT*; Taylor (2001); *IGLS* 17.1.; Yon (2013). Also, see Shifman 2014.
64. See Chapter 3.
65. See Chapter 3.
66. Meyer (2016).

67. See Chapter 1, and Hanson (2016) 769–770.
68. Schlumberger (1971); Gawlikowski (2003).
69. Raja et al. (forthcoming a).
70. See Chapter 1.
71. Such behavioral patterns are, for example, seen in the coin images of numerous cities across the Near East and beyond. See, for example, Lichtenberger (2003) for the Decapolis.
72. In general on the urban development of Palmyra and for in-depth discussions of the various monuments, see Starcky and Gawlikowski (1985); van Berchem (1976); Will (1983); Schlumberger (1935); Hammad (2010); Gabriel (1926); Frézouls (1976); Delplace (2017).
73. While this also seems to be the case at other sites, such as Gerasa, there are several sites where the urban layout seems to have been conceived on the basis of an overall plan in which a structured urban core made up the nucleus of urban fabric. Palmyrene coinage is discussed in Kristensen and Raja (forthcoming)
74. This is discussed in more detail above; see Chapter 1.
75. A number of recent accounts have discussed the urban development of Palmyra with various foci: Burns (2017) 233–251 (with a focus on the colonnaded streets); Smith (2013) 68–82 (also for the funding of the various monuments); Fortin et al. (1990); Gawlikowski (2019); Sommer (2017a), (2017b).
76. Gabriel (1926); Schnädelbach (2010) holds the most up-to-date map of the city.
77. Schnädelbach (2010), Gawlikowski (2019).
78. Schmidt-Colinet and al-As'ad (2013).
79. Février (1931); Kaizer (2002); Raja (2019i), (2019j).
80. Gawlikowski (2015). Also, see the collection of articles in Raja (2019i), prominently, Kaizer (2019c) as well as Sartre (2019).
81. *PAT* 0197; Kaizer (2002) 60–66.
82. See, for example, Gawlikowski (2014a).
83. For the main publication on the tesserae, see Ingholt et al. (1955); al-As'ad et al. (2005). These two articles contain important information on tesserae and about one crucial in-situ find of an entire series. For further detail see Raja (2015a), (2015d), (2019h), (2020b); Kaizer and Raja (2019). Also see Spoer (1905).
84. For further discussion of Palmyrenes worshipping outside of Palmyra, see Chapter 4. See also Dirven (1997), (1998a), (1998b), (1999), (2013).
85. Teixidor (1979) 79.
86. *PAT* no. 1524; Healey (2009).
87. Kaizer (2019b) 207.
88. Also see Raja (2016c), (2020b).
89. Kaizer (2019b) 209–211.
90. Kaizer (2019b) 208 and (2002) 108–116. The latter name should in fact read Fenebal, the name of an originally Phoenician deity, who was also worshipped in the Roman colony of Sarmizegetusa, in Dacia. Also see du Mesnil du Buisson (1966) 165–176; Gawlikowski (1973) 12–14. *PAT* 1523; *PAT* 1556 for the inscriptions as well as du Mesnil du Buisson (1966) 168–170.

91. Also see Raja (2019i) for a collection of articles on various aspects of Palmyrene religious life.

92. Seyrig (1939) 322–323, fig. 11, no. 28; (1940a); du Mesnil du Buisson (1966) esp. 179–185, figs. 5–6; Gawlikowski (1973) 53–66, esp. 54–56; Will (1992) 37–38; al-Maqdissi (2000); Bounni and al-Maqdissi (2001); Delplace and Dentzer-Feydy (2017) 73–74; Sommer (2017a) 61–62; Graf (2018) 483–489. Other evidence includes a subterranean tomb near the later temple of Baalshamin, which can be dated to the second century BCE (Fellmann (1970), (1975), (1976b); Gawlikowski (1973) 17–19; Kaizer (2017b) 35; Sommer (2017a) 62, and a Japanese team has excavated a coffin tomb of a young man in the southeast necropolis, which they date to the second century BCE (Saito (2002), (2005a) 34, figs. 42–44, (2016b) 351, fig. 4). These finds certainly point to more than sporadic activity in the Hellenistic period. Also see Kubiak-Schneider (2019).

93. Seyrig (1933), (1971); Abel (1938); Seyrig et al. (1968), (1975); Kaizer (2006); Jastrzębowska (2013); Gawlikowski (2015). See Kaizer (2002) 67–69 for a comprehensive overview of the development of the Sanctuary of Bel.

94. Seyrig et al. (1968), (1975); Seyrig (1932b), (1933). Also see Gawlikowski (2015) for an overview of the nature of the cult of Bel in Palmyra.

95. Downey (2017); Seyrig (1940a) for the sculptures and the epigraphic fragment.

96. Al-Maqdissi and Ishaq (in press).

97. Seyrig et al. (1975). Also see al-Maqdissi and Ishaq (in press).

98. Seyrig et al. (1975) 149.

99. Pietrzykowski (1997).

100. Seyrig et al. (1975) 170.

101. Schlumberger (1933) 114–132.

102. For comparison, see the Sanctuary of Zeus Olympios in Gerasa. Raja (2013), (2017j).

103. Gawlikowski (2019) 80–81.

104. Gawlikowski (1997a). Also Seyrig et al. (1968), (1975) in general as well as plan 1. See Will (1997).

105. Will (1997) 875–877; Tarrier (1995) 165 states that the hall could have accommodated only about fifty people. However, given that it measured more than 30 m in length, this estimation is possibly too low. See also Seyrig (1940b) 240 for the suggestion that a smaller temple had been converted into this banqueting hall at some—unknown—point in time.

106. Raja (2015a), (2015d), (2016c), (2019h), (2020b). Ingholt et al. (1955). For the mention of the finds of the tesserae in the drainage, see Seyrig et al. (1968), (1975) 241 s., album, pl. I; RTP, p. VII. See in particular Raja (2015d) for the evidence pertaining to the banqueting hall in the sanctuary of Bel and that of other banqueting halls in Palmyra.

107. See above for the wadi.

108. Gawlikowski (1977), (1983a), (1983b), (1990a), (2008), (2017); Starcky (1981); Wielgosz-Rondolino (2016).

109. *PAT* 0197; *PAT* 1944; Kaizer (2002) 124–143.

110. Gawlikowski (1973) 24. The divine name has been recognized by Gawlikowski on an old photo of a fragment discovered during the original excavation of the Agora.

111. *PAT* 0197; Kaizer (2002) 153–154.

112. Dirven (2011) 153–156, who also suggests that the imperial cult was celebrated there. But this is not certain.

113. du Mesnil du Buisson (1966) 161–162; Gawlikowski (1973) 25, 112–120; Kaizer (2002) 143–148.

114. The sanctuary was excavated in the 1960s by a joint French and Syrian team and published in two volumes: see Bounni et al. (1992); Bounni (2004).

115. Bounni 2004, B14/63, B16/63, B20/64, B10/63 for dedications to Nabu. Kaizer (2002) 91–94 on the sanctuary as well as the fact that none of the dedications mention the temple specifically. For other deities see Bounni (2004) 47–48.

116. Bounni (2004) 47–48.

117. For architectural fragments from the earlier phases, see Bounni et al. (1992) 18. For the Roman period phases, see Bounni (2004) 14, 18, B14/63, B10/63; *PAT* 009; Bounni et al. (1992) figs. 8–19, 99.

118. Bounni (2004) 5 and 13–14.

119. Bounni (2004) 11–13.

120. Bounni (2004) 46–49.

121. Bounni (2004) 16; Bounni et al. (1992) 85–86.

122. Bounni (2004) 13–14. For the suggested functions see Drijvers (1988) 175–176; Bounni (2004) 13; Dentzer (1990).

123. Drijvers (1976) 14–15; Gawlikowski (1990a) 2625–2627, particularly Durahle, e.g., Dunant (1971) 8–10.

124. Collart and Vicari (1969) 94–95; Dunant (1971) 10–11. *PAT* 0208; commentary in Dunant (1971) 72–75. Main publications of the sanctuary are Collart and Vicari (1969) and Dunant (1971).

125. Collart and Vicari (1969) 25, 89–90, plate III; Collart and Vincari (1969) 47–53.

126. Collart and Vicari (1969) 34–38, 54, 145–149, plate IV. Dunant (1971) 26–27, nos. 13–14.

127. Dunant (1971) 33–34; Collart and Vicari (1969) 30.

128. For the 90 CE evidence: Collart and Vicari (1969) 91–93, plate V. For the Rhodian peristyle in the north, Collart and Vicari (1969) 50. For the central court measuring c. 26 x 44 m (85 x 144 ft) dedicated by Malku who had previously given a column: Dunant (1971) 21–22; Collart and Vicari (1969) 145–149.

129. Collart and Vicari (1969) 71–73, 111, plates IX–X. On one of the consoles on the columns the dedicatory inscription of Malè was located (*PAT* 0305; Dunant (1971) 55–56, no. 44).

130. Collart and Vicari (1969) 108, 142, plates XIV–XV.

131. Collart and Vicari (1969) 121.

132. Gawlikowski and Pietrzykowski (1980) 426–430.

133. Collart and Vicari (1969) plates XCV–XCVI.

134. Collart and Vicari (1969) 129–132, plate XCVII.

135. Publication of excavations initiated in the 1970s is forthcoming, but see Gawlikowski (1973) 101–104, (1977) (1983b), (1983c), (1990b), (2006), (2007b), (2014b) and now also the final publication Gawlikowski (2017).

136. For Rahim and Shamash (*PAT* 0301; *PAT* 0297); a hamana was dedicated to Shamash in 31/30 BCE: Gawlikowski (2014b) 81.

137. *PAT* 1929; Gawlikowski (1997a).

138. Gawlikowski (1977) 271, (1990c) 102, Gawlikowski (2014b) 80–81.

139. Dedicatory inscriptions dating to 54 CE: Gawlikowski (1977) 263 and 64 CE (*PAT* 0312).

140. Gawlikowski (1977) 271; Drijvers (1995b). For the dedicatory inscription from the entrance gate, which dates to the mid-second century CE: *PAT* 0331; Gawlikowski (1977) 256.

141. Gawlikowski (2006) 534–535, (2007c) 520–521.

142. Gawlikowski (2006) 534–535; Gawlikowski (2007c) 520–521. For the name of the donor: *PAT* 1608; Gawlikowski (1977) 260–263.

143. Gawlikowski (1977) 258–259.

144. Gawlikowski (1977) 258–260, (2007c) 522. For the statue see, Gawlikowski (1996a).

145. Gawlikowski (1996a). Also see Stewart (2016), esp. 603–611.

146. Gawlikowski (1977) 264–271; (1996a), (2014b) 82.

147. Gawlikowski (2006) 535–536.

148. Kaizer (2002) 116–119.

149. Drijvers (1995a) 34–36.

150. Bounni (1995) 21; al-As'ad et al. (2005) 2–3.

151. al-As'ad and Teixidor (1985); al-As'ad et al. (2005).

152. Gawlikowski (2012).

153. Gawlikowski (2012).

154. In the Polish excavations in 2011, two stretches of the early paved street were uncovered, one in front of the agora and one in front of the Nabu sanctuary.

155. Burns (2017) 233–252 on Palmyra.

156. Burns (2017) 233.

157. Barański (1995), (1996).

158. Burns (2017) 238; Żuchowska (2000), (2006). This was also the case in other places, such as Gerasa of the Decapolis: see Raja (2012) 158–162.

159. Raja (2012) 158; Seigne (1989), (1992a), (1992b); Raja (2013), (2017j).

160. Raja (2019b), (2019f).

161. Raja (2017c), (2019k).

162. Żuchowska (2008); Juchniewicz and Żuchowska (2012).

163. Burns (2017) states the contrary. However, as I see it, this situation is very much a result of unpublished archeological material in several places.

164. Seigne (forthcoming); also see Raja (2012), chapter on Gerasa, as well as Lichtenberger and Raja (2015).

165. Gawlikowski (2019) 86.

166. Gawlikowski (2007a).

167. al-As'ad and Schmidt-Colinet (2013).

168. Raja (2019k).
169. Andrade (2013) 209.

Chapter 3

1. The main publications on these tombs remain Gawlikowski (1970) and Henning (2013b). For summaries of Henning's research, see Henning (2013a), (2019a).
2. Schnädelbach (2010) has maps with the location of all the graves that were known at this time, and these can be counted on the basis of the maps. Grave types can be divided as follows: tower tombs: 139; tower tombs with hypogea: 14; tower tombs with loculi on the outside of the tomb: 11; temple tombs: 68, tombs with special shapes: 3; tombs of unknown shape: 68; hypogea: 69; presumed hypogea: 101. I thank Julia Steding for counting and dividing the graves into types. This comes to 473 tombs recorded in Schnädelbach. However, Henning (2013b), records almost 180 tower tombs, a figure that is markedly higher than that given by Schnädelbach. Furthermore, since the conflict in Syria broke out, material from previously unknown tombs has appeared on both the art-historical market and the black market. It therefore seems certain that the total number of tombs in Antiquity was higher than the figure recorded by Schnädelbach. If Schnädelbach's figure is combined with that given by Henning (2013b) and the new material, this takes the number of graves to more than 500.
3. Raja (2019f).
4. Gilet (1994) 148.
5. The Getty Research Institute possesses a number of the original Cassas drawings and in 2017 made a permanent online exhibition about the site: https://www.getty.edu/research/exhibitions_events/exhibitions/palmyra/index.html.
6. See Chapter 6 for further detail of the earliest Western visitors to Palmyra.
7. See, for example, the travel reports by Østrup, who visited the site in the 1890s and described the looting and damage to many monuments: Østrup (1894), (1895). Also see the publications by Raja and Raja and Sørensen for more information in English on Østrup's travels and the significance of his reports to our knowledge about Palmyra in the late nineteenth century: Raja and Sørensen (2019). Also, see Raja (2018b).
8. Schnädelbach (2010) Annex.
9. Gawlikowski (1970) 147–166.
10. Henning (2013b) 11.
11. Fellmann (1970).
12. See, for example, fourteenth-century dating of a male burial in the southeastern necropolis (Tomb G) dating to between 380 and 160 BCE: Saito (2005a) 34. However, datings based on a single fourteenth-century sample should not be taken too seriously.
13. See De Jong (2017) for case studies from the region of Roman Syria and further literature. Also see the recent edited volume Blömer and Raja (2019a), as well as Eger and Mackersen (2018). Gawlikowski (1970) 9–33 also has an excellent overview of the monuments from the region but outside Palmyra. Henning (2013b) holds an updated bibliography relating to other tower tomb monuments in the region.

14. In general, see Gawlikowski (1970); Henning (2013a), (2013b), (2019a).
15. Henning (2013b) 14 for the earliest and latest dated tower tombs on the ground of their inscriptions. Tomb of Atenatan from 9 BCE and Tomb of Moqimu, son of Zebida from 128 CE. However, Henning also states that the earliest tower tombs must be earlier than 9 BCE due to their building techniques (Henning (2013b), 24). For all fourteen dated tower tombs, see Gawlikowski (1970) 45–46 as well as Gawlikowski (1975) 127–133, for tower tomb no. 83a.
16. Henning (2013b) 23–25 on the chronology of the tower tombs.
17. For an overview of other tower tombs in the region, see Henning (2013b) 101–118.
18. Henning (2013b) 96–98. The Palmyra Portrait Project has collected seven inscriptions mentioning freedmen in funerary contexts. It seems that these were of high societal standing. Funerary loculus relief depicting a female (100–150 CE), Palmyra Museum, Palmyra, inv. no. 2660/8943. al-As'ad et al. (2012) 167, no. 9; 2: funerary loculus relief depicting a male (120–150 CE), Bonhams Auction House (2012) lot 175; sarcophagus lid depicting two individuals and a box depicting three busts (170–200 CE), location: Palmyra, in situ, context: Southeast necropolis, Hypogeum F, east niche, Higuchi and Saito (2001) 24–25, pl. 20–22; Loculus relief depicting a female (200–273 CE), Palmyra Museum, Palmyra, inv. no. 3008/9549, context: found at the northern city wall (secondary context), al-As'ad et al. (2012) 170, cat. 19; 4: Sarcophagus lids depicting a banquet scene depicting seven individual figures (200–220 CE), Palmyra, in situ, context: Southeast necropolis, Hypogeum of Bôlḥâ, North exedra, last niche, al-As'ad and Al-Taha (1968) 101–106, cat. 29; Loculus relief depicting a male (200–250 CE), Vorderasiatisches Museum, Berlin, inv. no. VA 50, original context: unknown, Euting (1887) 414, cat. 106; Loculus relief depicting a male (240–273 CE), American University Museum, Beirut, inv. no. 2748, original context unknown, Porter and Torrey (1906) 262, 268–269, cat. 15, fig. 15; Ingholt (1928) 121–122. Also see Yon 2002, 186, 199, 207–210.
19. See in particular the two examples stemming from sarcophagi.
20. Cantineau (1932) 4.
21. Cantineau (1932) 4. Also see De Jong (2017) 288.
22. Neither Gawlikowski (1970) nor Henning (2013a) discusses non-elite burial monuments found outside monumental tombs. The wealth of material stemming from the monumental tombs is such that the less monumental tombs have been rather overshadowed, but it is certainly a research desideratum that work be undertaken on these. A study will collect this material in a publication by Raja et al. (forthcoming b).
23. See below.
24. Higuchi and Saito (2001) 98–101; Higuchi and Izumi (1994) 64–69; Michalowski (1960) 139–177.
25. On suggrundaria, see Carroll (2018) chapter 6.2.2; Fulminante (2018).
26. Henning (2013b) 87. Also see Amy and Seyrig (1936) 256; Schmidt-Colinet et al. (2000) 56 n. 233; Higuchi and Izumi (1994) 140; Saito (2005a) 33.
27. Henning (2013b, 87). For mummifications, see Amy and Seyrig (1936) 256; Higuchi and Izumi (1994) 17; Saito (2005b); Higuchi and Saito (2001) 49–51; Gawlikowski (1970) 178. Children's mummification: Pfister (1934) 9, pl. 2a.

28. Schmidt-Colinet et al. (2000) for a comprehensive publication of the textiles found in the graves in Palmyra.

29. Palmyra Portrait Project database accessed 8 October 2020: 1,360 funerary inscriptions in Palmyrene Aramaic divided among 1,077 objects. Of these, 22 are bilingual Greek and Palmyrene Aramaic. Additionally there are 12 Greek and 5 Latin inscriptions as well as a single inscription in Greek and Latin.

30. Discussed further below.

31. Also see below. Gawlikowski (1970) 22–30; (1972) 10; Will (1990) 435; Mouton (1997); Triebel (2004); Henning (2013b) 86–87.

32. See Saito (2005b) for images of objects: 114–125. The publication is largely in Japanese but has comprehensive summary sections in English. Higuchi and Izumi (1994) and Higuchi and Saito (2001) also include important material pertaining to grave goods.

33. Schmidt-Colinet et al. (2000). Also see al-As'ad and Chehade (2005); Pfister (1934–1940); Schmidt-Colinet (1995a), (1996), (2000a), (2000b), (2016); Stauffer (1996), (2000), (2005), (2007a), (2007b), (2010). For jewelry from a tower tomb see Witecka (1994).

34. Henning (2013b) is today the standard work on the tower tombs, but the first chronological outline for the dating of the tower tombs was produced by Will (1949). Gawlikowski (1970) 52–106 also remains an important contribution.

35. Henning (2013b) 33.

36. Henning (2013b) 24. These are the tombs of Atenatan, of Moqimu (son of Hagegu), of Hairan, of Kitot, of Ogeilu, of the sons of Taimisa, of Maliku, of the BeneBaa, of Iamliku, of Thaimisas, of Elahbel and his brothers, of Obaihan, of Nebuzabad and of Moqimu (son of Zebida).

37. The quarries with the hard limestone were situated about 12 to 15 km (roughly 7 to 9 miles) northeast of Palmyra. The quarries and the routes between them and the city have most recently been studied by Schmidt-Colinet (2017) 169, fig. 7, also for further references. However, also see Schmidt-Colinet (1990), (1995b).

38. See Henning (2013b) 27–39 for a detailed description of the limestone that was used for the various parts of the graves; he concludes that the soft limestone had lost its significance even as an interior material by the last quarter of the first century CE at the latest (p. 27).

39. Henning (2013b) 27.

40. Henning (2013b) 14.

41. Henning (2013) 35. Sarcophagi were introduced in the second century CE: Colledge (1976) 77–78; Makowski (1985); Wielgosz (1997).

42. Henning (2013b) 35.

43. Henning (2013b) 27–39.

44. Henning (2013b) 14, Tower tomb no. 13 where Henning counts 285 loculi and 12 sarcophagi. In Antiquity, the sarcophagi would have held more than one burial. There are cases from the ancient world in which sarcophagi held more than 20 burials in one box.

45. Henning (2013b) 37.

46. Henning (2013b) 35.
47. Henning (2013b) 13. See Gawlikowski (1970) 48–52, 107–128 for the hypogea. See also Sardurska and Bounni (1994), who surveyed all in-situ portraits from the hypogea in Palmyra; and the publications of excavations undertaken by the Japanese mission that offered detailed insights into the complexes the Japanese excavated: Higuchi and Izumi (1994); Higuchi and Saito (2001); Saito (2005a).
48. See numbers above. Also see Dentzer and Saupin (1996); Schnädelbach (2010).
49. Gawlikowski (1970) 125–126; 2005, 53; Schnädelbach (2010).
50. Fellmann (1970).
51. For 81 CE see Cantineau (1931a) no. 15. For the 87 CE inscription: *PAT* no. 1784.
52. Gawlikowski (1970) 201; (2005) 59; *PAT* no. 0569.
53. Higuchi and Saito (2001) 12.
54. Amy and Seyrig (1936) 246; Sadurska and Bounni (1994) 174–177, figs. 248–253, plan 14.
55. Saito (2005a) 35, fig. 45; Krag and Raja (2018), (2019a).
56. Gawlikowski (1970) 110–128; Sadurska and Bounni (1994); Schnädelbach (2010) 93–100.
57. Michałowski (1963) 206; Higuchi and Saito (2001) 36–39.
58. See Ingholt (1935) for five tombs that all contain inscriptions recording the sale of existing burial niches. The adjectives "profane" and "undefiled" that appear in two of the inscriptions (Ingholt (1935) 96–97, no. V, and 97–98, no. VI respectively) indicate that the Palmyrenes differentiated between the sale of burial niches that had been used, and burial niches that had been constructed but not used for burials before their sale. Also see Gawlikowski (1970) 204–16; Cussini (1995); Yon (2002) 223. For burial niches used several times see Fellmann (1970) 122; Higuchi and Izumi (1994) 108.
59. For architectural decoration see Amy and Seyrig (1936); Higuchi and Saito (2001); for wall paintings see Ingholt (1932b), (1935); Kraeling (1961–1962); Sørensen (2016); Raja and Sørensen (2019). Also see Eristov et al. (2019) for the wall paintings in the grave.
60. Raja (2021d); Ingholt (1932b).
61. Sadurska and Bounni (1994) plans 4, 7; Schnädelbach (2010) 93–100.
62. For the definition, see Schmidt-Colinet (1992).
63. Schmidt-Colinet (1987), (1992).
64. Gawlikowski (1970) 51; *PAT* no. 0519, 0569.
65. For a discussion of the tomb and previous bibliography see Andrade (2018) 158–159.
66. For the pseudo-pediment: Schmidt-Colinet (1992) 23–24. For facades including pilasters: Schmidt-Colinet (1992) 42–52; for half-column decorations: Saito (2016a), (2016b); for elaborate tabernacle architecture, as reconstructed in tomb no. 36: Schmidt-Colinet (1992).
67. See, for example, Schmidt-Colinet (1992) 47.
68. von Hesberg (1992) 182–201.
69. No number is given in Schnädelbach (2010); however, the graves can be counted on the maps and at the time that Schnädelbach carried out his survey, it was possible to identify 473.

70. Will (1990) 438; *PAT* p. 346.
71. Henning (2013b) 85–86.
72. See, for example, Sadurska (1988) 14–23, (1995); Sadurska and Bounni (1994).
73. Kaizer (2002) 242–256, in particular 242–245. Also see Kaizer (2000) in particular p. 227 for the importance of wall paintings in graves. These are often lost to us, but we should assume that they reflect important information that would further our understanding of the connection between Graeco-Roman and Palmyrene mythology. See, for example, the wall paintings in the tomb of the three brothers. A new publication deals with these in detail from a variety of aspects: Eristov et al. (2019) 59–64. See also Raja (2019f).
74. See, for example, Krag (2018), for the mourning mothers: 90–93. Krag and Raja (2016), (2017), (2018), Henning (2019b); Raja (2017a), (2017b), (2019c).
75. Kropp and Raja (2014) 405–406 for overview of the discussions on the topic. See Triebel (2004); Kühn (2005) for overviews. For breath or soul: Triebel (2004) 7–19, 53–61, 117–226; Kühn (2005) 109–233. For spirit: Triebel (2004) 241–246, 252–255. On afterlife and funerary beliefs, see also Kaizer (2010); Yon (2018).
76. Triebel (2004) 253.
77. Gawlikowski (1972) lists more than 100 attestations; Petra: Kühn (2005) passim. Palestine: Triebel (2004) 151–166; Palmyra: Triebel (2004) 142–147, 207–220. Architectural examples in Gawlikowski (1970) 22–43.
78. Tomb 66a: *PAT* no. 1134. Two further bilingual inscriptions, *PAT* no. 1221 and no. 2819, translate it as μνημεῖον. Tombs called nefesh in monolingual inscriptions: *PAT* 0516; 1896; 0509 (*nmš'*, thought to be scribal error for *npš'*, cf. Gawlikowski (1972) n. 39.
79. Gawlikowski (1972).
80. Raja (2015c), (2019b), (2019e). The first corpus of these portraits was published in 1928 by the Danish scholar Harald Ingholt: Ingholt (1928). Also see Raja (2021b). Currently the database holds the following numbers: objects in total: 2,713, portraits: 3,704, thereof male portraits: 1,643; priest portraits: 481; female portraits: 1,205; children's portraits: 216; unknown gender (due to fragmentation): 151.
81. Long and Sørensen (2017); Krag and Raja (2019a).
82. Raja et al. (forthcoming a).
83. See, for example, a loculus relief with a male bust from 150–200 CE (Palmyra, Palmyra Museum, inv. no. A 164), which features the following inscription on the plinth at the bottom of the relief. Latin: Iulius Bassu[s eq(ues?)] alae | Ulp(iae) sing(ularium) uix[it] | annes XX[- - -], translation: Iulius Bassus, rider from the wing | Ulpia I singularium, | who lived XX[- - -] years; see Seyrig (1933) 161–162, cat. 5; Cantineau (1932) 123, cat. 204; Soltan (1969) 28. For discussion of similar examples, see Seyrig (1933); Cantineau (1936); Soltan (1969); Colledge (1976); Parlasca (1982a) (1995); Gawlikowski (1998); al-As'ad and Delplace (2002) 397–398.

84. See, for example, the sarcophagus lid with a standing female, inv. no. IN 1065, at the Ny Carlsberg Glypotek, Copenhagen (230–250). This features three inscribed keys: on the right, Greek: ΛΝΥ, possibly ΑΝΥ, signifying the date 451 (139/140 CE) in the middle key: Palmyrene Aramaic: BT ʿLMʾ, translation: The house of eternity; on the left, Greek: ΦΗΕΛΙ, possibly meaning Θ(εοῦ) Ηελί(ου) (Theou Eliou), possible translation: belonging to the Helios. For further details, see CIS 4490, Ingholt Archive, PS 458; Simonsen (1889) 37, no. 43; Poulsen (1921) 87–88, fig. 11; Chabot (1922) 120, cat. 34, pl. XXX.3; Ingholt (1928) 143, PS 458; Ronzevalle (1934) 127, pl. 6.1; Mackay (1949) 167, pl. LII.1; Drijvers (1982) 711–712, 720; Parlasca (1988) 217–218, pl. 46.d; Hvidberg-Hansen and Ploug (1993) 135–136, cat. 89; Ploug (1995) 216–218, cat. 89; PAT 0851, Hvidberg-Hansen (1998) 77–78, cat. 89; IGLS 17.1, 417–148, cat. 560; Sokolowski (2014) 281, 399, fig. 14; Krag (2015) 111–113, fig. 3; Krag (2018) esp. cat. 804.

85. For further examples, consult IGLS or PAT. For wider reading, see Ingholt (1928); Cantineau (1929), (1930), (1936); Vermeule (1964); Michałowski (1966); Parlasca (1969–1970), (1982a), (1987), (1988); Milik (1972); Comstock and Vermeule (1976); Colledge (1976); Drijvers (1976), (1982); Makowski (1983); Tanabe (1986); Deppert-Lippitz (1987); Gawlikowski (1987a), (1998); Schmidt-Colinet (1992); Dentzer-Feydy and Teixidor (1993); Yon (2002–2003); Sartre-Fauriat and Sartre (2008); Heyn (2010); Farhat (2012); Sokolowski (2014); Krag and Raja (2016); Wielgosz-Rondolino (2016); Davies (2017); Krag (2018).

86. Kropp and Raja (2014), (2015). Sadurska and Bounni (1994); Krag (2019).

87. Hence the name loculus reliefs for the portrait reliefs.

88. See, for example, the founder reliefs at the tower tombs of Kitot, from 40 CE: Henning (2013b) 312–313, or ʿOgeîlû, from 73 CE: Henning (2013b) 286.

89. Raja (2015c), (2019b). The earliest datable fragment from a sarcophagus stems from the tower tomb no. 85d: Henning (2013b) 233. It has been dated to between 50 and 150 CE. On the basis of the chronology developed within the Palmyra Portrait Project, it seems most likely that it stems from the later first century CE or the early second century CE.

90. Bobou and Raja (forthcoming).

91. For graves with in-situ portraits, see Ingholt (1935); Gawlikowski (1970); Sadurska and Bounni (1994); Henning (2013b), Raja (2018b), (2019e). In particular see, Raja (2019e) 11–59.

92. Parlasca (1976) 34–39, (1982b) 22–23. Also see Raja (2017e).

93. For example, stele with full-standing male and female figure from the Hypogeum of Bôlḥâ: Sadurska and Bounni (1994) 81, cat. 110, fig. 11; stele with full-standing male figure from the Hypogeum of Bôlḥâ: Sadurska and Bounni (1994) 80, cat. 109, fig. 16; stele with full-standing child from the Hypogeum of Bôlḥâ: Sadurska and Bounni (1994) 73–74, cat. 95, fig. 15.

94. Kockel (1993). From Italy, there are some 270 reliefs with 450 portraits; a remarkable 85 percent come from Rome and date to the time of Augustus.

95. For Greek honorific statues, see Dillon (2006); Ma (2013).

96. Kockel (1993) 11, for the observation of freedmen reliefs being excerpts of Roman honorific toga-statues.

97. Heyn (2010), (2012); Krag (2016), (2017a), (2017b), (2018). Krag and Raja (2018); Heyn and Raja (2019).

98. Kropp and Raja (2014) 394. Parlasca (1985) 350, quotes a bust in Frankfurt as the sole funerary portrait of a togatus. To this must be added a relief on the front of a recently found, very large third-century sarcophagus in the Palmyra Museum, Schmidt-Colinet (2004) 193–194, (2009) 223–225 fig. 1–8; al-As'ad and Schmidt-Colinet (2005) 42–43 fig. 60, 63; Sartre-Fauriat and Sartre (2008) 39.

99. Raja (2015c) 335. Furthermore, see Parlasca (1976) 34–39 as well as Parlasca (1982b) 22–23.

100. Also see Raja (2019g) for a discussion on a particular attribute that had been associated with funerary iconography in the past.

101. Ingholt (1932). Also see Sørensen (2016) for the first attempt at recontextualizing the paintings within the larger unpublished tomb context as well as Raja et al. (2020).

102. Raja et al. (2021); Raja (2021d).

103. Krag (2018).

104. Raja (2019f).

105. Dentzer-Feydy and Teixidor (1993) 66. Also see Raja (2017c), (2019b).

106. Audley-Miller (2016); Cussini (2016a); Krag and Raja (2017).

107. Kropp and Raja (2014).

108. Curtis (2017); Heyn and Raja (2019).

109. Stucky (1973); Heyn (2008); Raja (2017d), (2017i), (2018a).

110. Heyn (2008); Raja (2017h); Raja (2021a); in general also see Heyn and Raja (2021) for a recent volume on attributes in the sculpture from Palmyra.

111. Raja (2016d), (2018a).

112. Raja (2016d), (2017h), (2017i), (2021c).

113. Raja and Sørensen (2015a).

114. Sadurska and Bounni (1994); Sadurska (1995).

115. For the complexities involved in the reconstruction and overall interpretations of grave situations, see, for example, Higuchi and Saito (2001). See also Krag (2019) for a contribution that highlights the methodological issues involved when reconstructing family genealogies in the Palmyrene graves.

116. Long and Sørensen (2017).

117. Raja et al. (forthcoming a).

118. The Persians launched attacks on Dura-Europos in 239 CE and on Hatra in 240 CE; see Edwell (2008).

Chapter 4

1. Butcher (2003). While Palmyra is certainly not comparable to other places, it was not necessarily unique. However, the evidence from the city is in many ways quite different from what is found in other sites in the Near East.
2. Yon (2002), (2019).
3. See, in general, Edwell (2008), (2013), (2019); Millar (1993) 319–336; Sartre (2001) 971–983; Smith (2013) chapters 2–3; Sommer (2017a) chapter 4.
4. See Chapter 1.
5. For further discussion of the concept of the "Middle Ground" and its application in a Palmyrene context, see White (2010); Ulf (2009), (2014). I have termed this "knowledge culture" in other publications: Raja (2015c).
6. Raja (2021d).
7. Sommer (2017a) 65 with reference to the excavations by Schmidt-Colinet and colleagues. For the English version of Sommer's German book, see Sommer (2017b).
8. Plattner (2013) 97–99.
9. Sommer (2017a) 65.
10. Römer-Strehl (2013) 7–80, here 33–80 in passim.
11. Sommer (2017a) 66–68. Also see Sommer (2005).
12. Sommer (2017a) 68.
13. Perkins (1973); Millar (1998b); Sommer (2005); Brody and Hoffman-Salz (2011); Baird (2014); Kaizer (2017a).
14. Millar (1998b); Brody and Hoffman (2011); James (2019). Also see Downey (1988), (1998), (2003).
15. Luther (2004), Sommer (2005) 58–65; Kaizer (2017a) 71–72.
16. See Chapter 1.
17. See Kaizer (2017a) 71–72.
18. Yon (2010) in particular 233 and 239.
19. Raja (2016d), (2019h).
20. Sommer (2017a) 107–108.
21. Kaizer (2002) 37. For the inscription: *PAT* 2754. See also Seyrig (1932a) 267–268, and Millar (1993) 34 n. 25. For later evidence for trade relations in the Gulf see: *PAT* 1584 (70 CE—perhaps), and second-century inscriptions: *PAT* 0262, 0274, 0294. See also Schörle (2017), as well as earlier publications by Will (1992) 66–81; Schoul (2000) 47–90 and 380–387; as well as Young (2001) 139–148.
22. Cantineau (1933a) no. 2.
23. Kaizer (2002) 37–38 n. 14. *AE* (1933) no. 205 for the milestone and Millar (1993) 83 n. 15 for further references.
24. *PAT* 1352.
25. Cantineau (1933c) 174, n. 2b (this inscription is not included in *PAT*).
26. *PAT* 0305 (130/1 CE). Boatwright (2000) 104–105.
27. Pro: Gawlikowski (1973) 47 and Matthews (1984) 175 n. 10. Contra: Millar (1993) 430–432, (1993) 324–325, and Savino (1999) 60–61. See also Kaizer (2020) 29–31.
28. Rey-Coquais (1978) 68–69, and Savino (1999) 59 n. 64.

29. See Edwell (2008) 54–62 for an account of the evidence connected to Palmyrene military presence within the Roman army after Lucius Verus's Persian conquest.

30. *Dig.* 50.15.1.4–5. Millar (1990) 42–46, (1993) 143–144 and 326–327. Sartre (1996) 394; Edwell (2008) 60. See also Sommer (2017a) 137–147 for an account of the time from 161 up to the reign of Caracalla; and Kaizer (2002) 39–40 for further evidence of Roman presence and Palmyra's integration.

31. For Palmyra as a *colonia*, see Kaizer (2020) 31–32.

32. Millar (1990) 42–46, (1995) 143–144, 326–327; Sartre (1996) 394–395; Yon (2002) 38–40, 243–244; Smith (2013) 130–132; Hartmann (2016) 54–59.

33. Hartmann (2016) 53–65.

34. Young (2001) 157–166; Sommer (2005) 155–157. *IGLS* 17.1, 53, 67, 97, 224.

35. *PAT* 0278.

36. *IGLS* 17.1, 53.

37. For example: *IGLS* 17.1, 53; Millar (1990) 43–44, (1994) 327; Smith (2013) 130. An inscription dating to 231/232 CE, recording that Zenobius was *strategos* and had accompanied the emperor Severus Alexander (222–235 CE), and the governor Rutilius Pudens Crispinus. In this inscription, Yarhibol as well as a representative of Rome were cited as witnesses to the dedication. Here the praetorian prefect Iulius Priscus, brother of the Emperor Philippus Arabus (244–249 CE). Also, see Hartmann (2016) for further inscriptions as well as Hartmann (forthcoming).

38. Sommer (2017a) 135.

39. Sommer (2017a) 132–136, and Edwell (2008) 61–62.

40. Dirven (1998b) and Smith (2013) 150–174 remain important overviews of the evidence for Palmyrenes outside of Palmyra.

41. Dirven (1996), (1998b); Seland (2011), (2013), (2015a), (2015b), (2016), (2019); Meyer and Seland (2016); Schörle (2017), (forthcoming b), (forthcoming d). For the only Palmyrene known from Roman Britain, see *RIB* 1065; the inscription, on a grave stele found at Arbeia (South Shields) tells us that Barates, who dedicated the stele to his deceased wife, was a *vexillarius* (flag-bearer) at Corbridge.

42. For a good overview of the scholarship on the topic and the biases that this text has created in scholarship, see Hekster and Kaizer (2004). For some of the earlier scholarship underlining the early trade of Palmyra, see Richmond (1963) 44; Frézouls (1996) 149; Dirven (1999) 19. However, see Hekster and Kaizer (2004) for a full overview of articles and books. Importantly, this latter work also lists two publications that have argued against Palmyra's having any large-scale involvement in trade in the earlier first century BCE: namely, Seyrig (1950b), and Isaac (1992) 141–142.

43. The inscription *PAT* 1067 (see below) from Dura-Europos related to the dedication of the Temple of Bel, might suggest trade links to the Euphrates in the second half of the first century BCE (see Edwell (2008) 36; Dirven (2013) 52 for this interpretation).

44. Rostovtzeff (1932); Millar (1998a).

45. Graf (2018) 443–530, particularly 481–507. Graf's bibliography includes all the most important contributions, though oddly enough not those by Seland: Seland (2011), (2013), (2015a), (2015b), (2016). See also Schörle (2017). These should be consulted in order to gain a complete overview, while only a summary of the most important

evidence is given here. Graf's paper goes way beyond the scope of Palmyra and includes important evidence from farther east about trade relations with the West in general.

46. Dirven (1996), (1999).
47. Smith (2013) 64; *PAT* 1067.
48. Dura-Europos collection 1938.5313 and 5314; Andrade (2013) 225–227.
49. For various locations in Dacia: *IDR* 3.2.20 = *AE* 1927, 00056 = *AE* 1977, 00668 = *AE* 2004, 01212; *AE* 2006, 01129; *CIL* III, 00907 = *CIL* III, 07693; *IDR* 3.5.2.559 = *AE* 1914, 00102.
50. *CIL* VIII, 02505 = *CIL* VIII, 18005.
51. Evers (2016).
52. Bron (1986).
53. Schörle (2017); Seland (2011).
54. The two earliest inscriptions referring to trade with Palmyra stem from 19 CE and 24 CE, respectively and mention Babylon and Seleucia: Rostovtzeff (1932) 796–798. Inscription *PAT* 0270 (19 CE) mentions the Greeks from Seleucia, and *PAT* 1352 (24 CE) mentions the merchants from Babylon.
55. Young (2001) 126–129. The above-mentioned inscription from 19 CE might also indicate an earlier interest in these places than has often been assumed: Cantineau (1931b) 139–141 n. 18; Gawlikowski (1994) 28; Healey (1996) 33.
56. Drexhage (1988) n. 17.
57. Compare to Steve (2003) for Kharg and the disputed evidence. For Tylos, see Young (2001) 144; Delplace and Dentzer-Feydy (2005) VI.04. For a potential Palmyrene official in the Janussan cemetery on Bahrain, see Healey (1996) 36.
58. *SEG* XXXIV, 1593 = *I.Portes* 103; Bingen (1984); Young (2001) 80–81.
59. *CIS* II, 3190.
60. Schörle (forthcoming c).
61. Cuvigny (2012) 48–49: I.did.5.
62. Notitia dignitatum for *Ala VIII Palmyrenorum* in the late fourth century (Or. 31, 49) at Phoinikon, a fort close to the Nile along the Myos Hormos: Cuvigny (2003). A statue base of Hierobol included a Palmyrene dedication by the prefect and the second-in-command of the *Ala Thracum Herculiana*, a cavalry division stationed at Palmyra until c. 185 CE, at which point it was transferred to Koptos: *OGIS* 639. There are several dedications listed from Egypt's eastern desert: Didymoi from the early third century CE: Cuvigny (2012) 48–49; I.did.5. Dedicatory inscription from female bronze statue from 215 CE by Marcus Aurelius Mokimos, a Palmyrene archer.
63. Rajak (1998) 358.
64. Visconti (1860) 415–450; Lanciani (1901) 112.
65. Translation is taken from S. Morton Braund's translation from the Loeb series, Juvenal and Persius.
66. Papi (1996) 55–56; Ensoli (2003) 46–47; Manetta (2012) 538.
67. Marble fragment with a bilingual Latin-Greek inscription: *CIL* VI, 50; *ILS* 4334; *IGUR* 117; *IG* XIV, 969; *IGR* I, 43, and fragment of a marble relief: *CIL* VI, 51; *IGUR* 118; *IG*

XIV, 970; *IGR* I, 44. Chausson (1995) 661–705; Fowlkes-Childs (2016) 195–196 with bibliography.

68. Adams (2003) 249.

69. Vincenti (2012) 554–557. This is also where a marble fragment of a relief with a woman's head with a *calathos* and a veil (Capitoline Museums inv. no. 2970) was found. A Greek inscription identifies her as Astarte, assimilated to Allat.

70. *IG* XIV, 962; *IGR* I, 33; *IGUR* 122.

71. Fowlkes-Childs (2016) 200–201, with previous bibliography.

72. Capitoline Museums, inv. no. 105, Chausson (1995) 669; Adam (2003) 251; Fowlkes-Childs (2016) 197. The inscription: *IGUR* 120; *IG* XIV, 972; *IGRR* I, 46; *CIS* II, 3, 3904.

73. Even earlier dates going back to the Julio-Claudian period have been suggested: Ensoli (2003) 46–59; (2004) 193–194.

74. Ensoli (2002) 138; Vincenti (2012) 553. A marble head of the priest might stem from this area as well: Montemartini inv. no. 2971, Manetta (2012) 534–537 with bibliography.

75. *CIL* VI, 31034, dated to 102 CE. Of the same period *CIL* VI, 52 = *ILS* 4335. See Chausson (1995) 664–666 with previous bibliography; Hijmans (2010) 416–418 for these inscriptions.

76. Lanciani (1902) 112; Palmer (1981) 372–381; Ensoli (2001) 123–128; Panciera (2006) 365. Capitoline Museums, inv. no. 2412 and inv. no. 1206.

77. Equini Schneider (1987) 78; Dirven (1999) 161–162.

78. Equini Schneider (1987) 77; Chausson (1995) 675–677; Belayche (2007) 208; Adam (2003) 250–253; Velestino (2017) 96–97; *contra* Houston (1990) 189–193; Dirven (1999) 179–180; Noy (2000) 242–245, who do not hold that Tiberius Claudius Felix was of Syrian origin.

79. Equini Schneider (forthcoming).

80. Cumont (1928) 101–109.

81. Contra Fowlkes-Childs (2016) 203–212, who proposes that the altar commemorates two different dedications: one to the Roman cult of Sol, and one to Malakbel and to Palmyrene gods. Equini Schneider does not agree based on a marble fragment stemming from the riverbed near the Aemilius Bridge: *CIL* VI, 31036 = *ILS* 4338, since this commemorates one dedication only, to one god *deo Soli invicto Malachibelo* on behalf of a (*P*) Aelius Longinus (centurio) frumentarius. Equini Schneider (forthcoming). For the Palmyrene family of *Publii Aelii* who owed their right to citizenship to Hadrian: Equini Schneider (1987) 72.

82. De Romanis (2008) 149–169; Filippi and Luigia (2008) 175–183; Papini and Cuccurullo (2015) 171–172; Goddard (2008) 165–174 for the Late Antique villa and the potential Osiris cult.

83. *IGUR* 119; *IG* XIV, 971; *IGR* I, 45; *CIS* II, 3, 3962.

84. Chausson (1995) 677–678; Ensoli (2001) 124; Fowlkes-Childs (2016) 201–203.

85. *CIL* VI, 3174; Milik (1972) 229–321 is particularly significant. See "Fragment of a Roman Votive Relief," now in Sir John Soane's Museum in London; collection online. Also see Terpstra (2013) 152–160 for this relief.

86. Palmieri (1982) 119–121, no. 55.
87. *CIL* VI, 19134; *CIS* I, 3, 3905; *PAT* 55; Adams (2003) 253.
88. Zos. 1.61.5. Wine was supposedly also distributed after the dedication of the trophies: Muzzioli (2008) 50.
89. Terpstra (2016).
90. Raja (2015c) for the term "knowledge culture."
91. Raja et al. (forthcoming a).
92. Hartmann (2001) remains the standard work on the third century with a wealth of sources and detailed analysis.
93. Hartmann (2001) 162–185; 242–258.
94. Hartmann (2001) 427–466; contra Sommer (2005) 159–170, 220–224, (2008) who explains parts of the reasons differently.
95. Hartmann (2001) 466, seen on the background of his entire chapter 12 (427–466).
96. Edwell (2008) 54–62 and for the third century activities 63–92; Pollard (2000).
97. Edwell (2008) 63–92. Also see Pollard (2000), as well as the edited volume by Ted Kaizer on Dura-Europos, Kaizer (2016).
98. See Hartmann (2001) 65–66. The battle is conveyed by al-Tabari in Arabic, p. 818f/ translation p. 14f.
99. Vologesias apparently existed until 247 CE.
100. See Graf (2017) for an amazing overview and discussion of the evidence pertaining to trade from China to the Roman Empire. Also McLaughlin (2016).
101. Kettenhofen (1982) 50–51; Kennedy (1986).
102. Hartmann (2001) 76–85; Smith (2013) 175–177; but see Sommer (2005) 158–159.
103. Gawlikowski (1983a) 67–68, (1996b) 143; Millar (1993) 331–332; Young (2001) 173–175. Also see Sommer (2017a) 200–220.
104. *IGLS* 17.1, 67.
105. Hartmann (2001) 86–230; Sommer (2017a) 154–168.
106. One inscription is dedicated to Odaenathus's son, Septimius Ḥairān, in October 251 CE, *IGLS* 17.1, 58; another, dating from April 252, is dedicated to himself: *IGLS* 17.1, 54. In these inscriptions, both Odaenathus and his son are called "Roman senator" and *exarchos*. In a third, undated, inscription, "Ogeilū, son of Maqqaī, refers to Odaenathus only as "head of Tadmōr"; it is therefore likely that this inscription is earlier: Cantineau (1931b) 138, no. 17; cf. *HA Trig. tyr.* 15.1.
107. Hartmann (2001) 90–96; Sommer (2017a) 156–158; but see Millar (1995) 417–419.
108. Fest. 24; Zos. 1.50.3; Hartmann (2001) 98–100.
109. For Odeanathus: *IGLS* 17.1, 54, 545; and his son: *IGLS* 17.1, 58–60. Hartmann (2001) 97–98; Hächler (2019) 581–588, no. 260; but see Gawlikowski (1985) 261; Strobel (1993) 248–249.
110. Fest. 23; Zos. 1.39.1; Hartmann (2001) 86–90, 108–111. Odaenathus was the son of Ḥairān, the grandson of Wahballāt and the great-grandson of Naṣōr: Cantineau (1931b) 138, no. 17; *IGLS* 17.1, 54, 545.
111. We do not have the name of his first wife. *HA Trig. tyr.* 16.1.
112. Most likely known from two inscriptions: *IGLS* 17.1, 61; Seyrig (1937) 3.

113. For *exarchos*, and in 263, following the victory over the Persians, the title "king of kings": *IGLS* 17.1, 61; Seyrig (1937) 3. Also see Hartmann (2001) 112–128 for these titles.

114. *CIS* II, 3971; Milik (1972) 318; *OGIS* 650–651; *CIL* III, 6727.

115. *HA Aurel.* 38.1; Pol. Silv. 521.49; cf. Zos. 1.59.1.

116. *IGLS* 17.1, 55–56, 59–60, 143; Gross (2005) 94–97, no. 2. Also, see an undated inscription from Tyre on the Mediterranean coast: Chéhab (1962) 19–20, plate VI, 1.

117. Ingholt (1976) 119; Gawlikowski (1985) 258; Hartmann (2001) 102–108.

118. Glas (2014) 163–167, 219–224.

119. Glas (2014) 167–186, 319–341; Geiger (2013) 93–125.

120. Hartmann (2001) 133–135; Glas (2014) 326–327 on Macrinus's campaign. Sources report that he collected Palmyrene troops and those left of Valerian's army: Zos. 1.39.1; cf. Fest. 23; *HA Valer.* 4.2; *Trig. tyr.* 15.2. On the Persian defeat on the Euphrates: Sync. 466.24–25; Zon. 12.23 p. 595.18–21; Kettenhofen (1982) 122–126; Hartmann (2001) 138–140. On the mutiny see Hartmann (2001) 141–145; Geiger (2013) 120–125.

121. Cantineau (1930) no. 19; cf. Zon. 12.24 p. 600.7–9; *HA Gall.* 1.1, 3.3, 10.1; Clermont-Ganneau (1920) 386–401; Potter (1990) 391–394, (1996) 272–274; Hartmann (2001) 147–156; only an honorific title without political power according to Cantineau (1933b) 217–220; Millar (1993) 170; Swain (1993).

122. Hartmann (2001) 162–185.

123. Hartmann (2001) 175; Geiger (2013) 133; Sommer (2017a) 165.

124. The title *rex regum* Herodianus was inscribed on the tripylon of Palmyra, erected in 263/64 by the *duumvir* of the *colonia Palmyra*, Vorodes. A Palmyrene inscription for rex Odaenathus on a krater, probably from 266/67, and the posthumous inscription honoring *rex regum* Odaenathus in the Great Colonnade of Palmyra in 271 confirm this: *IGLS* 17.1, 61; Schlumberger (1951) 60, no. 36; 151, no. 21; Cantineau (1930) no. 19; cf. *HA Trig. tyr.* 15.2; Hartmann (2001) 176–185; but see Gawlikowski (2007b) 305; Gnoli (2007) 81–94.

125. Hartmann (2001) 180–200, 440–469. For a recent assessment of Odaenathus and his career, see Kaizer (2020) 33–34.

126. *IGLS* 17.1, 67. See Hartman (2001) 200–211 for a description of this rapid development and the evidence connected to it. Also see Yon (2002) 35, 70–71 for the "royal" power.

127. Hartmann (2001) 221–222.

128. Hartmann (2001) 211–218.

129. Hartmann (2001) 218–230.

130. Hartmann (2001) 242–271. On Zenobia: Equini Schneider (1993); Kotula (1997) 89–144; Hartmann (2001); Sommer (2017a) 168–179; Andrade (2018); more popular accounts in Stoneman (1992); Southern (2008); Winsbury (2010). Andrade (2018) is the most comprehensive general narrative of Zenobia along with the French Sartre-Fauriat and Sartre (2014).

131. For a carefully researched and insightful book see Andrade (2018). For a short overview of the knowledge we have about her, see Andrade (2019). Also see Simiot (1978) and Sartre-Fauriat and Sartre (2014).

132. Paschoud (2002), (2011).
133. Paschoud (2003) xxxvi–xlvi. Both *HA* and Zosimus drew on contemporary sources, but still cannot be counted on for reliability: Mallan and Davenport (2015).
134. These are summarized in Andrade (2018) as well as Hartmann (2001) 342–394. The most important of these are the Byzantine sources, namely, Continuator Dionis, John of Antioch (seventh century), George Syncellus (ninth century), and Zonaras (twelfth century). These drew on Zosimus: Banchich (2015) 3–9; Potter (1990) 356–369, 395–397; Bleckmann (1992); Brecht (1999); Mariev (2008). Fragments of the correspondence between Paul of Samosata and Zenobia survive: Declerck (1984) 134. Paul of Samosata was a Christian bishop of Antioch who denied the divinity of Jesus: Eus., *Hist. Ecc.* 7.27 and 30; de Riedmatten (1952) 135–158. The most important rabbinical Jewish text to offer information about Zenobia is TJ Ter. 8: 10.46b in Guggenheimer (2000); Appelbaum (2011) 452. Legends about a Palmyrene queen named Tadi or Thadamor appear in later Manichaean texts, while the figure from medieval Arabic literature named al-Zabba ("the hairy one") also seems to refer to Zenobia: Gardner and Lieu (2004) 111–114; Weststeijn (2013), (2016); Hartmann (2001) 308–315, and 332–351; Woltering (2014) 38–40 Sommer 2015, 114–115.
135. Gawlikowski (2010), (2016). See also Kaizer (2020) 34 for a brief but significant discussion of Zenobia's agenda.
136. *PAT* 0317.
137. *ILS* 8924.
138. *IGR* 3.1065.
139. Lichtenberger and Raja (2020b).
140. "The sands of Palmyra are full of little copper coins. After strong winds the people of Palmyra gather them in handfuls. I bought hundreds of them for a few piasters. They are generally adorned with radiated heads, gazelles, fishes, zodiacal signs, and such like emblems. They are probably specimens of the currency with which Zenobia resisted the siege": Wright (1895) 155–156. Krzyzanowska (1976), (1979), (1982), (2002), (2014).
141. Bland (2011); Estiot (2004) 113–120, and 222–223.
142. Sartre-Fauriat and Sartre (2014) 75–76; Equini Schneider (1993) 95–96. Also, see Andrade (2018) chapter on dynasty, 166–190.
143. *ILS* 8924; for the coinage see Bland (2011).
144. Hartmann (2001) 242–394; Sommer (2017a) 168–179. It is not certain that Zenobia was present at the battles.
145. Zos. 1.54.2; 55–56.2; *HA Aurel.* 28.3; Sync. 470.5; Equini Schneider (1993) 85–86; Watson (1999) 76–77; Hartmann (2001) 375–386, (2008) 370–372. For the garrison: *HA Aurel.* 31.2; Hartmann (2001), 391.
146. *HA Aurel.* 30.1–3; Zos. 1.56.2–3, Hartmann (2001) 391–394.
147. Fest. 24; Eutr. 9.13.2; *HA Trig. tyr.* 24.4, 30.3, 30.24–26; *Aurel.* 30.2, 32.4, 33–34)
148. *HA Trig. tyr.* 30.27.
149. Sync. 470.5–7; Zon. 12.27 p. 607.6–11; Hartmann (2001) 411–424.
150. Sartre-Fauriat and Sartre (2014); Andrade (2018), (2019); Shapley (1974), Stoneman (1992); Gabucci (2002); Hvidberg-Hansen (2002); Southern (2008).
151. Zos. 1.60.1; Hartmann (2001) 371–373, 393.

152. Zos. 1.60.1; *IGLS* 17.1, 77; Kotula (1997) 141–142; Hartmann (2001) 395–396, (2008) 372–373; Yon (2002) 143–144, 149–150, 284; Sommer (2005) 165.
153. Zos. 1.60, 61.1; *HA Aurel.* 31.2; *Pol. Silv.* 521.49; Hartmann (2001) 117–124.
154. Hartmann (2001) 375–384; *HA Aurel.* 31; Zos. 1.60–61.1; Equini Schneider (1993) 85–86; Kotula (1997) 140–144; Watson (1999) 80–82; Hartmann (2001) 395–402, (2008) 372–374.
155. *Not. Dig.* or. 32.15, 32.30; Hartmann (2001) 409–410.
156. Smith (2013) 175–181; Will (1992) 167–197; Kaizer (2020) 35.

Chapter 5

1. Gibbon (1831).
2. Kowalski (1997); Genequand (2012); Intagliata (2018).
3. Kowalski (1997).
4. Sartre-Fauriat and Sartre (2014); Sartre-Fauriat and Sartre (2016); Sartre-Fauriat (2019).
5. Zos. 1.61.1*HA Aurel.* 31.3.
6. For the northwest quarter: Gawlikowski (2004) 323, the Great Colonnade: Żuchowska (2000) 187; the sanctuary of Allat: Gawlikowski (1983b) 61; the agora: Seyrig (1940b) 242; and the theater: Will (1966) 1413–1414; Kowalski (1997) 44.
7. Kowalski (1997) 39–44; Hartmann (2001) 398–401.
8. Schmidt-Colinet, al-Asʿad, and al-Asʿad (2013) 303;
9. Barański (1994) 9; Żuchowska (2000) 191–192, fig. 7.
10. Kowalski (1997) 42–46; Hartmann (2001) 400–402, 425–426, (2016) 65–67.
11. For the city's status under Emperor Diocletian (284–305 CE): *CIL* III, 6049; *CIS* II, 3971, note = *AE* 1921, 92; *AE* 1934, 262; *CIL* III, 14177/4, 1–2 = Bauzou (1989) vol. 2, 416, no. 113; *AE* 1993, 1606.
12. For the inscription from 272 CE: Cantineau (1933a), fasc. IX, 40, no. 28. This inscription was engraved on the wall of a chamber between the main door and the south lateral door of the propylaea in the Sanctuary of Bel. For the inscription from 273 CE: Gawlikowski (1971) 412–42, published it as a stray find. For Haddudan (and the inscriptions), see also Yon (2002) 119, 144, 15, 244, 287. A Greek–Palmyrene inscription, earlier dated to 279/80 CE, recounts that in that year, the *phyle* (tribe) of the Maththabolians honored Malchus/Malkō, son of Mocimus/Moqīmō, with a statue, because he rebuilt the roof of the great basilica of the god Ares/Arsu with his own resources, together with those of his son, Mucianus. However, this inscription has been redated by Yon to 179/180 CE and can therefore not support a theory that Palmyrene Aramaic was extensively used in the public sphere after the sack of Palmyra. For this inscription see *IGLS* 17.1, 81 = al-Asʿad and Gawlikowski (1986–1987) 167–168, no. 8; cf. *IGLS* 17.1, 80 = al-Asʿad and Gawlikowski (1986–1987) 167, no. 7; Kaizer (2002) 122–123; Yon (2002) 70, 76–77, 252–253, (2012) 95–96.

13. al-As'ad and Gawlikowski (1986–1987) 167–168, n. 7–8.
14. For Baalshamin, see *IGLS* 17.1, 154; Kowalski (1997) 45; Kaizer (2002) 86. For Allat see Barański (1994) 11 and Gawlikowski 2017.
15. Gawlikowski (1973) 76–78 for the two inscriptions. *IGLS* 17.1, 154 for the inscription from the sanctuary of Baalshamin. See also Kaizer (2020) 35–36.
16. Gawlikowski (2004) 318, and Raja (2019f) 352–353, cat. 136, with previous bibliography.
17. Hartmann (2016) 65–67.
18. *HA Aurel.* 31.1–2.
19. On this via militaris, see Bauzou (1992), (1993). Also see Dunand (1931); Mouterde (1930).
20. *Not. Dig., Or.* 32.30.
21. Kowalski (1998).
22. Fellmann (1976a) 190. For the bathhouse: Ostratz (1969) 114–115; more recently, Fournet (2009a), (2009b) for the renovation of the bathhouse by the governor of Syria Sossianus Hierocles between 293 and 303 CE.
23. For the earlier date, see von Gerkan (1935) 28; Seyrig (1950a) 240.
24. *CIL* III, 133 = 6661; Gawlikowski (1984) 10; Kowalski (1997) 44; Zos. 2.34.1, Ammianus Marcellinus 23.5.2.
25. von Gerkan (1935); Crouch (1975a) 12, 30; Juchniewicz et al. (2010); Hammad (2010) 115–117; *IGLS* 17.1, 445 for the latest tombs, which had a date of 215 CE. Seyrig (1950a) 239–242. Recently it has been suggested that these towers also could date to the Diocletianic period. See Juchniewicz (2013).
26. Barański (1994) 9–13 and Gawlikowski (2019).
27. Malalas, *Chr.* 17.2; Procopius, *Aed.* 2.9.10–12); and the later Theophanes, *Chr.* 1.174.
28. Gawlikowski (1984) 10–11, (1986).
29. *Kitāb* 1.140–142.
30. *IGLS* 17.1, 101 tells us about the curator Flavius Diogenes, who restored parts of the colonnade. For the paving and its chronology: Żuchowska (2000) 187.
31. al-As'ad and Stępniowski (1989) 211.
32. Delplace (2006–2007) 106–109.
33. Sanctuary of Nabu: Bounni et al. (1992) plate 8, fig. 12; Bounni (2004) 6, and the sanctuary of Baalshamin: Kowalski (1996); Intagliata (2017).
34. Bounni and Saliby (1968), plate I.
35. Potentially a ninth church can be identified in the structures in and around the cella of the sanctuary of Baalshamin: Kowalski (1996).
36. Le Quien (1740) 845; Devreesse (1945) 206.
37. Gąssowska (1982).
38. Żuchowska (2006) 447.
39. Gawlikowski (2001); Majcherek (2013) with further references.
40. Żuchowska (2006) 448–450.
41. Gawlikowski (1990b) 40–43. Also, see Intagliata (2015) 144–151 for a summary of these churches.

42. For more on the three chapels, see Majcherek (2005). For discussion of the church dedicated to the Virgin Mary in the Temple of Bel, see Jastrzębowska (2013), with further references.
43. Gawlikowski (1999) 192–194, (2000) 254–255.
44. Delplace (2013) 40.
45. al-Asʿad and Ruprechtsberger (1987) 137–146.
46. Schlumberger (1939a), (1939b); Schlumberger et al. (1986) 26–28; Jalabert and Mouterde (1959) 240–243; Genequand (2006) 69–70.
47. *De Bel.* 2.1.6.
48. Wright (1872) 2, 468 n. 585; Millar (2013) 24–25.
49. Intagliata (2018) 103–104; Gawlikowski (2009) 89.
50. al-Wāqidī, *al-Maghāzī* 1.44—747/748–822 (Kitab al-Tarikh wa al-Maghazi).
51. Donner (1981) 121, 124.
52. For example, al-Ṭabarī, *Taʾrikh* 9.1796; b. ʿAsakir, *Taʾrikh* 63.337. For the small size of the army: al-Balādhurī, *Futūḥ* 110, and al-Ṭabarī, *Tāʾrīkh* 4.2108–2110: just some 500 to 800 soldiers. However, also see Donner (1981) 126, 314 n. 185 who cites sources that indicate larger numbers.
53. al-Muqaddasī, *Aḥsan* 159.
54. al-Ṭabarī, *Tāʾrīkh* 7.482; also see Ibn ʿAsākir, *Tāʾrīkh* 55.261.
55. al-Iṣfahānī (897–967), *al-Aghānī* 17.112–113; 20.120–121.
56. Michałowski (1962) 60–66, 223–236; Skowronek (2014) 60–64. The date of deposition is uncertain, since later intrusions were found.
57. Skowronek (2014) 71–120.
58. The caliph subdued the rebel cities one by one, including Homs, which had been reinforced by a contingent of Kalbites from Palmyra led by Dhuʾāla b. al-Aṣbagh b. Dhuʾāla al-Kalbī: al-Ṭabarī, *Tāʾrīkh* 9.1892–1893. Tadmor was left until last.
59. *Kitāb* 1.829.
60. Intagliata (2017).
61. Genequand (2008), (2012) 52–57, (2013).
62. al-Asʿad and Stępniowski (1989).
63. Genequand (2012) 64.
64. Michałowski (1960) 62–78, (1962) 64–77, (1963) 41–60. For the Islamic structures in the courtyard of the Baalshamin sanctuary, see Intagliata (2016).
65. Genequand (2008) 13.
66. See Stucky (2008) 507–508.
67. See Geoffrey Chaucer's *The Monk's Tale* (ll. 2247–2374) composed in the last quarter of the fourteenth century.
68. See Sartre-Fauriat (2019).
69. Sommer (2017a) 8.
70. Sartre-Fauriat and Sartre (2008) 14–16, for the description of Godinho's travel, who presumably came so close to Palmyra that he could see its ruins from afar.
71. *Zenobia* by Tomaso Albinoni (1694); *Zenobia in Palmira* by Leonardo Leo (1725); *Zenobia* by Johann Adolph Hasse (1761); *Zenobia in Palmira* by Pasquale Anfossi (1789); *Zenobia in Palmira* by Giovanni Paisiello (1790); *Aureliano in Palmira* by

Gioachino Rossini (1813); *Zenobia, Queen of Palmyra* by Silas G. Pratt (1882); *Zenobia* by Mansour Rahbani (2007).

72. Lanoy and Goodyear (1695–1697) 130–138.

73. Lanoy and Goodyear (1695–1697) 138–160.

74. Halifax (1695–1697) 83–110. Also see the recent Astengo (2016).

75. Sartre-Fauriat (2019) 67–68. They did not publish accounts of their visits, but we know of them from other publications. Giraud and Sautet: cf. Perdrizet (1901) n. 3. 225–264. For Granger see Chabot (1897).

76. Barthélemy (1754).

77. The manuscript describing Cassas's travel in at the Getty Centre (Ca), 14 (unpublished). Cassas's drawings: Cassas (1799).

78. Buckingham (1825) 428–429.

79. De Vogüé (1865), (1877); Waddington (1870).

80. Raja (2018b), (2019e).

81. Shifman (2014) 1.

82. Nielsen (2019).

83. Wiegand (1932). It is less well known that the team headed by Puchstein at Baalbek also went to Gerasa one summer to do archeological soundings: for further detail, see Lichtenberger and Raja (2020a).

84. Raja (2015b), (2019c); Raja and Sørensen (2015a), (2015b), (2019).

85. For this work see Sartre-Fauriat (2019), with detail of further references. Both missions published extensively on the work that they have undertaken.

Chapter 6

1. Østrup (1894) 62–63. Translation by the author.

2. Østrup (1895). Raja and Sørensen (2019); Raja (2017b).

3. Østrup (1894) 90–91. For an introduction to the trajectories between archeology and politics, see the edited book with about sixty contributions, which accompanied the exhibition at the Ruhr Museum in 2010 entitled *Das Grosse Spiel—Archäologie und Politik*: Trümpler (2008).

4. Despite the fact that Puttmann is noted as the acquirer of some of the pieces for the Ny Carlsberg Glyptotek, it was most likely Østrup who was the initiator of the acquisition of these during his travels in Syria. Raja (2019e) cat. 4, cat. 6, cat. 25, cat. 86, cat. 76, cat. 14, cat. 63, cat. 78, cat. 74, cat. 114, cat. 137.

5. Østrup does not cover up the fact that he bought objects, but in fact writes openly about it.

6. The field on this topic is vast and expanding rapidly. For introductions to various aspects see, Renfrew (2000); Brodie et al. (2006); Diaz-Andreu (2007); La Follette (2013); Kila and Zeidler (2013); Mackenzie and Green (2009); Miles (2008); Soderland and Lilley (2015).

7. See, for example, Young and Tarlow's chapters in Scarre and Scarre (2006).

8. Nielsen (2019).

9. Nielsen (2019) 33–34.

10. For opposing views, see, for example, Jenkins (2016) contra Feeley (2012). For discussion of cultural and national identities, see Hitchens (1987); Jenkins (2016).

11. Gibbon (2005) and Cuno (2010).

12. See Stucky (2010)—also p. 508 for images.

13. Christie (1946).

14. UNESCO, "World Heritage List."

15. See Stucky (2010) 510 for the hotel Zenobia. Also, see Chevalier (2008) 317–323 for a comprised overview of the French involvement in the archeology of the Near East, as well as Gelin (2002) for a comprehensive overview of the French involvement in the archeology of Syria under the Mandate.

16. See Sartre-Fauriat (2019).

17. See Greenhalgh (2016), in particular 409–422 on the monuments of Syria in 2016. In general, the book gives a good introduction to the recent history of the region from the period of the early European travelers until today and also gives insights into the earlier destruction of monuments in the region. On the Arab Spring, its origins, and background, there is a wealth of literature in many languages. See, for example, Brownlee et al. (2013); Dabashi (2012). For many, the beginning of the Arab Spring was marked by a Tunisian street seller who set himself on fire due to growing desperation over poor living conditions and the oppressive political regime. Also Sartre-Fauriat (2016).

18. The most prominent international conventions are UNESCO convention (1970), as well as the Hague Convention; see UNESCO (1954).

19. For some of these, see the list at UNESCO, "Observatory of Syrian Cultural Heritage. Damage Assessment: Reports," which, however, holds reports only up until October 2018. For one of the early reports, see Bjørgo et al., "Satellite-based Damage Assessment." Also, see the webpage of the Directorate General of Antiquities and Museums for reports of damage and lootings.

20. See, for example, the recent short report done by the Palmyra Portrait Project for Syrians for Heritage (SIMAT). In this report, several portraits were assigned to their original graves in Palmyra, while others could not be assigned to their original contexts, most likely because they stemmed from recent illicit excavations and have not been documented before: see Syrians for Heritage (2020).

21. UNESCO, "World Heritage List." A total of six of the fifty-three sites are located in Syria. Apart from Palmyra they include Aleppo in Northern Syria; Bosra in the Hauran; Damascus; the so-called Dead Villages in Northern Syria; the medieval fortress of Crac des Chevaliers and Qal'at Salah El-Din. These were all added to the list in 2013 emphasizing that damages were already taking place before ISIS's foothold became strong in the region. Only fifty-three locations are inscribed on the "world heritage in danger list," underlining the importance that UNESCO ascribes to Palmyra.

22. UNITAR-UNOSAT (2017); UNESCO (2017).

23. UNESCO, "Unite4Heritage."

24. See, for example, UNESCO, "Safeguarding Syrian Cultural Heritage"; and UNESCO, "Observatory of Syrian Cultural Heritage." Both websites have useful information about a variety of initiatives in and outside UNESCO, although they are not currently kept up to date.
25. Taylor (2015); Raja (2015b), (2016a), (2016b).
26. Salibi et al. "Syria," Shorrock (1970); "French Mandate for Syria and the Lebanon" (1923). For a general history of the region in this period, see Fisk (2005).
27. Amnesty International (2001).
28. Sarraj (2016).
29. See, for example, interviews with the Syrian writer Yassin al-Haj Saleh: Mroue (2015). See also his extensive writings on his experiences of prison in Syria, as well as his discussions of the ongoing situation in the country: al-Haj Saleh (2012), (2014), (2017).
30. See, for example, UNESCO, "Observatory of Syrian Cultural Heritage. Damage Assessment: Reports," for numerous international reports on the various destructions wrought in Palmyra over the last few years. While these make for useful—if devastating—reading, they also make clear that as of yet, there is no complete overview of the situation.
31. Freeman (2015).
32. Sartre-Fauriat and Sartre (2016) 11–12.
33. See, for example, Shaheen and Black (2015).
34. BBC News (2015).
35. John (2016). Also, see Plets (2017) 18.
36. The article by Plets (2017) provides a useful and nuanced contribution to the wider discussion about the politics of cultural heritage management in conflict and post-conflict zones. It also provides a solid overview of Russian involvement in Palmyra up to the time of its publication
37. BBC News (2017); Al-Jazeera (2017). For an earlier attempt: BBC News (2016).
38. See, for example, Barford (2016) and The New Arab (2016) for visits by members of the Polish mission. French architects and archeologists have also visited the site.
39. See, for example, Weiss and Connelly (2017), also with reference to the earlier UNESCO conventions (1954) (1970) on the protection of cultural heritage in the event of armed conflict.
40. See, for example, Denker, (2017) 27. For a useful but not particularly in-depth consideration of the way cultural heritage protection and digital initiatives are riven by Western academics and foundations, resulting in a new era of digital colonialism of the cultural heritage of the Middle East, see Samad (2020). This PhD dissertation was submitted at Bowling Green State University in May 2020, and though it is not published, can be accessed online.
41. #New Palmyra.
42. See also the recent reconstruction of the tomb of Hairan in Palmyra based on the unpublished sketches in the excavation diaries of Harald Ingholt by McAvoy and Raja (2020).

43. Turner (2016), "Triumphal Arch in the News." The arch has since traveled to several other sites. There have been discussions about the appropriateness of this expensive project in marble. However, the project has done much to raise awareness of the impact of the destruction of cultural heritage in Syria.

44. Terpak and Bonfitto, "The Legacy of Palmyra," with further links to more resources.

45. ALIPH Foundation Project. "Collart—Palmyra"; ALIPH Foundation Project, "Preserving and Sharing Palmyra's Cultural Heritage."

46. Raja (2020a), (2015b), (2019a), for contributions on the work of Harald Ingholt in Palmyra and beyond. Also, see Raja and Sørensen (2015 a and b).

47. Syrians for Heritage (2020). This report was written through the documentation undertaken within the Palmyra Portrait Project.

48. Museum of Islamic Art, "The Cultural Heritage of Syria in Danger" and "Syrian Heritage Archive Project."

49. For details of two recent conferences, see University of Lausanne, "Project Collart—Palmyre"; University of Warsaw "Life in Palmyra, Life for Palmyra." For exhibitions, see The J. Paul Getty Museum, "The Classical World in Context"; Ny Carlsberg Glyptotek, "The Road to Palmyra"; The Metropolitan Museum of Art, "The World between Empires."

Postludium

1. Palmyra Portrait Project, "Bibliography."

Historical Sources

Abū al-Fidā. *Taqwīm al-Buldān*, ed. by Heinrich Leberecht Fleischer (Leipzig: Vogel, 1831).

Adler, Marcus Nathan. *The Itinerary of Benjamin of Tudela* (London: Frowde, 1907).

al-Balādhurī. *Futūḥ al-Buldān*, ed. by Michael Jan de Goeje (Leiden: Brill, 1866).

al-Iṣfahānī. *Kitāb al-Aghānī*, ed. by Nasr al-Hurini (Cairo: Bulaq, 1867–1869).

al-Muqaddasī. *Aḥsan al-taqāsīm fī maʿrifat al-aqālīm*, ed. by Michael Jan de Goeje (Leiden: Brill, 1906).

al-Ṭabarī. *Tāʾrīkh al-rusul wa-al-mulūk*, ed. by Michael Jan de Goeje et al. (Leiden: Brill, 1879–1901).

al-Wāqidī. *Kitāb al-Maghāzī*, ed. by William Nassau Lees (Calcutta: Bengal Military Orphan Press, 1854).

Chronicle of Zuqnīn, ed. by Jean-Baptiste Chabot (Leuven: Peeters, 1933).

Ḥamza al-Iṣfahānī. *Tāʾrīkh sinī mulūk al-arḍ waʾl-anbiyaʾ*, ed. and trans. by Joseph M. E. Gottwald (Leipzig: Leopoldum Voss, 1844–1848).

Ibn ʿAsākir. *Tāʾrīkh madīnat Dimashq*, ed. by ʿUmar G. al-ʿAmrawi (Beirut: Dar al-Fikr, 1995–2000).

Ibn Aʿtham al-Kūfī. *Kitāb al-futūḥ*, ed. by Muhammad ʿA. Khān and ʿA. W. al-Bukhari (Hyderabad: Osmania Oriental Publications Bureau, 1968–1975).

John Malalas. *Chronographia*, ed. by Ludwig August Dindorf (Bonn: Weber, 1831).

John Malalas. *The Chronicle of John Malalas: A Translation*, ed. and trans. by Elizabeth Jeffreys, Michael Jeffreys, and Roger Scott. Byzantina Australiensia 4 (Melbourne: Australian Association for Byzantine Studies, 1986).

John of Ephesus. *Ecclesiastical History*, ed. by William Cureton (Oxford: Oxford University Press, 1853).

John of Ephesus. *The Third Part of the Ecclesiastical History of John, Bishop of Ephesus*, trans. by Robert Payne Smith (Oxford: Oxford University Press, 1860).

Michael the Syrian. *Chronique de Michel le Syrien*, ed. and trans. by Jean-Baptiste Chabot (Paris: Leroux, 1899–1910).

Notitia dignitatum, ed. by Otto Seeck (Berlin: Weidmann, 1876).

Procopius. *Constructions de Justinien Ier: Peri ktismaton = De aedificiis*, ed. and trans. by Denis Roques. Hellenica 39 (Alessandria: Edizioni dell'Orso, 2011).

Procopius. *De aedificiis*, ed. and trans. by Henry Bronson Dewing (London: William, 1961).

Procopius. *De bellis*, ed. by Jakob Haury (Leipzig: Teubner, 1963–1964).

Theophanes. *The Chronicle of Theophanes Confessor: Byzantine and Near Eastern History, A.D. 284–813*, trans. by Cyril Mango and Roger Scott (Oxford: Clarendon Press, 1997).

Theophanes. *Chronographia*, ed. by Carolus de Boor (Leipzig: Teubner, 1884).

Vies d'Aurélien et de Tacite, vol. 5.1, *Histoire Auguste*, ed. and trans. by François Paschoud. Collection des universités de France Série latine—Collection Budé 335 (Paris: Les Belles Lettres, 1996).

Yāqūt. *Kitāb muʿjam al-buldān*, ed. by Ferdinand Wüstenfeld (Leipzig: Brokhaus, 1866–1873).

Zosimus. *Histoire nouvelle: livres I et II*, vol. 1, *Zosime*, ed. and trans. by François Paschoud. Collection des universités de France Série grecque—Collection Budé 401 (Paris: Les Belles Lettres, 2000).

Bibliography

Abdul-Hak, Selim. 1952. "L'hypogée de Taai à Palmyre." *Les Annales archéologiques de Syrie* 2: 193–251.

Abel, Félix-Marie. 1938. *Géographie de la Palestine. Géographie politique. Les villes* (Paris: Gabalda).

Adams, James Noel. 2003. *Bilingualism and the Latin Language* (Cambridge: Cambridge University Press).

al-Asʻad, Khaled, and Obaid Al-Taha. 1968. "Bolha, Palmyrene Grave." *Syria* 18: 83–108 [in Arabic]

al-Asʻad, Khaled, Françoise Briquel-Chatonnet, and Jean-Baptiste Yon. 2005. "The Sacred Banquets at Palmyra and the Functions of the Tesserae: Reflections on the Tokens Found in the Arṣu Temple." In *A Journey to Palmyra: Collected Essays to Remember Delbert R. Hillers*, ed. by Eleonora Cussini. Culture and History of the Ancient Near East 22 (Leiden: Brill), pp. 1–10.

al-Asʻad, Khaled, and Jawdat Chehade. 2005. "Die Textilien aus Palmyra. Ein internationales und interdisziplinäres Projekt." In *Palmyra: Kulturbegegnung im Grenzbereich*, ed. by Andreas Schmidt-Colinet. Sonderbände der Antike Welt, Zaberns Bildbände zur Archäologie 27, 3rd ed. (Mainz am Rhein: von Zabern), pp. 64–66.

al-Asʻad, Khaled, and Christiane Delplace. 2002. "Inscriptions latines de Palmyre." *Revue des Études Anciennes* 104.3–4: 363–400.

al-Asʻad, Khaled, and Michał Gawlikowski. 1986–1987. "New Honorific Inscriptions in the Great Colonnade of Palmyra." *Annales archéologiques arabes syriennes* 36–37: 164–171.

al-Asʻad, Khaled, Michał Gawlikowski, and Jean-Baptiste Yon. 2012. "Aramaic Inscriptions in the Palmyra Museum. New Acquisitions." *Syria* 89: 162–183.

al-Asʻad, Khaled, and Erwin Maria Ruprechtsberger. 1987. "Palmyra in spätantiker, oströmischer (byzantinischer) und frühislamischer Zeit." In *Palmyra: Geschichte, Kunst und Kultur der syrischen Oasenstadt*, ed. by Erwin Maria Ruprechtsberger. Linzer Archäologische Forschungen Band 16 (Linz: Gutenberg), pp. 137–148.

al-Asʻad, Khaled, and Andreas Schmidt-Colinet. 1985. "Das Tempelgrab Nr. 36 in der Westnekropole von Palmyra: Ein Vorbericht." *Damaszener Mitteilungen* 2: 17–36.

al-Asʻad, Khaled, and Andreas Schmidt-Colinet. 2005. "Kulturbegegnung im Grenzbereich." In *Palmyra: Kulturbegegnung im Grenzbereich*, ed. by Andreas Schmidt-Colinet. Sonderbände der Antike Welt, Zaberns Bildbände zur Archäologie 27, 3rd ed. (Mainz am Rhein: von Zabern), pp. 36–64.

al-Asʻad, Khaled, and Franciszek Stępniowski. 1989. "The Umayyad Suq in Palmyra." *Damaszener Mitteilungen* 4: 205–223.

al-Asʻad, Khaled, and Javier Teixidor. 1985. "Un culte arabe préislamique à Palmyre d'après une inscription inédite." *Comptes rendus des séances de l'Académie des inscriptions et belles-lettres* 129. 2: 286–293.

al-As'ad, Khaled, and Jean-Baptiste Yon. 2007. "Nouveaux textes palmyréniens." *Semitica* 52–53: 101–110.

al-Haj Saleh. 2012. *Salvation O Boys: 16 Years in Syrian Prisons* (Beirut: Dar al-Saqi) [in Arabic].

al-Haj Saleh (ed.). 2014. *Deliverance or Destruction? Syria at a Crossroads* (Cairo: Cairo Institute for Human Rights Studies) [in Arabic].

al-Haj Saleh. 2017. *The Impossible Revolution: Making Sense of the Syrian Tragedy*, trans. by Ibtihal Mahmood (London: Hurst).

ALIPH Foundation Project. "Collart—Palmyra: The Digital Restoration of the Baalshamîn Temple on Syrian Heritage." https://www.aliph-foundation.org/en/projects/collart-palmyra-the-digital-restoration-of-the-baalshamin-temple [accessed 29 July 2020].

ALIPH Foundation Project. "Preserving and Sharing Palmyra's Cultural Heritage Through Harald Ingholt's Digital Archives." https://www.aliph-foundation.org/en/projects/preserving-and-sharing-palmyras-cultural-heritage-through-harald-ingholts-archives [accessed 29 July 2020].

Al-Jazeera. 2017 (3 March). "Palmyra: Russia-backed Syrian Army Retakes Ancient City." https://www.aljazeera.com/news/2017/03/palmyra-russia-backed-syria-army-retakes-ancient-city-170303050427702.html.

Al-Maqdissi, Michel. 2000. "Note sur les sondages réalisés par Robert du Mesnil du Buisson dans la cour du sanctuaire de Bêl à Palmyre." *Syria* 77: 137-158.

Al-Maqdissi, Michel, and Eva Ishaq. In press. "Les phases anciennes du temple de Bêl d'après les archives de R. du Mesnil du Buisson et les travaux de la Mission syrienne." In *Life in Palmyra, Life for Palmyra*, ed. by Dagmara Wielgosz and Marta Żuchowska (Warsaw: Uniwersytet Warszawski).

Amnesty International. 2001 (18 September). "Syria: Torture, Despair and Dehumanization in Tadmur Military Prison." https://www.amnesty.org/en/documents/MDE24/014/2001/en/ [accessed March 2021].

Amy, Robert, and Henri Seyrig. 1936. "Recherches dans la nécropole de Palmyre." *Syria* 17.3: 229-266.

Andrade, Nathanael John. 2013. *Syrian Identity in the Greco-Roman World*. Greek Culture in the Roman World (Cambridge: Cambridge University Press).

Andrade, Nathanael John. 2018. *Zenobia: Shooting Star of Palmyra* (Oxford: Oxford University Press).

Andrade, Nathanael John. 2019. "Zenobia of Palmyra." In *The Road to Palmyra*, ed. by Anne Marie Nielsen and Rubina Raja (Copenhagen: Ny Carlsberg Glyptotek), pp. 193-204.

Anfinset, Nils. 2009. *Palmyrena: Palmyra and Surrounding Territory. Joint Syrian-Norwegian Project. Surface Survey North of Palmyra, April and May 2009. Preliminary Report, Prehistorical Period*. Palmyrena. City, Hinterland and Caravan Trade Between Occident and Orient (Bergen: University of Bergen). http://bora.uib.no/handle/1956/10472 [accessed March 2021].

Anfinset, Nils, and Kristina Josephson Hesse. 2013. *Palmyrena: Palmyra and the Surrounding Territory. Joint Syrian-Norwegian Project. Surface Survey North of Palmyra, April and May 2011. Preliminary Report, Prehistorical Period*. Palmyrena. City, Hinterland and Caravan Trade Between Occident and Orient (Bergen: University of Bergen). http://bora.uib.no/handle/1956/10476 [accessed March 2021].

Anfinset, Nils, and Jørgen Christian Meyer. 2010. "The Hinterland of Palmyra." *Antiquity Project Gallery* 84.324. http://antiquity.ac.uk/projgall/anfinset324/ [accessed March 2021].

Appelbaum, Alan. 2011. "The Rabbis and Palmyra: A Case Study on (Mis-)Reading Rabbinics for Historical Purposes." *Jewish Quarterly Review* 101.4: 527–544.

Arbeitman, Yoël L. 1988. *A Linguistic Happening in Memory of Ben Schwartz: Studies in Anatolian, Italic, and Other Indo-European Languages.* Bibliotheque des Cahiers de l'Institut de Linguistique de Louvain 42 (Leuven: Peeters).

Astengo, Gregorio. 2016 (16 March). "The Rediscovery of Palmyra and Its Dissemination in Philosophical Transactions." *Notes and Records of the Royal Society of Publishing*: 1–21.

Audley-Miller, Lucy. 2016. "The Banquet in Palmyrene Funerary Contexts." In *Dining and Death: Interdisciplinary Perspectives on the "Funerary Banquet" in Ancient Art, Burial and Belief*, ed. by Catherine Mary Draycott and Maria Stamatopoulou. Colloquia Antiqua 16 (Leuven: Peeters), pp. 553–590.

Baird, Jennifer A. 2014. *The Inner Lives of Ancient Houses: An Archaeology of Dura-Europos* (Oxford: Oxford University Press).

Ball, Warwick. 2016. *Rome in the East: The Transformation of an Empire* (London: Routledge).

Banchich, Thomas M. 2015. *The Lost History of Peter the Patrician: An Account of Rome's Imperial Past from the Age of Justinian.* Routledge Classical Translations (London: Routledge).

Barański, Marek. 1994. "The Roman Army in Palmyra: A Case of Adaptation of a Pre-existing City." In *The Roman and Byzantine Army in the East: Proceedings of a Colloquium Held at the Jagiellonian University, Krakow in September 1992*, ed. by Edward Dąbrowa (Krakow: Jagiellonian University Press), pp. 9–17.

Barański, Marek. 1995. "The Great Colonnade of Palmyra Reconsidered." *ARAM Periodical* 7: 37–46.

Barański, Marek. 1996. "Development of the Building Techniques in Palmyra." *Annales archéologiques arabes syriennes* 42: 379–384.

Barański, Marek. 1997. "Western Aqueduct in Palmyra." *Studia Palmyreńskie* 10: 7–17.

Barford, Paul. 2016 (16 April). "Polish Mission in Palmyra." *Portable Antiquity Collecting and Heritage Issues Blog.* http://paul-barford.blogspot.com/2016/04/polish-mission-in-palmyra.html [accessed March 2021].

Barker, Graeme. 2002. "A Tale of Two Deserts: Contrasting Desertification Histories on Rome's Desert Frontiers." *World Archaeology* 33.3: 488–507.

Barrett, Anthony A. 2008. "Herod, Augustus, and the Special Relationship: The Significance of the Procuratorship." In *Herod and Augustus: Papers Presented at the IJS Conference, 21st–23rd June 2005*, ed. by David Jacobson and Nikos Kokkinos. IJS Studies in Judaica 6 (Leiden: Brill), pp. 281–302.

Barthélemy, Jean-Jacques. 1754. *Réflexions sur l'alphabet et sur la langue don't on se servoit autrefois a Palmyre* (Paris: Guérin).

Bauzou, Thomas. 1989. "A finibus Syriae: Recherches sur les routes des frontières orientales de l'Empire Romain." 3 vols. (Unpubl. PhD dissertation, Université de Paris I).

Bauzou, Thomas. 1992. "Activité de la mission archéologique 'Strata Diocletiana' en 1990 et 1992." *Chronique archéologique en Syrie* 1: 136–140.

Bauzou, Thomas. 1993. "Épigraphie et toponymie: le cas de la Palmyrène du sud-ouest." *Syria* 70.1–2: 27–50.

BBC News. 2015 (4 July). "Islamic State 'Murders 25 Men in Palmyra.'"https://www.bbc.com/news/world-middle-east-33397305.

BBC News. 2016 (11 December). "Palmyra: IS Retakes Ancient Syrian City." https://www.bbc.com/news/world-middle-east-38280283.

BBC News. 2017 (2 March). "Palmyra: Syrian Forces 'Completely Retake' IS-held Town." https://www.bbc.com/news/world-middle-east-39147612.

Belayche, Nicole. 2007. "Les immigrés orientaux à Rome et en Campanie: Fidélité aux *patria* et intégration sociale." *Cahiers de la Villa Kérylos* 18.1: 243–260.

Bingen, Jean. 1984. "Une dédicace de marchands Palmyréniens à Coptos." *Chroniques d'Égypte* 59: 355–358.

Bjørgo, Einar et al. "Satellite-based Damage Assessment to Cultural Heritage Sites in Syria." UNITAR. https://unitar.org/unosat/chs-syria [accessed 28 July 2020].

Bland, Roger. 2011. "The Coinage of Vabalathus and Zenobia from Antioch and Alexandria." *Numismatic Chronicle* 171: 133–186.

Bleckmann, Bruno. 1992. *Die Reichskrise des III. Jahrhunderts in der spätantiken und byzantinischen Geschichtsschreibung* (Munich: Tuduv).

Blömer, Michael, Achim Lichtenberger, and Rubina Raja (eds.). 2015. *Religious Identities in the Levant from Alexander to Muhammad*. Contextualizing the Sacred 4 (Turnhout: Brepols).

Blömer, Michael, and Rubina Raja (eds.). 2019a. *Funerary Portraiture in Greater Roman Syria*. Studies in Classical Archaeology 6 (Turnhout: Brepols).

Blömer, Michael, and Rubina Raja. 2019b. "Shifting the Paradigms: Towards a New Agenda in the Study of the Funerary Portraiture of Greater Roman Syria." In *Funerary Portraiture in Greater Roman Syria*, ed. by Michael Blömer and Rubina Raja. Studies in Classical Archaeology 6 (Turnhout: Brepols), pp. 5–26.

Boatwright, Mary T. 2000. *Hadrian and the Cities of the Roman Empire* (Princeton: Princeton University Press).

Bobou, Olympia, and Rubina Raja. Forthcoming. *Palmyrene Sarcophagi*. Sarkofagen Studien.

Bobou, Olympia, Rubina Raja, and Iza Romanowska. 2021. "Historical Trajectories of Palmyra's Elites through the Lens of Archaeological Data." *Journal of Urban Archaeology* 4: 153–166.

Bobou, Olympia et al. (eds.). 2021. *Studies on Palmyrene Sculpture. A Translation of Harald Ingholt's "Studier over Palmyrensk Skulptur," Edited and with Commentary*. Studies in Palmyrene Archaeology and History 1 (Turnhout: Brepols).

Bonhams Auction House. 2012 (25 April). *Antiquities* (London: Bonhams).

Bowersock, Glen Warren. 1990. *Hellenism in Late Antiquity* (Ann Arbor: University of Michigan Press).

Bounni, Adnan. 2004. *Le sanctuaire de Nabū à Palmyre*, vol. 1. Bibliothèque archéologique et historique 131 (Beirut: Institut d'archéologie du Proche-Orient).

Bounni, Adnan, and Michel al-Maqdissi. 2001. "Note sur un sondage dans la cour du sanctuaire de Bêl à Palmyra." *Topoi* 11: 17–34.

Bounni, Adnan, and Nassib Saliby. 1968. "Fouilles de l'annxe de l'agora à Palmyre." *Annales Archéologiques Arabes Syriennes* 18: 93–102.

Bounni, Adnan, Jacques Seigne, and Nassib Saliby. 1992. *Le sanctuaire de Nabū à Palmyre*, vol. 2. Bibliothèque archéologique et historique 131 (Paris: Geuthner).

Brecht, Stephanie. 1999. *Die römische Reichskrise von ihrem Ausbruck bis zu ihrem Höhepunkt in der Darstellung byzantinischer Autoren*. Althistorische Studien der Universität Würzburg 1 (Rahden/Westfalen: Leidorf).

Brodie, Neil et al. (eds.). 2006. *Archaeology, Cultural Heritage, and the Antiquities Trade* (Gainesville: University of Florida Press).

Brody, Lisa R., and Gail L. Hoffman (eds.). 2011. *Dura-Europos: Crossroads of Antiquity* (Boston: McMullen Museum of Art).

Bron, François. 1986. "Palmyréniens et Chaldéens en Arabie du Sud." *Studi epigrafici e linguistici sul Vicino Oriente antico* 3: 95–98.

Brownlee, Jason, Tarek Masoud, and Andrew Reynolds. 2013. *The Arab Spring: The Politics of Transformation in North Africa and the Middle East* (Oxford: Oxford University Press).

Buckingham, James Silk. 1825. *Travels Among the Arab Tribes* (London: Longman).

Burns, Ross. 2017. *Origins of the Colonnaded Streets in the Cities of the Roman East* (Oxford: Oxford University Press).

Butcher, Kevin. 2003. *Roman Syria and the Near East* (Los Angeles: J. Paul Getty Museum).

Cantineau, Jean. 1929. "Fouilles à Palmyre." *Mélanges de l'Institut Français de Damas* 1: 1–15.

Cantineau, Jean. 1930. *Inventaire des inscriptions de Palmyra*, tome 3, *La grande colonnade*. Publications du musée national syrien de Damas 1 (Beirut: Imprimerie Catholique).

Cantineau, Jean. 1931a. *Inventaire des inscriptions de Palmyra*, tome 7, *Les nécropoles nord-ouest et nord*. Publications du musée national syrien de Damas 1 (Beirut: Imprimerie Catholique).

Cantineau, Jean. 1931b. "Textes palmyréniens provenant de la fouille du Temple de Bêl." *Syria* 12.2: 116–141.

Cantineau, Jean. 1932. *Inventaire des inscriptions de Palmyra*, tome 8, *Le dépot des Antiquités*. Publications du musée national syrien de Damas 1 (Beirut: Imprimerie Catholique).

Cantineau, Jean. 1933a. *Inventaire des inscriptions de Palmyra*, tome 9, *Le sanctuaire de Bêl*. Publications du musée national syrien de Damas 1 (Beirut: Imprimerie Catholique).

Cantineau, Jean. 1933b. "Un *restitutor orientis* dans les inscriptions de Palmyre." *Journal Asiatique* 222: 217–233.

Cantineau, Jean. 1933c. "Tadmorea." *Syria* 14: 169–202.

Cantineau, Jean. 1936. "Tadmorea." *Syria* 17.4: 346–355.

Carroll, Maureen. 2018. *Infancy and Earliest Childhood in the Roman World* (Oxford: Oxford University Press).

Cassas, Louis-François. 1799. *Voyage pittoresque de la Syrie, de la Phénicie et de la Basse-Aegypte* (Paris: Imprimerie de la République).

Cassas, Louis-François. Unpubl. "Materials for Voyage pittoresque de la Syrie, de la Phoenicie, de la Palaestine, et de la Basse Aegypte, 1795–1823" (Getty Research Center).

Chabot Jean-Baptiste. 1897. "Les ruines de Palmyre en 1735." *Journal Asiatique* (Sept.–Oct.): 335–355.

Chabot Jean-Baptiste. 1922. *Choix d'inscriptions de Palmyre* (Paris: Imprimerie nationale).

Charles-Gaffiot, Jacques, Henri Lavagne, and Jean-Marc Hofman (eds.). 2001. *Moi, Zénobie, reine de Palmyre* (Milan: Skira).

Chausson, François. 1995. "Vel Iovi vel Soli: Quatre études autour de la Vigna Barberini (191–354). *Mélanges de l'Ecole française de Rome, Antiquité* 107.2: 661–765.

Chéhab, Maurice. 1962. "Tyr à l'époque romaine." *Mélanges de l'Université Saint-Joseph* 38: 13–40.

Chevalier, Nicole. 2008. "Die französische Archäologie zwischen 1860 und 1940." In *Das Große Spiel: Archäologie und Politik zur Zeit des Kolonialismus (1860–1940)*, ed. by Charlotte Trümpler (Cologne: DuMont), pp. 316–323.

Christie, Agatha. 1946. *Come, Tell Me How You Live: An Archaeological Memoir* (Glasgow: William Collins and Sons).

Clarke, Graeme Wilber et al. 2016. *Report on Excavations 2000–2010*, vol. 5, *Jebel Khalid on the Euphrates*. Mediterranean Archaeology supplement 10 (Sydney: Sydney University Press).

Clermont-Ganneau, Charles Simon. 1920. "Odeinat et Vaballat, rois de Palmyre, et leur titre romain de corrector." *Revue biblique* 29: 382–419.

Cohen, Getzel M. 2006. *The Hellenistic Settlements in Syria, the Red Sea Basin, and North Africa*. Hellenistic Culture and Society 46 (Berkeley: University of California Press).

Collart, Paul, and Jacques Vicari. 1969. *Topographie et architecture*, vols. 1–2, *Le Sanctuaire de Baalshamîn à Palmyre*. Bibliotheca Helvetica Romana 10 (Rome: Institut Suisse de Rome).

Colledge, Malcolm A. R. 1976. *The Art of Palmyra* (London: Thames and Hudson).

Colledge, Malcolm A. R. 1987. "Parthian Cultural Elements at Roman Palmyra." *Mesopotamia* 22: 19–28.

Colledge, Malcolm A. R. 1996. "Roman Influence in the Art of Palmyra." *Annales Archéologiques Arabes Syriennes* 42: 363–370.

Comstock, Mary B., and Cornelius C. Vermeule. 1976. *Sculpture in Stone. The Greek, Roman and Etruscan Collections of the Museum of Fine Arts* (Boston: Museum of Fine Arts).

Creason, Stuart. 2004. "Aramaic." In *The Cambridge Encyclopedia of the World's Ancient Languages*, ed. by Roger D. Woodard (Cambridge: Cambridge University Press), pp. 391–426.

Crouch, Dora P. 1975a. "The Ramparts of Palmyra." *Studia Palmyreńskie* 6–7: 6–44.

Crouch, Dora P. 1975b. "The Water System of Palmyra." *Studia Palmyreńskie* 6–7: 151–186.

Cumont, Franz. 1928. "L'autel palmyrénien du Musée du Capitole." *Syria* 9: 101–109.

Cuno, James. 2010. *Who Owns Antiquity? Museums and the Battle over Our Ancient Heritage* (Princeton: Princeton University Press).

Curtis, Vesta Sarkhosh. 2017. "The Parthian Haute-Couture at Palmyra." In *Positions and Professions in Palmyra*, ed. by Tracey Long and Anette Højen Sørensen. Palmyrene Studies 2 (Copenhagen: Det Kongelige Danske Videnskabernes Selskab), pp. 52–67.

Cussini, Eleonora. 1995. "Transfer of Property at Palmyra." *ARAM Periodical* 7: 233–250.

Cussini, Eleonora. 2005. "Beyond the Spindle: Investigating the Role of Palmyrene Women." In *A Journey to Palmyra. Collected Essays to Remember Delbert R. Hillers*, ed. by Eleonora Cussini. Culture and History of the Ancient Near East 22 (Leiden: Brill), pp. 26–43.

Cussini, Eleonora. 2012. "What Women Say and Do (in Aramaic Documents)." In *LEGGO! Studies Presented to Prof. Frederick Mario Fales on the Occasion of His 65th Birthday*, ed. by Giovanni B. Lanfranchi et al. Leipziger altorientalistische Studien 2. (Wiesbaden: Harrassowitz), pp. 161–172.

Cussini, Eleonora. 2016a. "Family Banqueting at Palmyra. Reassessing the Evidence." In *Libiamo ne' lieti calici. Ancient Near Eastern Studies Presented to Lucio Milano on the*

Occasion of His 65th Birthday by Pupils, Colleagues and Friends, ed. by Paolo Corò et al. Alter Orient und Altes Testament 436 (Münster: Ugarit-Verlag), pp. 139–159.

Cussini, Eleonora. 2016b. "Reconstructing Palmyrene Legal Language." In *The World of Palmyra*, ed. by Andreas Kropp and Rubina Raja. Palmyrene Studies 1 (Copenhagen: Det Kongelige Danske Videnskabernes Selskab), pp. 42–52.

Cussini, Eleonora. 2019. "Daughters and Wives: Defining Women in Palmyrene Inscriptions." In *Women, Children, and the Family in Palmyra*, ed. by Signe Krag and Rubina Raja. Palmyrene Studies 3 (Copenhagen: Det Kongelige Danske Videnskabernes Selskab), pp. 67–81.

Cuvigny, Hélène (ed.). 2003. *La route de Myos Hormos: L'armée romaine dans le désert Oriental d'Égypte* (Cairo: Institut français d'archéologie orientale du Caire).

Cuvigny, Hélène (ed.). 2012. *Didymoi: Une garnison romaine dans le désert Oriental d'Égypte*, vol. 2, *Les textes*. Fouilles de l'IFAO, 67 (Cairo: Institut français d'archéologie orientale du Caire).

Davies, G. 2017. "The Body Language of Palmyra and Rome." In *Positions and Professions in Palmyra*, ed. by Tracey Long and Annette Højen Sørensen. Palmyrene Studies 2 (Copenhagen: Det Kongelige Danske Videnskabernes Selskab), pp. 20–51.

Dabashi, Hamid. 2012. *The Arab Spring: The End of Postcolonialism* (London: Zed Books).

Declerck, José H. 1984. "Deux nouveaux fragments attribués à Paul de Samosate." *Byzantion* 54: 116–140.

de Jong, Lidewijde. 2017. *The Archaeology of Death in Roman Syria: Burial, Commemoration, and Empire* (Cambridge: Cambridge University Press).

Delplace, Christiane. 2006–2007. "La fouille du marché suburbain de Palmyre (2001–2005)." *Annales Archéologiques Arabes Syriennes* 49–50: 91–111.

Delplace, Christiane. 2013. "Les recherches de la mission archéologique Française à Palmyre." *Studia Palmyreńskie* 12: 37–48.

Delplace, Christiane. 2017. *Palmyre: Histoire et archéologie d'une cité caravanière à la croisée des cultures* (Paris: Éditions du Centre national de la recherche scientifique).

Delplace, Christiane, and Jacqueline Dentzer-Feydy. 2005. *L'Agora de Palmyre*. Mémoires 14, Bibliothèque archéologique et historique 175 (Bordeaux: Institut Ausonius).

Delplace, Christiane, and Jacqueline Dentzer-Feydy. 2017. "Topographie cultuelle et urbanisation à Palmyre." In *Les archives au secours des temples détruits de Palmyre. Actes du colloque international organisé par l'Académie des Inscriptions et Belles-Lettres à l'Académie des Inscriptions et Belles-Lettres, le 19 mai 2017*, ed. by Paul Ducrey, Pierre Gros, and Stephan Zink (Paris: De Boccard), pp. 73–91.

Denker, Ahmet. 2017. "Rebuilding Palmyra Virtually: Recreation of Its Former Glory in Digital Space." *Virtual Archaeology Review* 8.17: 20–30. doi: 10.4995/var.2017.5963.

Dentzer-Feydy, Jacqueline, and Javier Teixidor. 1993. *Les antiquités de Palmyre au Musée du Louvre* (Paris: Réunion des musées nationaux), pp. 57–81.

Dentzer, Jean-Marie. 1990. "Edicules d'epoque Hellenistico-Romaine et tradition des pierres cultuelles en Syrie et en Arabie." In *Resurrecting the Past: A Joint Tribute to Adnān Bounnī*, ed. by Paolo Matthiae, Maurits Nanning van Loon, and Harvey Weiss (Leiden: Nederlands Historisch-Archaeologisch Instituut te Istanbul), pp. 65–83.

Dentzer, Jean-Marie, and René Saupin. 1996. "L'espace urbain à Palmyre: remarques sur des photographies aériennes anciennes." In *Documenting the Activities of the International Colloquium Palmyra and the Silk Road, Palmyra, 7–11 April 1992*, ed. by Directorate-General of Antiquities and Museums, Syria. *Special Issue Annales Archéologiques Arabes Syriennes* 42: 303–318.

Deppert-Lippitz, Barbara. 1987. "Die Bedeutung der palmyrenischen Grabreliefs für die Kenntnis römischen Schmucks." In *Palmyra: Geschichte, Kunst und Kultur der syrischen Oasenstadt*, ed. by Erwin M. Ruprechtsberger (Linz: Gutenberg), pp. 179–192.

de Riedmatten, Henri. 1952. *Les Actes du proces de Paul de Samosate: étude sur la Christologie du IIIe au IVe siècle*. Paradosis: Etudes de littérature et de théologie ancienne 6 (Fribourg: Éditions St-Paul).

De Romanis, Federico. 2008. "Cultores huius loci: Sulle coabitazioni divine del *lucus Furrinae*." In *Culti orientali: Tra scavo e collezionismo*, ed. by Beatrice Palma (Rome: Artemide), pp. 149–157.

De Vogüé, Melchior. 1865. *La Syrie centrale: architecture civile et religieuse de Ier au VII siècle*. Tome 2, *Planches* (Paris: Baudry).

De Vogüé, Melchior. 1877. *La Syrie centrale: architecture civile et religieuse de Ier au VII siècle*. Tome 1, *Texte* (Paris: Baudry).

Devreesse, Robert. 1945. *Le patriarcat d'Antioche: depuis la paix de l'eglise jusqu' à la conquête arabe*. Études palestiniennes et orientales (Paris: Gabalda).

Díaz-Andreu, Margarita. 2007. *A World History of Nineteenth-Century Archaeology: Nationalism, Colonialism, and the Past*. Oxford Studies in the History of Archaeology (Oxford: Oxford University Press).

Dillon, Sheila. 2006. *Ancient Greek Portrait Sculpture: Contexts, Subjects, and Styles* (Cambridge: Cambridge University Press).

Directorate General of Antiquities and Museums, Ministry of Culture, Syrian Arab Republic. http://www.dgam.gov.sy/index.php?m=315 [accessed March 2021].

Dirven, Lucinda. 1996. "The Nature of the Trade Between Palmyra and Dura-Europos." *ARAM Periodical* 8: 39–54.

Dirven, Lucinda. 1997. "The Exaltation of Nabû: A Reision of the Relief Depicting the Battle Against Tiamat from the Temple of Bel in Palmyra." *Die Welt des Orientes* 28: 96–116.

Dirven, Lucinda. 1998a. "The Arrival of the Goddess Allat in Palmyra." *Mesopotamia* 33: 297–307.

Dirven, Lucinda. 1998b. "The Palmyrene Diaspora in East and West. A Syrian Community in the Diaspora in the Roman Period." In *Strangers and Sojourners: Religious Communities in the Diaspora*, ed. by Gerrie ter Haar (Leuven: Peeters), pp. 77–94.

Dirven, Lucinda. 1999. *The Palmyrenes of Dura-Europos: A Study of Religious Interaction in Roman Syria*. Religions in the Graeco-Roman World 138 (Leiden: Brill).

Dirven, Lucinda. 2011a. "The Imperial Cult in the Cities of the Decapolis, Caesarea Maritima, and Palmyra." *ARAM Periodical* 23: 141–156.

Dirven, Lucinda. 2013. "Palmyrenes in Hatra: Evidence for Cultural Relations in the Fertile Crescent." *Studia Palmyrenskie* 12: 49–60.

Donner, Fred McGraw. 1981. *The Early Islamic Conquest*. Princeton Studies on the Near East (Princeton: Princeton University Press).

Dossin, Georges. 1951. "Quelques textes inédits de Mari." In *Compte rendus de la première rencontre assyriologique internationale (Paris, 26–28 juin 1950)* (Leiden: Brill), pp. 19–21.

Downey, Susan B. 1988. *Mesopotamian Religious Architecture. Alexander Through the Parthians* (Princeton: Princeton University Press).

Downey, Susan B. 1998. "Cult Reliefs at Dura-Europos: Problems of Interpretation and Placement." *Damaszener Mitteilungen* 10: 201–210

Downey, Susan B. 2003. *Terracotta Figuines and Plaques from Dura-Europos* (Ann Arbor: University of Michigan Press).

Downey, Susan B. 2017. "Degrees of Access to Temples at Palmyra." In Contextualizing the Sacred in the *Hellenistic and Roman Near East. Religious Identities in Local, Regional, and Imperial Settings,* ed. by Rubina Raja. Contextualizing the Sacred 8 (Turnhout: Brepols), pp. 99–108.

Drexhage, Raphaela. 1988. *Untersuchungen zum römischen Osthandel* (Bonn: Habelt).

Drijvers, Han J. W. 1976. *The Religion of Palmyra* (Leiden: Brill).

Drijvers, Han J. W. 1982. "Afterlife and Funerary Symbolism in Palmyrene Religion." In *La soteriologia dei culti orientali nell'impero romano: atti del colloquio internazionale su la soteriologia dei culti orientali nell'impero romano, Roma 24–28 settembre 1979,* ed. by Ugo Bianchi and Maarten Jozef Vermaseren (Leiden: Brill), pp. 709–733.

Drijvers, Han J. W. 1988. "Aramaic HMN and Hebrew HMN: Their Meaning and Root." *Journal of Semitic Studies* 33.2: 165–180.

Drijvers, Han J. W. 1995a. "Greek and Aramaic in Palmyrene Inscriptions." In *Studia Aramaica: New Sources and New Approaches,* ed. by Markham J. Geller, Jonas C. Greenfield, and Michael Weitzman (Oxford: Oxford University Press), pp. 31–42.

Drijvers, Han J. W. 1995b. "Inscriptions from Allat's Sanctuary." *ARAM Periodical* 7: 109–119.

du Mesnil du Buisson, Robert. 1966. "Première campagne des fouilles à Palmyre." *Comptes rendus de l'Académie des Inscriptions et Belles-Lettres* 110.1: 158–190.

Dunand, Maurice. 1931. "La Strata Diocletiana." *Revue biblique* 40: 227–248.

Dunant, Christiane. 1971. *Le sanctuaire de Baalshamin à Palmyre: Inscriptions* (Rome: Institut suisse de Rome).

Dupont-Sommer, André. 1942. "Un buste palmyrénien inédit." *Syria* 1.2: 78–85.

Dupont-Sommer, André. 1970. "Une nouvelle inscription araméenne d'Asoka trouvée dans la vallée du Laghman (Afghanistan)." *Comptes rendus de l'Académie des Inscriptions et Belles-Lettres* 114.1: 158–173.

Edwell, Peter M. 2008. *Between Rome and Persia: The Middle Euphrates, Mesopotamia and Palmyra Under Roman Control.* Routledge Monographs in Classical Studies (London: Routledge).

Edwell, Peter M. 2013. "The Euphrates as a Boundary Between Rome and Parthia in the Late Republic and Early Empire." *Antichthon* 47: 191–206.

Edwell, Peter M. 2019. "Palmyra Between Rome and the Parthians." In *The Road to Palmyra,* ed. by Anne Marie Nielsen and Rubina Raja (Copenhagen: Ny Carlsberg Glyptotek), pp. 109-126.

Eger, Christoph, and Michael Mackensen. 2018. *Death and Burial in the Near East from Roman to Islamic Times: Research in Syria, Lebanon, Jordan and Egypt.* Münchner Beiträge zur Provinzialrömischen Archäologie 7 (Wiesbaden: Reichert).

Ensoli, S. 2002. "Comunità e culti siriani a Roma: i santuari della regio XIV Transtiberim." In *Zenobia. Il sogno du una regina d'Oriente* ed. by Ada Gabucci, Angela Benotto, and Fondazione Palazzo Bricheriasio (Milan: Electa), pp. 137–143.

Ensoli, Serena. 2003. "Il santuario della Dea Syria e i culti palmireni nell'area meridionale di Trastevere." *Orizzonti rassegna di archeologia* 4: 45–59.

Ensoli, Serena. 2004. "Deae Syriae Templum." *Lexicon topographicum urbis Romae: Suburbium,* vol. 2, *D–G,* ed. by Eva Margareta Steinby (Rome: Quasar), pp. 191–196.

Equini Schneider, Eugenia. 1987. "Il santuario di Bel e delle divinità di Palmira. Comunità e tradizioni religiose dei Palmireni a Roma." *Dialoghi di archeologia* 1: 69–85.

Equini Schneider, Eugenia. 1993. *Septimia Zenobia Sebaste*. Studia archaeologica 61 (Rome: L'Erma di Bretschneider).

Equini Schneider, Eugenia. Forthcoming. "Palmyrenes in Rome." In *The Oxford University Press Handbook of Palmyra*, ed. by Rubina Raja (Oxford: Oxford University Press).

Eristov, Hélène et al. (eds.). 2019. *Le tombeau des Trois Frères à Palmyre: Mission archéologique franco-syrienne 2004-2009*. Bibliothèque archéologique et historique 215 (Beirut: Institut français du Proche-Orient).

Estiot, Sylviane. 2004. *D'Aurélian à Florien (270–276 après J.-C.)*, vol. 12, *Catalogue des monnaies de l'Empire romain*. 2 vols. (Paris: Bibliothèque nationale de France).

Euting, Julius. 1887. "Epigraphische Miscellen." *Sitzungsberichte der königlich preussischen Akademie der Wissenschaften zu Berlin* 25: 407–426.

Evers, Kasper Grønlund. 2016. "Cave of Revelations: Indian Ocean Trade in Light of the Socotra Graffiti." *Journal of Indian Ocean Archaeology* 10–11: 19–37.

Farhat, May. 2012. "A Mediterraneanist's Collection: Henri Pharaon's 'Treasure House of Arab Art.'" *Ars Orientalis* 42: 102–113.

Feeley, Kathryn-Magnolia. 2012. *How the Greeks Can Get Their Marbles Back. The Legal Argument for the Return of the Parthenon Marbles to Greece* (Canberra: self-published).

Fellmann, Rudolf. 1970. *Die Grabanlage*, vol. 5, *Le Sanctuaire de Baalshamîn à Palmyre* (Rome: Institut Suisse de Rome).

Fellmann, Rudolf. 1975. "Die Lampen." In *Le Sanctuaire de Baalshamin à Palmyre*, vol. 6, *Die Kleinfunde: Objets divers*, ed. by Rudolf Fellmann and Christiane Dunant (Rome: Institut suisse de Rome), pp. 9–59.

Fellmann, Rudolf. 1976a. "Le 'camp de Dioclétien' à Palmyre et l'architecture militaire du Bas empire." In *Mélanges d'histoire ancienne et d'archéologie offerts à Paul Collart*, ed. by Pierre Ducrey et al. Cahiers d'archéologie romande de la Bibliothèque historique vaudoise 5 (Lausanne: Bibliothèque historique vaudoise), pp. 173–191.

Fellmann, Rudolf. 1976b. "Le tombeau prés du temple du Ba'alšamên, témoin de deux siècles d'histoire palmyrénienne." In *Palmyre: Bilan et Perspectives. Colloque de Strasbourg 18–20 Octobre 1973, à la mémoire de Daniel Schlumberger et de Henri Seyrig*, ed. by Edmond Frézouls. Université des Sciences Humaines de Strasbourg. Travaux du Centre de Recherche Sur le Proche-Orient et la Grèce Antiques 3 (Strasbourg: Association pour l'étude de la civilisation romaine), pp. 213-231.

Février, J. G. 1931. *La religion des Palmyréniens* (Paris: Vrin).

Filippi, Fedora, and Attilia Luigia. 2008. "Tra Gianicolo e Tevere: le fonti documentarie sui culti orientali." In *Culti orientali: Tra scavo e collezionismo*, ed. by Beatrice Palma (Rome: Artemide), pp. 174–188.

Fisk, Robert. 2005. *The Great War for Civilisation: The Conquest of the Middle East* (London: Fourth Estate).

Fowlkes-Childs, Blair. 2016. "Palmyrenes in Transtiberim: Integration in Rome and Links to the Eastern Frontier." In *Rome and the Worlds Beyond Its Frontiers*, ed. by Daniëlle Slootjes and Michael Peachin. Impact of Empire 21 (Leiden: Brill), pp. 193–212.

Fortin, Michel et al. 1990. "Chronique archéologique." *Syria* 67.2: 435–482.

Fournet, Thibaut. 2009a. "Les bains de Zénobie à Palmyre. Rapport préliminaire—août 2009." Rapports des Opérations Balnéorient. https://balneorient.hypotheses.org/604 [accessed 6 August 2020].

Fournet, Thibaut. 2009b. "Résumé de T. Fournet." Rapports des Opérations Balnéorient. https://balneorient.hypotheses.org/1124 [accessed 6 August 2020].

"Fragment of a Roman Votive Relief to Fortuna Redux." Sir John Soane's Museum, London, inv. no. M1446. http://collections.soane.org/object-m1446 [accessed March 2021]

Freeman, Colin. 2015 (23 June). "Islamic State Fighters Blow Up Two Burial Sites at Palmyra." *The Telegraph*. https://www.telegraph.co.uk/news/worldnews/islamic-state/11693510/Islamic-State-fighters-blow-up-two-burial-sites-at-Palmyra.html [accessed March 2021].

"French Mandate for Syria and the Lebanon." 1923. *American Journal of International Law* 17.3: 177–182. doi: 10.2307/2212963.

Frézouls, Edmond. 1952. "Les theätres romains de Syrie." *Annales archéologiques arabes syriennes* 2: 87—91.

Frézouls, Edmond. 1959. "Recherches sur les theätres de Orient Syrien." *Syria* 36: 202–228.

Frézouls, Edmond. 1976. "Questions d'urbanisme palmyrénien." In *Palmyre: Bilan et Perspectives. Colloque de Strasbourg 18–20 Octobre 1973, à la mémoire de Daniel Schlumberger et de Henri Seyrig*, ed. by Edmond Frézouls. Université des Sciences Humaines de Strasbourg. Travaux du Centre de Recherche Sur le Proche-Orient et la Grèce Antiques 3 (Strasbourg: Association pour l'étude de la civilisation romaine), pp. 191–207.

Frézouls, Edmond. 1996. "Palmyre et les conditions politiques du développement de son activité commerciale." *Annales archéologiques arabes syriennes* 42: 147–155.

Fulminante, Francesca. 2018. "Infancy and Urbanization in Central Italy During the Early Iron Age and Beyond." In *The Archaeology of Death: Proceedings of the Seventh Conference of Italian Archaeology Held at the National University of Ireland, Galway, April 16–18, 2016*, ed. by Edward Herring and Eóin O'Donoghue. Papers in Italian Archaeology 7 (Oxford: Archaeopress), pp. 197–207.

Gabriel, Albert. 1926. "Recherches archéologiques à Palmyre." *Syria* 7: 71–92.

Gabucci, Ada. 2002. *Zenobia. Il sogno di una regina d'Oriente* (Milan: Electa).

Gardner, Iain, and Samuel N. C. Lieu (eds.). 2004. *Manichaean Texts from the Roman Empire* (Cambridge: Cambridge University Press).

Gąssowska, Barbara. 1982. "Maternus Cynegius, Praefectus Praetorio Orientis and the Destruction of the Allat Temple in Palmyra." *Archeologia: Rocznik Instytutu historii kultury materialnej Polskiej akademii nauk* 22: 107–123.

Gawlikowski, Michał. 1970. *Monuments funéraires de Palmyre*. Travaux du Centre d'Archéologie Méditerranéenne de l'Académie Polonaise des Sciences 9 (Warsaw: Editions Scientifiques de Pologne).

Gawlikowski, Michał. 1971. "Inscriptions de Palmyre." *Syria* 48.3–4: 407–426

Gawlikowski, Michał. 1972. "La notion de tombeau en syrie romaine." *Berytus* 21: 5–15.

Gawlikowski, Michał. 1973. *Le temple palmyrénien. Étude d'épigraphie et de topographie historique*. Palmyra 6 (Warsaw: Państwowe Wydawnictwo Naukowe).

Gawlikowski, Michał. 1975. "Trois inscriptions funéraires du camp de Dioclétien." *Studia Palmyrenskie* 6–7: 127–133.

Gawlikowski, Michał. 1977. "Le Temple d'Allat a Palmyre." *Revue Archéologique* 2: 253–274.

Gawlikowski, Michał. 1983a. "Palmyre et l'Euphrate." *Syria* 60.1–2: 53–68.

Gawlikowski, Michał. 1983b. "Réflexions sur la chronologie du sanctuaire d'Allat à Palmyre." *Damaszener Mitteilungen* 1: 59–67.

Gawlikowski, Michał. 1983c. "Le sanctuaire d'Allat à Palmyre. Aperçu préliminaire." *Les annales archéologiques arabes syriennes* 33: 179–198.

Gawlikowski, Michał. 1984. *Les principia de Dioclétien ("Temple des Enseignes")*, vol. 8, *Palmyre* (Warsaw: Państwowe Wydawnictwo Naukowe).

Gawlikowski, Michał. 1985. "Les princes de Palmyre." *Syria* 62.3–4: 251–261.

Gawlikowski, Michał. 1986. "Palmyre (mission Polonaise)." *Chronique Archéologique* 63: 397–399.

Gawlikowski, Michał. 1987a. "Objektbeschreibungen, nr. 1–76." In *Palmyra: Geschichte, Kunst und Kultur der syrischen Oasenstadt*, ed. by Erwin M. Ruprechtsberger (Linz: Gutenberg), pp. 287–339.

Gawlikowski, Michał. 1987b. "Palmyre." *Syria* 64.1: 158–160.

Gawlikowski, Michał. 1990a. "Les dieux de Palmyre." In *Aufstieg und Niedergang der römischen Welt*, vol. 2, ed. by Wolfgang Haase. Principat no. 18, Religion 4 (Berlin: De Gruyter), pp. 2605–2658.

Gawlikowski, Michał. 1990b. "Palmyra." *Polish Archaeology in the Mediterranean* 1: 38–44.

Gawlikowski, Michał. 1990c. "Le premier temple d'Allat." In *Resurrecting the Past: A Joint Tribute to Adnan Bounni*, ed. by Paolo Matthiae, Maurits van Loon, and Harvey Weiss (Leiden: Nederlands Historisch-Archaeologisch Instituut te Istanbul), pp. 101–108.

Gawlikowski, Michał. 1993. "Palmyra 1992." *Polish Archaeology in the Mediterranean* 4: 111–118.

Gawlikowski, Michał. 1994. "Palmyra as a Trading Centre." *Iraq* 56: 27–33.

Gawlikowski, Michał. 1995a. "Les arabes en Palmyrène." In *Présence arabe dans le croissant fertile avant l'Hégire*, ed. by Hélène Lozachmeur (Paris: Éditions recherche sur les Civilisations), pp. 103–108.

Gawlikowski, Michał. 1995b. "Les arabes de Syrie dans l'antiquité." In *Immigration and Emigration Within the Ancient Near East: Festschrift for E. Lipinski*, ed. by Karel van Lerberghe and A. Schoors (Leuven: Peeters), pp. 83–92.

Gawlikowski, Michał. 1996a. "The Athena of Palmyra." *Archeologia* 47: 21–32.

Gawlikowski, Michał. 1996b. "Palmyra and Its Caravan Trade." *Annales archéologiques arabes syriennes* 42: 139–145.

Gawlikowski, Michał. 1996c. "Les sculptures funéraires de Palmyre by Anna Sadurska; Adnan Bounni." *American Journal of Archaeology* 100.2: 437–438.

Gawlikowski, Michał. 1997a. "Du ḥamānā au naos. Le temple palmyrénien hellénisé." *Topoi. Orient-Occident* 7.2: 837–849.

Gawlikowski, Michał. 1997b. "The Syrian Desert Under the Romans." In *The Early Roman Empire in the East*, ed. by Susan B. Alcock (Oxford: Oxbow), pp. 37–54.

Gawlikowski, Michał. 1998. "Deux publicains et leur tombeau." *Syria* 75: 145–151.

Gawlikowski, Michał. 1999. "Palmyra, Excavations 1998." *Polish Archaeology in the Mediterranean* 10: 189–196.

Gawlikowski, Michał. 2000. "Palmyra, Season 1999." *Polish Archaeology in the Mediterranean* 11: 249–260.

Gawlikowski, Michał. 2001. "Le groupe épiscopal de Palmyre." In *Rome et ses provinces. Genèse et diffusion d'une image du pouvoir. Hommages à Jean-Charles Balty*, ed. by Cécile Evers and Athéna Tsingarida. Lucernae Novantiquae: Études d'archéologie classique de l'Université Libre de Bruxelles (Brussels: Le Livre Timperman), pp. 119–127.

Gawlikowski, Michał. 2003. "Palmyra: From a Tribal Federation to a City." In *Kulturkonflikte im Vorderen Orient an der Wende vom Hellenismus zur römischen Kaiserzeit*, ed. by Klaus Stefan Freyberger, Agnes Henning, and Henner von Hesberg (Rahden/Westfalen: Leidorf), pp. 7–10.

Gawlikowski, Michał. 2004. "Palmyra: Season 2003 Preliminary Report." *Polish Archaeology in the Mediterranean* 15: 313–324.

Gawlikowski, Michał. 2006. "Palmyra: Excavations in the Allat Sanctuary, 2005–2006." *Polish Archaeology in the Mediterranean* 18: 531–541.

Gawlikowski, Michał. 2007a. "Beyond the Colonnades: Domestic Architecture in Palmyra." In *From Antioch to Alexandria: Recent Studies in Domestic Architecture*, ed. by Katharina Galor and Tomasz Waliszewski (Warsaw: University of Warsaw), pp. 79–93.

Gawlikowski, Michał. 2007b. "Odainat et Hérodien, rois des rois." *Mélanges de l'Université Saint-Joseph* 60: 289–311.

Gawlikowski, Michał. 2007c. "Palmyra: Preliminary Report on the Forty-Fifth Season of Excavations." *Polish Archaeology in the Mediterranean* 19: 517–526.

Gawlikowski, Michał. 2008. "The Statues of the Sanctuary of Allat in Palmyra." In *The Sculptural Environment of the Roman Near East. Reflections on Culture, Ideology, and Power*, ed. by Yaron Z. Eliav, Elise A. Friedland, and Sharon C. Herbert (Leuven: Peeters), pp. 397–411.

Gawlikowski, Michał. 2009. "Palmyra in the Early Islamic Time." In *Residences, Castles, Settlements: Transformation Processes from Late Antiquity to Early Islam in Bilad al-Sham: Proceedings of the International Conference Held at Damascus, 5–9 November 2006*, ed. by Karin Bartl and Abd al-Razzaq Moaz (Rahden/Westfalen: Leidorf), pp. 89–96.

Gawlikowski, Michał. 2010. "The Royalty from Palmyra Once Again." In *Zeitreisen Syrien – Palmyra – Rom: Festschrift für Andreas Schmidt-Colinet zum 65. Geburtstag*, ed. by Beatrix Bastl, Verena Gassner, and Ulrike Muss (Vienna: Phoibos), pp. 67–72.

Gawlikowski, Michał. 2012. "Le Tarif de Palmyre et le temple de Rab'asirê." *Comptes rendus des séances de l'Académie des inscriptions et belles-lettres* 156.2: 765–780.

Gawlikowski, Michał. 2013. "In the Footsteps of Prince Abamelek in Palmyra." *Studia Palmyreńskie* 12: 87–96.

Gawlikowski, Michał. 2014a. "Gods and Temples of Palmyra." *Miscellanea Anthropologica et Sociologica* 15.3: 76–91

Gawlikowski, Michał. 2014b. "Palmyra: Reexcavating the Site of the Tariff (Fieldwork in 2010 and 2011)." *Polish Archaeology in the Mediterranean* 23.1: 415–430.

Gawlikowski, Michał. 2015. "Bel of Palmyra." In *Religious Identities in the Levant from Alexander to Muhammad: Continuity and Change*, ed. by Michael Blömer, Achim Lichtenberger, and Rubina Raja. Contextualizing the Sacred 4 (Turnhout: Brepols), pp. 247–254.

Gawlikowski, Michał. 2016. "The Portraits of Palmyrene Royalty." In *The World of Palmyra*, ed. by Andreas Kropp and Rubina Raja. Palmyrene Studies 1 (Copenhagen: Det Kongelige Danske Videnskabernes Selskab), pp. 126–134.

Gawlikowski, Michał. 2017. *Le sanctuaire d'Allat à Palmyre* (Warsaw: University of Warsaw).

Gawlikowski, Michał. 2019. "The Making of a City." In *The Road to Palmyra*, ed. by Anne Marie Nielsen and Rubina Raja (Copenhagen: Ny Carlsberg Glyptotek), pp. 77–90.

Gawlikowski, Michał. Forthcoming. "Palmyra: The Development of an Ancient City." In *The Oxford University Press Handbook of Palmyra*, ed. by Rubina Raja (Oxford: Oxford University Press).

Gawlikowski, Michał, and Michał Pietrzykowski. 1980. "Les sculptures du temple de Baalshamin à Palmyre." *Syria* 57.2–4: 421–452.

Geiger, Michael. 2013. *Gallienus* (Frankfurt am Main: Peter Lang).

Genequand, Denis. 2006. "Some Thoughts on Qasr al-Hayr al Gharbi, Its Dam, Its Monastery and the Ghassanids." *Levant* 38.1: 63–84.

Genequand, Denis. 2008. "An Early Islamic Mosque in Palmyra." *Levant* 40.1: 3–15.

Genequand, Denis. 2012. *Les établissements des élites omeyyades en Palmyène et au Proche-Orient*. Bibliotheque archéologique et historique 200 (Beirut: Institut français du Proche-Orient).

Genequand, Denis. 2013. "Between Rome and Islam: Recent Research on the So-Called Caesareum of Palmyra." *Studia Palmyreńskie* 12: 97–114.

Gelin, Mathilde. 2002. *L'archéologie en Syrie et au Liban à l'époque du mandat, 1919–1946: Histoire et organisation*. Varia (Paris: Geuthner).

Gibbon, Edward. 1831. *The History of the Decline and Fall of the Roman Empire. A New Edition, in One Volume, with Some Account of the Life and Writings of the Author*, by Alexander Chalmers (London: Longman Green).

Gibbon, Kate Fitz (ed.). 2005. *Who Owns the Past? Cultural Policy, Cultural Property, and the Law* (New Brunswick: Rutgers University Press).

Gibson, Roy, and Ruth Morello (eds.). 2011. *Pliny the Elder: Themes and Contexts*. Mnemosyne, Supplements 329 (Leiden: Brill).

Gilet, Annie. 1994. "Die Durchquerung der Syrischen Wüste – Aufenthalt in Palmyra, 4. Mai–25. Juni 1785." In *Louis-François Cassas 1756–1827: Dessinateur – voyageur. Im Banne der Sphinx. Ein französischer Zeichner reist nach Italien und in den Orient*, ed. by Annie Gilet and Uwe Westfehling (Mainz am Rhein: von Zabern), pp. 145–158.

Glas, Toni. 2014. *Valerian: Kaisertum und Reformansätze in der Krisenphase des Römischen Reiches* (Paderborn: Schöningh).

Gnoli, Tommaso. 2007. *The Interplay of Roman and Iranian Titles in the Roman East (1st–3rd Century A.D.)*. Österreichische Akademie der Wissenschaften, Philosophisch-Historische Klasse, Sitzungsberichte 765, Veröffentlichungen zur Iranistik 43 (Vienna: Österreichische Akademie der Wissenschaften).

Gnoli, Tommaso. 2016. "Banqueting in Honour of the Gods: Notes on the Marzeah of Palmyra." In *The World of Palmyra*, ed. by Andreas Kropp and Rubina Raja. Palmyrene Studies 1 (Copenhagen: Det Kongelige Danske Videnskabernes Selskab), pp. 31–41.

Goddard, Christophe J. 2008. "Nuove osservazioni sul Santuario cosiddetto 'siriaco' al Gianicolo." In *Culti orientali: Tra scavo e collezionismo*, ed. by Beatrice Palma (Rome: Artemide), pp. 165–173.

Graf, David Frank. 2018. "The Silk Road Between Syria and China." In *Trade, Commerce, and the State in the Roman World*, ed. by Andrew Wilson and Alan Bowman (Oxford: Oxford University Press), pp. 443–530.

Graf, David Frank. 2019. "Palmyra: The Indigenous Factor." In *Roman Imperial Cities in the East and in Central-Southern Italy*, vol. 1, *Ancient Cities*, ed. by Nathanael Andrade et al. (Rome: L'Erma di Bretschneider), pp. 295–318.

Grainger, John D. 1990. *The Cities of Seleukid Syria* (Oxford: Clarendon Press).

Greenhalgh, Michael. 2016. *Syria's Monuments: Their Survival and Destruction*. Heritage and Identity 5 (Leiden: Brill).

Gross, Andrew D. 2005. "Three New Palmyrene Inscriptions." In *A Journey to Palmyra: Collected Essays to Remember Delbert R. Hillers*, ed. by Eleonora Cussini. Culture and History of the Ancient Near East 22 (Leiden: Brill), pp. 89–102.

Gruen, Erich S. 2009. "Herod, Rome, and the Diaspora." In *Herod and Augustus: Papers Presented at the IJS Conference, 21st–23rd June 2005*, ed. by David Jacobson and Nikos Kokkinos. IJS Studies in Judaica 6 (Leiden: Brill), pp. 11–28.

Günther, Linda-Marie (ed.). 2008. *Herodes und Rom* (Stuttgart: Steiner).

Guggenheimer, Heinrich Walter. 2000. *The Jerusalem Talmud* (Berlin: De Gruyter).

Gurukkal, Rajan. 2016. *Rethinking Classical Indo-Roman Trade. Political Economy of Eastern Mediterranean Exchange Relations* (Oxford: Oxford University Press).

Gzella, Holger. 2011. "Late Imperial Aramaic." In *The Semitic Language—An International Handbook*, ed. by Stefan Weninger. Handbücher zur Sprach- und Kommunikationswissenschaft 36 (Berlin: De Gruyter), pp. 598–609.

Hächler, Nikolas. 2019. *Kontinuität und Wandel des Senatorenstandes im Zeitalter der Soldatenkaiser: Prosopographische Untersuchungen zu Zusammensetzung, Funktion und Bedeutung des amplissimus ordo zwischen 235–284 n. Chr.* Impact of Empire 33 (Leiden: Brill).

Haider, Peter W. 1987. "Vor- und Frühgeschichte der Oase von Palmyra." In *Palmyra: Geschichte, Kunst und Kultur der syrischen Oasenstadt*, ed. by Erwin Maria Ruprechtsberger (Linz: Guternberg), pp. 115–118.

Halifax, William. 1695–1697. "A Relation of a Voyage from Aleppo to Palmyra in Syria; Sent by the Reverend Mr. William Halifax to Dr. Edw. Bernard (Late) Savilian Professor of Astronomy in Oxford, and by Him Communicated to Dr. Thomas Smith. Reg. Soc. S." *Philosophical Transactions* 19: 83–110.

Hammad, Manar. 2010. *Palmyre: Transformations urbaines: développement d'une ville antique de la marge aride syrienne* (Paris: Geuthner).

Hammad, Manar. 2013. "Morphologie des environs de Palmyre: relief, enceintes, pistes." *Studia palmyreńskie* 12: 129–148.

Hannestad, Niels. 1988. *Roman Art and Imperial Policy*. Jutland Archaeological Society Publications 19 (Aarhus: Aarhus University Press).

Hanson, John William. 2016. *An Urban Geography of the Roman World*. Roman Archaeology 18 (Oxford: Archaeopress).

Hartmann, Udo. 2001. *Das palmyrenische Teilreich* (Stuttgart: Steiner).

Hartmann, Udo. 2008. "Das palmyrenische Teilreich." In *Die Zeit der Soldatenkaiser: Krise und Transformation des Römischen Reiches im 3. Jahrhundert n. Chr. (235 –284)*, ed. by Klaus-Peter Johne, Udo Hartmann, and Thomas Gerhardt (Berlin: Akademie Verlag), pp. 343–78.

Hartmann, Udo. 2016 "What Was It Like to Be a Palmyrene in the Age of Crisis? Changing Palmyrene Identities in the Third Century AD." In *The World of Palmyra*, ed. by Andreas Kropp and Rubina Raja. Palmyrene Studies 1 (Copenhagen: Det Kongelige Danske Videnskabernes Selskab), pp. 53–69.

Hartmann, Udo. Forthcoming. "Palmyra and the Third-Century Crisis." In *The Oxford University Press Handbook of Palmyra*, ed. by Rubina Raja (Oxford: Oxford University Press).

Healey, John F. 1996. "Palmyra and the Arabian Gulf Trade." *ARAM Periodical* 8: 33–37.

Healey, John F. 2009. *Aramaic Inscriptions and Documents of the Roman Period*. Textbook of Syrian Semitic Inscriptions 4 (Oxford: Oxford University Press).

Hekster, Olivier, and Ted Kaizer. 2004. "Mark Antony and the Raid on Palmyra: Reflections on Appian, 'Bella Civilia' V, 9." *Latomus* 63.1: 70–80.

Henning, Agnes. 2013a. "The Tower Tombs of Palmyra: Chronology, Architecture, and Decoration." *Studia Palmyreńskie* 12: 159–176.

Henning, Agnes. 2013b. *Die Turmgräber von Palmyra: Eine locale Bauform im kaiserzeitlichen Syrien als Ausdruck kultureller Identität*. Orient-Archäologie 29 (Rahden/Westfalen: Leidorf).

Henning, Agnes. 2019a. "Houses of Eternity: The Funerary Monuments of Palmyra." In *The Road to Palmyra*, ed. by Anne Marie Nielsen and Rubina Raja (Copenhagen: Ny Carlsberg Glyptotek), pp. 155-172.

Henning, Agnes. 2019b. "The Representation of Matrimony in the Tower Tombs of Palmyra." In *Women, Children, and the Family in Palmyra*, ed. by Signe Krag and Rubina Raja. Palmyrene Studies 3 (Copenhagen: Det Kongelige Danske Videnskabernes Selskab), pp. 19-37.

Hesse, Kristina. J. 2016. "Palmyra, Pastoral Nomads, and City-State Kings in the Old Babylonian Period." In *Palmyrena: City, Hinterland and Caravan Trade Between Orient and Occident. Proceedings of the Conference Held in Athens, December 1– 3, 2012*, ed. by Jørgen Christian Meyer, Eivind Heldaas Seland, and Nils Anfinset (Oxford: Archaeopress), pp. 1–10.

Heyn, Maura Keane. 2008 "Sacerdotal Activities and Parthian Dress in Roman Palmyra." In *Reading a Dynamic Canvas: Adornment in the Ancient Mediterranean World*, ed. by Cynthia S. Colburn and Maura Keane Heyn (Newcastle: Cambridge Scholars Publishing), pp. 170–193.

Heyn, Maura Keane. 2010. "Gesture and Identity in the Funerary Art of Palmyra." *American Journal of Archaeology* 114.4: 631–661.

Heyn, Maura Keane. 2012. "Female Portraiture in Palmyra." In *A Companion to Women in the Ancient World*, ed. by Sharon L. James and Sheila Dillon (Chichester Malden, MA: Wiley-Blackwell), pp. 439–441.

Heyn, Maura Keane. 2019. "Valuable Impressions of Women in Palmyra." In *The Road to Palmyra*, ed. by Anne Marie Nielsen and Rubina Raja (Copenhagen: Ny Carlsberg Glyptotek), pp. 175–192.

Heyn, Maura Keane, and Rubina Raja. 2019. "Male Dress Habits in Roman Period Palmyra." In *Fashioned Selves: Dress and Identity in Antiquity*, ed. by Megan Cifarelli (Oxford: Oxbow), pp. 41–53.

Heyn, Maura Keane, and Rubina Raja (eds.). 2021. *Individualizing the Dead: Attributes in Palmyrene Funerary Sculpture*. Studies in Palmyrene Archaeology and History 3 (Turnhout: Brepols).

Higuchi, Takayasu, and Takura Izumi. 1994. *Tombs A and C: Southeast Necropolis, Palmyra, Syria, Surveyed in 1990–92*. Publication of Research Center for Silk Roadology 1 (Nara: Research Center for Silk Roadology).

Higuchi, Takayasu, and Kiyohide Saito (eds.). 2001. *Tomb F–Tomb of BWLH and BWRP–Southeast Necropolis, Palmyra, Syria*. Publication of Research Center for Silk Roadology 2 (Nara: Research Center for Silk Roadology).

Hitchens, Christopher. 1987. *Imperial Spoils: The Curious Case of the Elgin Marbles* (London: Chatto and Windus).

Hijmans, Steven. 2010. "Temples and Priests of Sol in the City of Rome." *Mouseion: Journal of the Classical Association of Canada* 54.3: 381–427.

Hoffmann-Salz, Julia. 2011. *Die wirtschaftlichen Auswirkungen der römischen Eroberung. Vergleichende Untersuchungen der Provinzen Hispania Tarraconensis, Africa Proconsularis und Syria*. Historia 218 (Stuttgart: Steiner).

Hoffmann-Salz, Julia. 2015. "The Local Economy of Palmyra. Organizing Agriculture in an Oasis Environment." In *Ownership and Exploitation of Land and Natural Resources in the Roman World*, ed. by Paul Erdkamp, Koenraad Verboven, and Arjan Zuiderhoek. Oxford Studies on the Roman Economy (Oxford: Clarendon Press), pp. 239–247.

Houston, George W. 1990. "The Altar from Rome with Inscriptions to Sol and Malakbel." *Syria* 67: 189–193.

Hvidberg-Hansen, Finn Ove. 1998. *The Palmyrene Inscriptions: Ny Carlsberg Glyptotek* (Copenhagen: Ny Carlsberg Glyptotek).

Hvidberg-Hansen, Finn Ove. 2002. *Zenobia – byen Palmyra og dens dronning* (Aarhus: Tidsskriftet SFINX).

Hvidberg-Hansen, Finn Ove, and Gunhild Ploug. 1993. *Palmyra Samlingen* (Copenhagen: Ny Carlsberg Glyptotek).

Ingholt, Harald. Ingholt Archive, Ny Carlsberg Glyptotek, Copenhagen.

Ingholt, Harald. 1928. *Studier over Palmyrensk Skulptur* (Copenhagen: Reitzel).

Ingholt, H. 1932a. Deux inscriptions bilingues de Palmyre, *Syria* 13,3: 278–292.

Ingholt, Harald. 1932b. "Quelques fresques récemment découvertes à Palmyre." *Acta Archaeologica* 3: 1–20.

Ingholt, Harald. 1935. "Five Dated Tombs from Palmyra." *Berytus* 2: 58–120.

Ingholt, Harald. 1976. "Varia Tadmorea." In *Palmyre: Bilan et Perspectives. Colloque de Strasbourg 18–20 Octobre 1973, à la mémoire de Daniel berger et de Henri Seyrig*, ed. by Edmond Frézouls. Université des Sciences Humaines de Strasbourg. Travaux du Centre de Recherche Sur le Proche-Orient et la Grèce Antiques, 3 (Strasbourg: Association pour l'étude de la civilisation romaine), pp. 115–137.

Ingholt, Harald, Henri Seyrig, and Jean Starcky. 1955. *Recueil des Tessères de Palmyre* (Paris: Geuthner).

Intagliata, Emanuele Ettore. 2015. "Palmyra/Tadmur in Late Antiquity and Early Islam: An Archaeological and Historical Reassessment" (Unpubl. PhD dissertation, University of Edinburgh).

Intagliata, Emanuele Ettore. 2016. "The Post-Roman Occupation of the Northern Courtyard of the Sanctuary of Baalshamin in Palmyra: A Reassessment of the Evidence Based on the Documents in the Fonds d'Archives Paul Collart, Université de Lausanne." *Zeitschrift für Orient-Archäologie* 9: 180–199.

Intagliata, Emanuele Ettore. 2017. "Palmyra and Its Ramparts During the Tetrarchy." In *New Cities in Late Antiquity: Documents and Archaeology*, ed. by Efthymios Rizos. Bibliothèque de l'Antiquité Tardive 35 (Turnhout: Brepols), pp. 71–83.

Intagliata, Emanuele Ettore. 2018. *Palmyra after Zenobia AD 273–750: An Archaeological and Historical Reappraisal* (Oxford: Oxbow).

Intagliata, Emanuele Ettore. 2019. "The City That Would Not Fall." In *The Road to Palmyra*, ed. by Anne Marie Nielsen and Rubina Raja (Copenhagen: Ny Carlsberg Glyptotek), pp. 235–250.

Isaac, Benjamin. 1992. *The Limits of Empire: The Roman Army in the East* (Oxford: Oxford University Press).

Jalabert, Louis, and René Mouterde. 1959. *Emésène*, vol. 5, *Inscriptions grecques et latines de la Syrie*. Bibliothèque archéologique et historique 66 (Paris: Geuthner).

James, Simon T. 2019. *The Roman Military Base at Dura-Europos, Syria: An Archaeological Visualisation* (Oxford: Oxford University Press).

Jastrzębowska, Elżbieta. 2013. "Christianisation of Palmyra: Early Byzantine Church in the Temple of Bel." *Studia Palmyreńskie* 12: 177–191.

Jenkins, Tiffany. 2016. *Keeping Their Marbles: How the Treasures of the Past Ended Up in Museums . . . and Why They Should Stay There* (Oxford: Oxford University Press).

Joannès, Francis. 1997. "Palmyre et les routes de desert au début du deuxième millénaire av. J.-C." *MARI: Annales de Recherches Interdisciplinaires* 8: 393–415.

202 BIBLIOGRAPHY

John, Tara. 2016 (6 May). "Russian Orchestra Plays Bach Amid Ruins of Palmyra."
Time Magazine. https://time.com/4320723/russia-orchestra-concert-syria-palmyra/
[accessed March 2021].

Jones, Arnold H. M. 1937. *Cities of the Roman Provinces* (Oxford: Oxford University
Press, repr. 1998).

J. Paul Getty Museum. "The Classical World in Context: Palmyra—Loss & Remembrance."
18 April 2018–27 May 2019, Los Angeles. https://www.getty.edu/art/exhibitions/pal-
myra_sculpture/index.html. [accessed 29 July 2020].

Juchniewicz, Karol. 2013. "Late Roman Fortifications of Palmyra." *Studia Palmyreńskie*
12: 193–202.

Juchniewicz, Karol, Khaled Asʿad, and Khalil al-Hariri. 2010. "The Defense Wall in
Palmyra after Recent Syrian Excavations." *Studia Palmyreńskie* 11: 55–73.

Juchniewicz, Karol, and Marta Żuchowska. 2012. "Water Supply in Palmyra: A
Chronological Approach." In *The Archaeology of Water Supply*, ed. by Marta Żuchowska
(Oxford: Archeopress), pp. 61–73.

Kaizer, Ted. 2000. "The 'Heracles Figure' at Hatra and Palmyra: Problems of
Interpretation." *Iraq* 62: 219–232.

Kaizer, Ted. 2002. *The Religious Life of Palmyra: A Study of the Social Patterns of Worship in
the Roman Period.* Oriens et Occidens 4 (Stuttgart: Steiner).

Kaizer, Ted. 2006. "Reflections on the Dedication of the Temple of Bel at Palmyra in
AD 32." In *The Impact of Imperial Rome on Religion: Ritual and Religious Life in the
Roman Empire. Proceedings of the Fifth Workshop of the International Network Impact
of Empire*, ed. by Lucas de Blois, Peter Funke, and Johannes Hahn. Impact of Empire 5
(Leiden: Brill), pp. 95–105.

Kaizer, Ted. 2007. "'Palmyre, cité grecque?' A Question of Coinage" *Klio* 89: 39–60.

Kaizer, Ted. 2010. "Funerary Cults at Palmyra." In *Cultural Messages in the Graeco-
Roman World: Acta of the BABESCH 80th Anniversary Workshop Radboud University
Nijmegen, September 8th 2006*, ed. by Oliver Hekster and Stephan A.M. Mols.
BABESCH Supplement 15 (Leuven: Peeters), pp. 23–31.

Kaizer, Ted (ed.). 2016. *Religion, Society and Culture at Dura-Europos.* Yale Classical
Studies 38 (Cambridge: Cambridge University Press).

Kaizer, Ted. 2017a. "Empire, Community, and Culture on the Middle Euphrates: Durenes,
Palmyrenes, Villagers, and Soldiers." In *Roman History: Six Studies for Fergus Millar*,
ed. by Nicholas Purcell (London: Institute of Classical Studies), pp. 63–95.

Kaizer, Ted. 2017b. "Trajectories of Hellenism at Tadmor-Palmyra and Dura-Europos."
In *Hellenism and the Local Communities of the Eastern Mediterranean: 400 BCE–
250 CE*, ed. by Boris Chrubasik and Daniel King (Oxford: Oxford University Press),
pp. 29–52.

Kaizer, Ted. 2019a. "Family Connections and Religious Life at Palmyra." In *Women,
Children, and the Family in Palmyra*, ed. by Signe Krag and Rubina Raja. Palmyrene
Studies 3 (Copenhagen: Det Kongelige Danske Videnskabernes Selskab),
pp. 82–94.

Kaizer, Ted. 2019b. "Gods, Temples, and Cults. Religious Life in Palmyra." In *The Road
to Palmyra*, ed. by Anne Marie Nielsen and Rubina Raja (Copenhagen: Ny Carlsberg
Glyptotek), pp. 207–220.

Kaizer, Ted. 2019c. "Patterns of Worship at Palmyra: Reflections on Methods and
Approaches." In *Revisiting the Religious Life of Palmyra*, ed. by Rubina Raja.
Contextualizing the Sacred 9 (Turnhout: Brepols), pp. 7–24.

Kaizer, Ted. 2020. "Tadmur-Palmyra as a Greek city in the Roman World (or not) in Five Episodes." In *Inter duo Imperia: Palmyra between East and West*, ed. by Michael Sommer (Stuttgart: Steiner), pp. 23–36.

Kaizer, Ted, and Rubina Raja. 2019. "Divine Symbolism on the Tesserae from Palmyra: Considerations about the So-Called 'Symbol of Bel' or 'Signe de la pluie.'" *Syria* 95: 297–315.

Kennedy, David Leslie. 1986. "Ana on the Euphrates in the Roman Period." *Iraq* 48: 103–104.

Kettenhofen, Erich. 1982. *Die römisch-persischen Kriege des 3. Jahrhunderts n. Chr.: nach der Inschrift Šāhpuhrs I. an der Ka'be-ye Zartošt (ŠKZ)*. TAVO-Beihefte B 55 (Wiesbaden: Reichert).

Kila, Joris D., and James A. Zeidler (eds.). 2013. *Cultural Heritage in the Crosshairs: Protecting Cultural Property During Conflict*. Heritage and Identity 2 (Leiden: Brill).

Klaver, Sanne. 2019. "The Participation of Palmyrene Women in the Religious Life of the City." In *Women, Children, and the Family in Palmyra*, ed. by Signe Krag and Rubina Raja. Palmyrene Studies 3 (Copenhagen: Det Kongelige Danske Videnskabernes Selskab), pp. 157–167.

Klengel, Horst. 1972. *Zwischen Zelt und Palast. Die Begegnung von Nomaden und Sesshaften im alten Vorderasien* (Vienna: Schroll).

Kockel, Valentin. 1993. *Porträtreliefs stadtrömischer Grabbauten: ein Beitrag zur Geschichte und zum Verständnis des spätrepublikanisch-frühkaiserzeitlichen Privatporträts*. Beiträge zur Erschließung hellenistischer und kaiserzeitlicher Skulptur und Architektur 12 (Mainz am Rhein: von Zabern).

Kotula, Tadeusz. 1997. *Aurélien et Zénobie: L'unité ou la division de l'Empire?* Acta Universitatis Wratislaviensis 1966 (Wrocław: University of Wrocław).

Kowalski, Sławomir P. 1996. "Doubtful Christian Reutilization of the Baalshamin Temple in Palmyra." *Damaszener Mitteilungen* 9: 217–226.

Kowalski, Sławomir P. 1997. "Late Roman Palmyra in Literature and Epigraphy." *Studia Palmyreńskie* 10: 39–62.

Kowalski, Sławomir P. 1998. "The Camp of the Legio I Illyricorum in Palmyra." *Novaensia: Badania ekspedycji archeologicznej Uniwersytetu Warszawskiego w Novae, Studia i materiały* 10: 189–209.

Kraeling, Carl H. 1961–1962. "Color Photographs of the Paintings in the Tomb of the Three Brothers at Palmyra." *Annales archéologiques arabes syriennes* 11–12: 13–18.

Krag, Signe. 2015. "The Secrets of the Funerary Buildings in Palmyra During the Roman Period." In *Revealing and Concealing in Antiquity: Textual and Archaeological Approaches to Secrecy*, ed. by Eva Mortensen and Sine Grove Saxkjær (Aarhus: Aarhus University Press), pp. 105–118.

Krag, Signe. 2016. "Females in Group Portraits in Palmyra." In *The World of Palmyra*, ed. by Andreas Kropp and Rubina Raja. Palmyrene Studies 1 (Copenhagen: Det Kongelige Danske Videnskabernes Selskab), pp. 180–193.

Krag, Signe. 2017a. "Changing Identities, Changing Positions: Jewellery in Palmyrene Female Portraits." In *Positions and Professions in Palmyra*, ed. by Tracey Long and Annette Højen Sørensen. Palmyrene Studies 2 (Copenhagen: Det Kongelige Danske Videnskabernes Selskab), pp. 36–51.

Krag, Signe. 2017b. "Women in Palmyra." In *Palmyra: Pearl of the Desert*, ed. by Rubina Raja (Aarhus: SUN-TRYK), pp. 56–66.

Krag, Signe. 2018. *Funerary Representations of Palmyrene Women from the First Century BC to the Third Century AD.* Studies in Classical Archaeology 3 (Turnhout: Brepols).

Krag, Signe. 2019. "Palmyrene Funerary Buildings and Family Burial Patterns." In *Women, Children, and the Family in Palmyra*, ed. by Signe Krag and Rubina Raja. Palmyrene Studies 3 (Copenhagen: Det Kongelige Danske Videnskabernes Selskab), pp. 38–66.

Krag, Signe, and Rubina Raja. 2016. "Representations of Women and Children in Palmyrene Funerary Loculus Reliefs, Loculus Stelae and Wall Paintings." *Zeitschrift für Orient-Archäologie* 9: 134–178.

Krag, Signe, and Rubina Raja. 2017. "Representations of Women and Children in Palmyrene Banqueting Reliefs and Sarcophagus Scenes." *Zeitschrift für Orient-Archäologie* 10: 196–227.

Krag, Signe, and Rubina Raja. 2018. "Unveiling Female Hairstyles: Markers of Age, Social Roles, and Status in Funerary Sculpture from Palmyra." *Zeitschrift für Orient-Archäologie* 11: 242–277.

Krag, Signe, and Rubina Raja. 2019a. "Families in Palmyra: The Evidence from the First Three Centuries CE." In *Women, Children, and the Family in Palmyra*, ed. by Signe Krag and Rubina Raja. Palmyrene Studies 3 (Copenhagen: Det Kongelige Danske Videnskabernes Selskab), pp. 7–18.

Krag, Signe, and Rubina Raja (eds.). 2019b. *Women, Children, and the Family in Palmyra.* Palmyrene Studies 3 (Copenhagen: Det Kongelige Danske Videnskabernes Selskab).

Krag, Signe, Rubina Raja, and Jean-Baptiste Yon. 2019. *The Collection of Palmyrene Funerary Portraits in Musei Vaticani: Notes and Observations*, with an introduction by Alessia Amenta. Bollettino dei monumenti musei e gallerie pontificie, supplemento 4 (Vatican: Edizioni Musei Vaticani).

Kristensen, Nathalia B., and Rubina Raja. Forthcoming. "Palmyrene Coinage." In *The Oxford University Press Handbook of Palmyra*, ed. by Rubina Raja (Oxford: Oxford University Press).

Kropp, Andreas, and Rubina Raja. 2014. "The Palmyra Portrait Project." *Syria* 91: 393–408.

Kropp, Andreas, and Rubina Raja. 2015. "The Palmyra Portrait Project." In *Centro y periferia en el Mundo Clásico: Actas XVIII Congreso internacional de arqueología clásica*, ed. by José María Álvarez Martínez, Trinidad Nogales Bassarrate, and Isabel Rodà de Llanza (Mérida: Museo Nacional De Arte Romano), pp. 1223–1226.

Kropp, Andreas, and Rubina Raja (eds.). 2016. *The World of Palmyra.* Palmyrene Studies 1 (Copenhagen: Det Kongelige Danske Videnskabernes Selskab).

Krzywinski, Knut, and Jonatan Krzywinski. 2016. "Agriculture in Byzantine Palmyrena." In *Palmyrena: City, Hinterland and Caravan Trade Between Orient and Occident. Proceedings of the Conference Held in Athens, December 1–3, 2012*, ed. by Jørgen Christian Meyer, Eivind Heldaas Seland, and Nils Anfinset (Oxford: Archaeopress), pp. 171–183.

Krzyzanowska, Aleksandra. 1976. "Tresor de monnaies palmyréniennes trouvé à Alexandrie." In *Actes du 8ème Congrés international de numismatique, New York–Washington, septembre 1973*, ed. by Herbert Adolph Cahn and Georges Le Rider. Publications de l'Association internationale des numismates professionnels 4. 2 vols. (Paris: Association internationale des numismates professionnels), pp. 327–332.

Krzyzanowska, Aleksandra. 1979. "La circulation monétaire à Palmyre d'aprés le materiel provenant des fouilles." *Wiadomości Numizmatyczne* 3: 44–52.

Krzyzanowska, Aleksandra. 1982. "Le monnayage de Palmyre." In *Actes du 9ème Congrès international de numismatique, Berne, septembre, 1979*, ed. by Tony Hackens and Raymond Weiller. Publications de l'Association internationale des numismates professionnels 7. 2 vols. (Louvain-la-Neuve: Association internationale des numismates professionnels), pp. 445–457.

Krzyzanowska, Aleksandra. 2002. "Les monnaies de Palmyre: leur chronologie et leur rôle dans la circulation monétaire e la region." In Les monnayages Syriens. Quel apport pour l'histoire du Proche-Orient hellenistique et romain? Actes de la table ronde de Damas, 10–12 novembre 1999, ed. by Christian Augé and Frédérique Duyrat. Bibliothèque Archéologique et Historique 162 (Beirut: Institut français du Proche- Orient), pp. 167–173.

Krzyzanowska, Aleksandra. 2014. "Monnaies grecques et romaines." Studia Palmyreńskie 13: 13–68.

Kubiak-Schneider, Aleksandra. 2019. "Bel the Merciful." In Revisiting the Religious Life of Palmyra, ed. by Rubina Raja. Contextualizing the Sacred 9 (Turnhout: Brepols), pp. 171–174.

Kühn, Dagmar. 2005. Totengedenken bei den Nabatäern und im Alten Testament: Eine religionsgeschichtliche und exegetische Studie. Alter Orient und Altes Testament 311 (Münster: Ugarit-Verlag).

La Follette, Laetitia. 2013. Negotiating Culture: Heritage, Ownership, and Intellectual Property (Amherst: University of Massachusetts Press).

Lanciani, Rodolfo A. 1901. Forma urbis Romae: Scala 1:2000 (Rome: Quasar, repr. 2007).

Lanciani, Rodolfo A. 1902. Storia degli scavi di Roma e notizie intorno le collezioni romane di antichità I (Rome: Ermanno Loescher).

Lanoy, Timothy and Aaron Goodyear. 1695–1697. "An Extract of the Journals of Two Several Voyages of the English Merchants of the Factory of Aleppo, to Tadmor, Anciently Call'd Palmyra." Philosophical Transactions 19: 129–160.

Le Quien, Michel. 1740. Oriens christianus, in quatuor patriarchatus digestus quo exhibentur ecclesiae, patriarchae, caeterique praesules totius orientis (Paris: Ex typographia regia).

Lichtenberger, Achim. 2003. Kulte und Kultur der Dekapolis. Untersuchungen zu nimismatischen, archäologischen und epigraphischen Zeugnissen (Wiesbaden: Harrassowitz).

Lichtenberger, Achim, and Rubina Raja. 2015. "New Archaeological Research in the Northwest Quarter of Jerash and Its Implications for the Urban Development of Roman Gerasa." American Journal of Archaeology 119.4: 483–500.

Lichtenberger, Achim, and Rubina Raja. 2020a. "Late Hellenistic and Roman Antioch on the Chrysorhoas, also called Gerasa. A Reappreciation of the Evidence in the Light of the Findings of the Danish-German Jerash Northwest Quarter Project (2011–2017)." In Hellenistic and Roman Gerasa. The Archaeology and History of a Decapolis City, ed. by Achim Lichtenberger and Rubina Raja. Jerash Papers 5 (Turnhout: Brepols), pp. 7–54.

Lichtenberger, Achim, and Rubina Raja. 2020b. "Roman City Coins of Gerasa: Contextualizing Currency and Circulation from the Hellenistic to the Late Roman Period." In Hellenistic and Roman Gerasa. The Archaeology and History of a Decapolis City, ed. by Achim Lichtenberger and Rubina Raja. Jerash Papers 5 (Turnhout: Brepols), pp. 369–382.

Long, Tracey. 2017. "The Use of Parthian Costume in Funerary Portraiture at Palmyra." In Positions and Professions in Palmyra, ed. by Tracey Long and Anette H. Sørensen. Palmyrene Studies 2 (Copenhagen: Det Kongelige Danske Videnskabernes Selskab), pp. 68–83.

Long, Tracey, and Anette Højen Sørensen (eds.). 2017. *Positions and Professions in Palmyra*. Palmyrene Studies 2 (Copenhagen: Det Kongelige Danske Videnskabernes Selskab).

Luther, Andreas. 2004. "Doura-Europos zwischen Palmyra und den Parthern: Der politische Status der Region am Mittleren Euphrat am 2. Jh. n. Chr. und die Organisation des palmyrenischen Fernhandels." In *Commerce and Monetary Systems in the Ancient World: Means of Transmission and Cultural Interaction*, ed. by Robert Rollinger and Christoph Ulf. Oriens et Occidens 6 (Stuttgart: Steiner), pp. 327–351.

Ma, John. 2013. *Statues and Cities: Honorific Portraits and Civic Identity in the Hellenistic World* (Oxford: Oxford University Press).

Mackay, Dorothy. 1949. "The Jewellery of Palmyra and Its Significance." *Iraq* 11.2: 160–187.

Mackenzie, Simon, and Penny Green (eds.). 2009. *Criminology and Archaeology: Studies in Looted Antiquities*. Oñati International Series in Law and Society (Oxford: Hart Publishing).

Majcherek, Grzegorz. 2005. "More Churches from Palmyra: An Inkling of the Late Antique City." In *Aux pays d'Allat: Mélanges offerts à Michal Gawlikowski*, ed. by Piotr Bieliński and Franciszek M. Stępniowski (Warsaw: University of Warsaw), pp. 141–150.

Majcherek, Grzegorz. 2013. "Excavating the Basilicas." *Studia Palmyreńskie* 12: 251–268.

Makowski, Krysztof. 1983. "Recherches sur le tombeau de A'ailamî et Zebîdâ." *Damaszener Mitteilungen* 1: 175–87.

Makowski, Krysztof. 1985. "La sculpture funéraire palmyrénienne et sa fonction dans l'architecture sépulcrale." *Studia Palmyreńskie* 8: 69–117.

Mallan, Christopher, and Caillan Davenport. 2015. "Dexippus and the Gothic Invasions: Interpreting the New Vienna Fragment (Codex Vindobonensis Hist. gr. 73, ff. 192v–193r)." *Journal of Roman Studies* 105: 203–226.

Manetta, Consuelo. 2012. "*Orientalia* da Villa Bonelli–Crescenzi–Mangani. Riesame e nuovi tentativi di contestualizzazione." *Horti Hesperidum* 2.1: 533–551.

Mariev, Sergei. 2008. *Ioannis Antiocheni Fragmenta quae supersunt omnia*. Corpus Fontium Historiae Byzantinae—Series Berolinensis 47 (Berlin: De Gruyter).

Matthews, John F. 1984. "The Tax Law of Palmyra: Evidence for Economic History in a City of the Roman East." *Journal of Roman Studies* 74: 157–180.

McAvoy, Scott, and Rubina Raja. 2020 (21 April). "Hairan Reconstruction Sketchup File." Figshare. doi: 10.6084/m9.figshare.9999767.v2.

McLaughlin, Raoul. 2016. *The Roman Empire and the Silk Routes: The Ancient World Economy and the Empires of Parthia, Central Asia and Han China* (Barnsley: Pen & Sword).

Meyer, Jørgen Christian. 2013. "City and Hinterland: Villages and Estates North of Palmyra. New Perspectives." *Studia Palmyreńskie* 12: 265–282.

Meyer, Jørgen Christian. 2016. "Palmyrena: Settlements, Forts and Nomadic Networks." In *The World of Palmyra*, ed. by Andreas Kropp and Rubina Raja. Palmyrene Studies 1 (Copenhagen: Det Kongelige Danske Videnskabernes Selskab), pp. 86–102.

Meyer, Jørgen Christian. 2017. *Palmyrena: Palmyra and the Surrounding Territory from the Roman to the Early Islamic Period* (Oxford: Archaeopress).

Meyer, Jørgen Christian, and Eivind Heldaas Seland. 2016. "Palmyra and the Trade Route to the Euphrates." *ARAM Periodical* 28: 497–523.

Meyer, Jørgen Christian, Eivind Heldaas Seland, and Nils Anfinset. 2016a. "Introduction." In *Palmyrena: City, Hinterland and Caravan Trade Between Orient and Occident.*

Proceedings of the Conference held in Athens, December 1–3, 2012, ed. by Jørgen Christian Meyer, Eivind Heldaas Seland, and Nils Anfinset (Oxford: Archaeopress), pp. 1–10.

Meyer, Jørgen Christian, Eivind Heldaas Seland, and Nils Anfinset (eds.). 2016b. *Palmyrena: City, Hinterland and Caravan Trade Between Orient and Occident; Proceedings of the Conference Held in Athens, December 1–3, 2012* (Oxford: Archaeopress).

Metropolitan Museum of Art, "The World Between Empires: Art and Identity in the Ancient Middle East." 18 March–23 June 2019, New York. https://www.metmuseum.org/exhibitions/listings/2019/world-between-empires-art-and-identity-ancient-middle-east [accessed 29 July 2020].

Michalowski, Kazimierz. 1960. *Palmyre: Fouilles Polonaises 1959* (Warsaw: Państwowe Wydawnictwo Naukowe).

Michalowski, Kazimierz. 1962. *Palmyre: Fouilles Polonaises, 1960* (Warsaw: Państwowe Wydawnictwo Naukowe).

Michalowski, Kazimierz. 1963. *Palmyre: Fouilles Polonaises 1961* (Warsaw: Państwowe Wydawnictwo Naukowe).

Michalowski, Kazimierz. 1966. *Palmyre V: Fouilles Polonaises 1963–1964* (Warsaw: Państwowe Wydawnictwo Naukowe).

Michelini Tocci, Franco. 1960. *La Siria nell'età di Mari* (Rome: Università di Roma).

Miles, Margaret Melanie. 2008. *Art as Plunder: The Ancient Origins of Debate About Cultural Property* (Cambridge: Cambridge University Press).

Milik, Józef Thadeusz. 1972. *Dédicaces faites par des dieux (Palmyra, Hatra, Tyr) et des thiases sémitiques à l'époque romaine*, vol. 1, *Recherches d'épigraphie Proche-Orientale* (Paris: Geuthner).

Millar, Fergus. 1987a. "Empire, Community, and Culture in the Roman Near East: Greeks, Syrians, Jews and Arabs." *Journal of Jewish Studies* 38: 143–164

Millar, Fergus. 1987b. "The Problem of Hellenistic Syria." In *Hellenism in the East: The Interaction of Greek and Non-Greek Civilizations from Syria to Central Asia After Alexander*, ed. by Amelie Kuhrt and Susan Scherwin-White (Berkeley: University of California Press), pp. 110–133.

Millar, Fergus. 1990. "The Roman Coloniae of the Near East." In *Roman Eastern Policy and Other Studies in Roman History*, ed. by Heikki Solin and Mika Kajava (Helsinki: Societas Scientiarum Fennica), pp. 7–58, 42–46.

Millar, Fergus. 1993. *The Roman Near East, 31 BC–AD 337* (Cambridge, MA: Harvard University Press).

Millar, Fergus. 1995. "Latin in the Epigraphy of the Roman Near East." In *Acta colloquii epigraphici latini: Helsingiae 3.-6. sept. 1991 habiti*, ed. by Heikki Solin, Olli Salomies, and Uta-Maria Liertz. Commentationes Humanarum Litterarum 104 (Helsinki: Societas Scientiarum Fennica), pp. 403–419.

Millar, Fergus. 1998a. "Caravan Cities: The Roman Near East and Long-Distance Trade by Land." In *Modus Operandi: Essays in Honour of Geoffrey Rickman*, ed. by Michel Austin, Jill Harries, and Christopher John Smith (London: University of London), pp. 119–137.

Millar, Fergus. 1998b. "Dura-Europos Under Parthian Rule." In *Das Partherreich und seine Zeugnisse*, ed. by Josef Wiesehöfer (Stuttgart: Steiner), pp. 473–492.

Millar, Fergus. 2013. "A Syriac Codex from Near Palmyra and the 'Ghassanid' Abokarib." *Hugoye: Journal of Syriac Studies* 16.1: 15–35.

Mouterde, René. 1930. "La Strata Diocletiana et ses bornes milliaires." *Mélanges de l'Université Saint-Joseph* 15: 221–233.

Mouton, Michel. 1997. "Les tours funéraires d'arabie, *nefesh* monumentales." *Syria* 74: 81–98.

Mroue, Bassem. 2015 (1 June). "Ex-inmates Regret Destruction of Notorious Syrian Prison." Associated Press. https://apnews.com/0649ccc6f76148d79adee593d06d0794 [accessed March 2021].

Murphy, Trevor. 2004. *Pliny the Elder's Natural History: The Empire in the Encyclopedia* (Oxford: Oxford University Press).

Museum of Islamic Art. "The Cultural Heritage of Syria in Danger" [flyer]. Syrian Heritage Archive Project, Museum of Islamic Art and the German Archaeological Institute, Berlin. https://project.syrian-heritage.org/wp-content/uploads/2017/10/flyer_en-1.pdf [accessed 29 July 2020].

Museum of Islamic Art. "Syrian Heritage Archive Project." Syrian Heritage Archive Project, Museum of Islamic Art and the German Archaeological Institute, Berlin. https://project.syrian-heritage.org/en/ [accessed 29 July 2020].

Muzzioli, Maria Pia. 2008. "I luoghi dei culti orientali a Roma: Problemi topografici generali e particolari." In *Culti orientali: Tra scavo e collezionismo*, ed. by Beatrice Palma (Rome: Artemide), pp. 49–56.

The New Arab. 2016 (22 April). "Polish Experts in Syria's Palmyra for Restoration Mission." https://english.alaraby.co.uk/english/society/2016/4/22/polish-experts-in-syrias-palmyra-for-restoration-mission [accessed March 2021].

#New Palmyra. "#NEWPALMYRA." https://newpalmyra.org/ [accessed 29 July 2020].

Nielsen, Anne Marie. 2019. "Palmyra in the Glyptotek." In *The Road to Palmyra*, ed. by Anne Marie Nielsen and Rubina Raja (Copenhagen: Ny Carlsberg Glyptotek), pp. 23-40.

Nielsen, Anne Marie, and Rubina Raja (eds.). 2019. *The Road to Palmyra* (Copenhagen: Ny Carlsberg Glyptotek).

Noy, David. 2000. *Foreigners at Rome: Citizens and Strangers* (London: Duckworth).

Ny Carlsberg Glyptotek. "The Road to Palmyra." 20 September 2019–1 March 2020, Copenhagen. https://www.glyptoteket.com/exhibition/the-road-to-palmyra/?_ga=2.196903212.1600499162.1596013330-499902488.1592560776 [accessed 29 July 2020].

O'Connor, M. 1988. "The Etymologies of Tadmor and Palmyra." In *A Linguistic Happening in Memory of Ben Schwartz: Studies in Anatolian, Italic, and Other Indo-European Languages*, ed. by Yoël L. Arbeitman. Bibliotheque des Cahiers de l'Institut de Linguistique de Louvain 42 (Leuven: Peeters), pp. 235–254.

Ostratz, A. 1969. "Note sur le plan de la partie médiane de la rue principale à Palmyre." *Annales Archéologiques Arabes Syriennes* 19: 109–120.

Palmer, Robert E. A. 1981. "The Topography and Social History of Rome's Trastevere (Southern Sector)." *Proceedings of the American Philosophical Society* 125: 368–397.

Palmieri, Raffaele. 1982. "Un *apparitor* ed arti e mestieri." In *Il Lapidario Zeri di Mentana*, ed. by Guido Barbieri. Studi pubblicati dall'Istituto Italiano per la storia antica 32.1 (Città di Castello: Arti Grafiche), pp. 119–121.

Palmyra Portrait Project. Aarhus University. https://projects.au.dk/palmyraportrait/ [accessed 25 July 2019].

Palmyra Portrait Project, "Bibliography." https://figshare.com/articles/Palmyra_Portrait_Project_full_bibliography_2013-2020_MAY_pdf/12272714 [accessed March 2021].

Panciera, Silvio. 2006. *Epigrafi, Epigrafia, Epigrafisti: Scritti vari e inediti (1956 – 2005) con note complementari e indici* (Rome: Quasar).

Papi, Emanuele. 1996. "Horti Caesaris (Transtiberim)." In *Lexicon topographicum urbis Romae*, vol. 3, *G–L*, ed. by Eva Margareta Steinby (Rome: Quasar), pp. 55–56.

Papini, Massimiliano, and Emanuele Cuccurullo. 2015. "Una nuova divinità siriana dalle Terme di Elagabalo: Un Apollo di Hierapolis Bambyce a Roma?" *Scienze dell'Antichità: Storia, archeologia, antropologia* 21: 153–180.

Parlasca, Klaus. 1969–1970. "A New Grave Relief from Syria." *Brooklyn Museum Annual* 11: 169–185.

Parlasca, Klaus. 1976. "Probleme palmyrenischer grabreliefs—chronologie und interpretation." In *Palmyre: Bilan et Perspectives. Colloque de Strasbourg 18–20 Octobre 1973, à la mémoire de Daniel Schlumberger et de Henri Seyrig*, ed. by Edmond Frézouls. Université des Sciences Humaines de Strasbourg. Travaux du Centre de Recherche Sur le Proche-Orient et la Grèce Antiques 3 (Strasbourg: Association pour l'étude de la civilisation romaine), pp. 33–43.

Parlasca, Klaus. 1982a. "Römische Kunst in Syrien." In *Land des Baal: Syrien, Forum der Völker und Kulturen*, ed. by Kay Kohlmeyer and Eva Strommenger (Mainz am Rhein: von Zabern), pp. 186–226.

Parlasca, Klaus. 1982b. *Syrische Grabreliefs hellenistischer und römischer Zeit: Fundgruppen und Probleme*. Trierer Winckelmannsprogramm 3 (Mainz am Rhein: von Zabern).

Parlasca, Klaus. 1985. "Das Verhältnis der palmyrenischen Grabplastik zur römischen Porträtkunst." *Mitteilungen des Deutschen Archäologischen Instituts Römische Abteilung* 92: 343–356.

Parlasca, Klaus. 1987. "Ein antoninischer Frauenkopf aus Palmyra in Malibu." In *Ancient Portraits in the J. Paul Getty Museum*, vol. 1, ed. by Jiří Frel, Arthur Houghton, and Marion True (Los Angeles: J. Paul Getty Museum), pp. 107–114.

Parlasca, Klaus. 1988. "Ikonographische Probleme palmyrenischer Grabreliefs." *Damaszener Mitteilungen* 3: 215–221.

Parlasca, Klaus. 1995. "Some Problems of Palmyrene Plastic Art." *ARAM Periodical* 7: 59–71.

Paschoud, François. 2002. *Vies d'Aurélien et de Tacite*, vol. 5.1, *Histoire Auguste*. Collection des universités de France Série latine—Collection Budé 335. 2nd ed. (Paris: Les Belles Lettres).

Paschoud, François. 2003. *Histoire nouvelle: livres I et II*, vol. 1, *Zosime*. Collection des universités de France Série grecque—Collection Budé 401. 2nd ed. (Paris: Les Belles Lettres).

Paschoud, François. 2011. *Vies des Trente Tyrans et de Claude*, vol. 4.3, *Histoire Auguste*. Collection des universités de France Série latine—Collection Budé 400 (Paris: Les Belles Lettres).

Perdrizet, Paul. 1901. "Les dossiers de P. J. Mariette sur Ba'albek et Palmyre." *Revue des Etudes Anciennes* 3.3: 225–264.

Perkins, Anne Louise. 1973. *The Art of Dura-Europos* (Oxford: Clarendon Press).

Perowne, Stewart. 1956. *The Life and Times of Herod the Great*. Sutton History Classics (New York: Abingdon Press; repr. Gloucestershire: Sutton, 2003).

Piersimoni, Palmira. 1995a. "Compiling a Palmyrene Prosopography: Methodological Problems." *ARAM Periodical* 7: 251–260.

Piersimoni, Palmira. 1995b. "The Palmyrene Prosopography" (Unpubl. PhD dissertation, University College London).

Pietrzykowski, Michał. 1997. *Adyta świątyń palmyreńskich*, ed. by Michał Gawlikowski (Warsaw: University of Warsaw) [Polish with a French summary].

Pfister, Rudolf. 1934. *Textiles de Palmyre découverts par le service des Antiquetés du haut-commissariat de la République Française dans la nécropole de Palmyre* (Paris: Les Éditions d'art et d'histoire).

Pfister, Rudolf. 1934–1940. *Textiles de Palmyre.* 3 vols. (Paris: Les Éditions d'art et d'histoire).

Plattner, Georg. 2013. "Sondage 1: Eine hellenistisch- römische Straßenkreuzung und angrenzende Wohnbebauung. Baubefund, Architektur, Chronologie." In *Palmyras Reichtum durch weltweiten Handel,* ed. by Andreas Schmidt-Colinet and Waleed al-As'ad (Vienna: Holzhausen), pp. 89–117.

Plets, Gertjan. 2017. "Violins and Trowels for Palmyra: Post-conflict Heritage Politics." *Anthropology Today* 33.4: 18–22. doi: 10.1111/1467-8322.12362.

Ploug, Gunhild. 1995. *Catalogue of the Palmyrene Sculptures, Ny Carlsberg Glyptotek* (Copenhagen: Ny Carlsberg Glyptotek).

Pollard, Nigel. 2000. *Soldiers, Cities and Civilians in Roman Syria* (Ann Arbor: University of Michigan Press).

Porter, Harvey, and Charles C. Torrey. 1906. "Inscribed Palmyrene Monuments in the Museum of the Syrian Protestant College, Beirut." *American Journal of Semitic Languages and Literatures* 22.4: 262–271.

Potter, David Stone. 1990. *Prophecy and History in the Crisis of the Roman Empire: A Historical Commentary on the Thirteenth Sibylline Oracle.* Oxford Classical Monographs (Oxford: Clarendon Press).

Potter, David Stone. 1996. "Palmyra and Rome. Odaenathus' Titulature and the Use of the imperium maius." *Zeitschrift für Papyrologie und Epigraphik* 113: 271–285.

Poulsen, Frederik. 1921. "De Palmyrenske Skulpturer." *Tidskrift för Konstvetenskap* 6: 79–105.

Raja, Rubina. 2012. *Urban Development and Regional Identity in the Eastern Roman Provinces, 50 BC–AD 250: Aphrodisias, Ephesos, Athens, Gerasa* (Copenhagen: Museum Tusculanum Press).

Raja, Rubina. 2013. "Changing Space and Shifting Attitudes: Revisiting the Sanctuary of Zeus in Gerasa." In *Cities and Gods: Religious Space in Transition,* ed. by Ted Kaizer et al. Babesch Supplement 22 (Leuven: Peeters), pp. 31–46.

Raja, Rubina. 2015a. "Cultic Dining and Religious Patterns in Palmyra. The Case of the Palmyrene Banqueting Tesserae." In *Antike. Kultur. Geschichte. Festschrift für Inge Nielsen zum 65. Geburtstag,* ed. by Stephan Faust, Martina Seifert, and Leon Ziemer. Gateways: Hamburger Beiträge zur Archäologie und Kulturgeschichte des antiken Mittelmeerraumes 2 (Aachen: Shaker), pp. 181–199.

Raja, Rubina. 2015b. "Introduction: From Studying Portraits to Documenting Syria's Cultural Heritage." In Rubina Raja and Annette Højen Sørensen, *Harald Ingholt and Palmyra* (Aarhus: Antikmuseet Aarhus University), pp. 10–13.

Raja, Rubina. 2015c. "Palmyrene Funerary Portraits in Context: Portrait Habit Between Local Traditions and Imperial Trends." In *Traditions: Transmission of Culture in the Ancient World,* ed. by Jane Fejfer, Mette Moltesen, and Annette Rathje. Acta Hyperborea 14 (Copenhagen: Museum Tusculanum Press), pp. 329–361.

Raja, Rubina. 2015d. "Staging 'Private' Religion in Roman 'Public' Palmyra. The Role of the Religious Dining Tickets (Banqueting Tesserae)." In *Public and Private in Ancient Mediterranean Law and Religion: Historical and Comparative Studies,* ed. by Clifford Ando and Jörg Rüpke. Religionsgeschichtliche Versuche und Vorarbeiten 65 (Berlin: De Gruyter), pp. 165–186.

Raja, Rubina. 2016a. "The History and Current Situation of World Heritage Sites in Syria: The Case of Palmyra." In *Cultural Heritage at Risk: The Role of Museums in War and Conflict*, ed. by Kurt Almqvist and Louise Belfrage (Stockholm: Axel and Margaret Ax:son Johnson Foundation), pp. 27–47.

Raja, Rubina. 2016b. "Illegal Trade and Export of Cultural Goods: The Case of the Palmyrene Funerary Portraiture." In *Fighting the Looting of Syria's Cultural Heritage. Report from the Sofia Conference 16 September: Initiatives to Stop Illicit Antiquities Trade Financing the Syrian Conflict. Awareness Rising*, ed. by Dima Chahin and Inge Lindblom (Sofia: Norwegian Institute for Cultural Heritage Research), pp. 11–12.

Raja, Rubina. 2016c. "In and Out of Contexts: Explaining Religious Complexity Through the Banqueting Tesserae from Palmyra." *Religion in the Roman Empire* 2.3: 340–371.

Raja, Rubina. 2016d. "Representations of Priests in Palmyra. Methodological Considerations on the Meaning of the Representation of Priesthood in Roman Period Palmyra." *Religion in the Roman Empire* 2.1: 125–146.

Raja, Rubina. 2017a. "Between Fashion Phenomena and Status Symbols: Contextualising the Wardrobe of the So-called 'Former Priests' of Palmyra." In *Textiles and Cult in the Ancient Mediterranean*, ed. by Cecilie Brøns and Marie-Louise Nosch. Ancient Textiles Series 31 (Oxford: Oxbow), pp. 209–229.

Raja, Rubina. 2017b. "Danish Pioneers at Palmyra: Historiographic Aspects of Danish Scholarship on Palmyra." In *Palmyra: Pearl of the Desert*, ed. by Rubina Raja (Aarhus: SUN-TRYK), pp. 21–29.

Raja, Rubina. 2017c. "Going Individual: Roman Period Portraiture in Classical Archaeology." In *The Diversity of Classical Archaeology*, ed. by Achim Lichtenberger and Rubina Raja. Studies in Classical Archaeology 1 (Turnhout: Brepols), pp. 271–286.

Raja, Rubina. 2017d. "Networking Beyond Death: Priests and Their Family Networks in Palmyra Explored Through the Funerary Sculpture." In *Sinews of Empire: Networks in the Roman Near East and Beyond*, ed. by Håkon Fiane Teigen and Eivind Heldaas Seland (Oxford: Oxbow), pp. 121–136.

Raja, Rubina. 2017e. "Powerful Images of the Deceased: Palmyrene Funerary Portrait Culture Between Local, Greek and Roman Representations." In *Bilder der Macht: Das griechische Porträt und seine Verwendung in der antiken Welt*, ed. by Dietrich Boschung and François Queryel. Morphomata 34 (Paderborn: Fink), pp. 319–348.

Raja, Rubina. 2017f. "Priesthood in Palmyra: Public Office or Social Status?" In *Palmyra: Pearl of the Desert*, ed. by Rubina Raja (Aarhus: SUN-TRYK), pp. 77–85.

Raja, Rubina. 2017g. "Representations of the so-called 'Former Priests' in Palmyrene Funerary Art. A Methodological Contribution and Commentary." *Topoi* 21: 51–81.

Raja, Rubina. 2017h. "To Be or Not to Be Depicted as a Priest in Palmyra: A Matter of Representational Spheres and Societal Values." In *Positions and Professions in Palmyra*, ed. by Tracey Long and Annette Højen Sørensen. Palmyrene Studies 2 (Copenhagen: Det Kongelige Danske Videnskabernes Selskab), pp. 115–130.

Raja, Rubina. 2017i. "You Can Leave Your Hat On. Priestly Representations from Palmyra: Between Visual Genre, Religious Importance and Social Status." In *Beyond Priesthood, Religious Entrepreneurs and Innovators in the Imperial Era*, ed. by Richard L. Gordon, Georgia Petridou, and Jörg Rüpke. Religionsgeschichtliche Versuche und Vorarbeiten 66 (Berlin: De Gruyter), pp. 417–442.

Raja, Rubina. 2017j. "Zeus Olympios, Hadrian and the Jews of Antiochia-on-the-Chrysorrhoas-formerly-called-Gerasa." In *Text and the Material World: Essays in Honour of Graeme Clarke*, ed. by Elizabeth Minchin and Heather Jackson (Uppsala: Åström), pp. 171–195.

Raja, Rubina. 2018a. "The Matter of the Palmyrene 'Modius': Remarks on the History of Research of the Terminology of the Palmyrene Priestly Hat." *Religion in the Roman Empire* 4.2: 237–259.

Raja, Rubina. 2018b. "Palmyrene Funerary Portraits: Collection Histories and Current Research." In *Palmyra: Mirage in the Desert*, ed. by Joan Aruz (New York: Metropolitan Museum of Art), pp. 100–109.

Raja, Rubina. 2019a. "Family Matters: Family Constellations in Palmyrene Funerary Sculpture." In *Family Lives: Aspects of Life and Death in Ancient Families*, ed. by Kristine Bøggild Johannsen and Jane Hjarl Petersen. Acta Hyperborea 15 (Copenhagen: Museum Tusculanum Press), pp. 245–270.

Raja, Rubina. 2019b. "Funerary Portraiture in Palmyra: Portrait Habit at a Cross-Road or a Signifier of Local Identity?" In *Funerary Portraiture in Greater Roman Syria*, ed. by Michael Blömer and Rubina Raja. Studies in Classical Archaeology 6 (Turnhout: Brepols), pp. 95–100.

Raja, Rubina. 2019c. "Harald Ingholt and Palmyra: A Danish Archaeologist and His Work at Palmyra." In *The Road to Palmyra*, ed. by Anne Marie Nielsen and Rubina Raja (Copenhagen: Ny Carlsberg Glyptotek), pp. 42–64.

Raja, Rubina. 2019d. "It Stays in the Family: Palmyrene Priestly Representations and Their Constellations." In *Women, Children and the Family in Palmyra*, ed. by Signe Krag and Rubina Raja. Palmyrene Studies 3 (Copenhagen: Det Kongelige Danske Videnskabernes Selskab), pp. 95–156.

Raja, Rubina. 2019e. *The Palmyra Collection* (Copenhagen: Ny Carlsberg Glyptotek).

Raja, Rubina. 2019f. "Portrait Habit in Palmyra." In *The Road to Palmyra*, ed. by Anne Marie Nielsen and Rubina Raja (Copenhagen: Ny Carlsberg Glyptotek), pp. 137–154.

Raja, Rubina. 2019g. "Reconsidering the Dorsalium or "Curtain of Death" in Palmyrene Funerary Sculpture: Significance and Interpretations in Light of the Palmyra Portrait Project Corpus." In *Revisiting the Religious Life of Palmyra*, ed. by Rubina Raja. Contextualizing the Sacred 9 (Turnhout: Brepols), pp. 67–151.

Raja, Rubina. 2019h. "Religious Banquets in Palmyra and the Palmyrene Banqueting Tesserae." In *The Road to Palmyra*, ed. by Anne Marie Nielsen and Rubina Raja (Copenhagen: Ny Carlsberg Glyptotek), pp. 221–234.

Raja, Rubina (ed.). 2019i. *Revisiting the Religious Life of Palmyra*. Contextualizing the Sacred 9 (Turnhout: Brepols).

Raja, Rubina. 2019j. "Revisiting the Religious Life of Palmyra: Or Why It Still Matters to Focus on Ancient Religious Life Within the Context of a Single Site." In *Revisiting the Religious life of Palmyra*, ed. by Rubina Raja. Contextualizing the Sacred 9 (Turnhout: Brepols), pp. 1–6.

Raja, Rubina. 2019k. "Stacking Aesthetics in the Syrian Desert: Displaying Palmyrene Sculpture in the Public and Funerary Sphere." In *Visual Histories of the Classical World: Essays in Honour of R. R. Smith*, ed. by Catherine M. Draycott et al. Studies in Classical Archaeology 4 (Turnhout: Brepols), pp. 281–298.

Raja, Rubina. 2020a. "Archive Archaeology: Preserving and Sharing Palmyra's Cultural Heritage Through Harald Ingholt's Digital Archives." Aarhus University. https://projects.au.dk/archivearcheology/ [accessed 29 July 2020].

Raja, Rubina. 2020b. "Come and Dine with Us: Invitations to Ritual Dining as Part of Social Strategies in Sacred Spaces in Palmyra." In *Lived Religion in the Ancient Mediterranean World: Approaching Religious Transformations from Archaeology, History and Classics*, ed. by Valentino Gasparini et al. (Berlin: De Gruyter), pp. 385–404.

Raja, Rubina. 2021a. "Adornment and Jewellery as a Status Symbol in Priestly Representations in Roman Palmyra: The Palmyrene Priests and Their Brooches." In *Individualizing the Dead: Attributes in Palmyrene Funerary Sculpture*, ed. by Maura Keane Heyn and Rubina Raja. Studies in Palmyrene Archaeology and History 3 (Turnhout: Brepols), pp. 75–118.

Raja, Rubina. 2021b. "Harald Ingholt and Palmyrene Sculpture: Continuing a Lifelong Relationship a Century Later." In *Studies on Palmyrene Sculpture. A Translation of Harald Ingholt's "Studier over Palmyrensk Skulptur," Edited and with Commentary*, ed. by Olympia Bobou et al. Studies in Palmyrene Archaeology and History 1 (Turnhout: Brepols), pp. 1–27.

Raja, Rubina. 2021c. "Negotiating Social and Cultural Interaction Through Priesthoods: The Iconography of Priesthood in Palmyra." In *The Middle East as Middle Ground? Cultural Interaction in the Ancient Middle East Revisited*, ed. by Julia Hoffman-Salz (Vienna: Holzhausen), pp. 129–146.

Raja, Rubina. 2021d. "Populating Public Palmyra: Display of Statues and Their Impact on the Perception of Public Space in Roman Palmyra." In *Public Statues Across Time and Cultures*, ed. by Christopher Paul Dickenson (London: Routledge).

Raja, Rubina. Forthcoming. *Palmyrene Priests* (Turnhout: Brepols).

Raja, Rubina, Olympia Bobou, and Iza Romanowska. Forthcoming. "Three Hundred Years of Palmyrene History. Unlocking Archaeological Data for Studying Past Societal Transformations." *PLOS ONE*.

Raja, Rubina, Olympia Bobou, and Jean-Baptiste Yon. Forthcoming. *The Palmyrene Funerary Portraits* (Turnhout: Brepols).

Raja, Rubina, and Eivind Heldaas Seland. 2021. "Horses and Camels in Palmyrene Art: Iconography, Contexts and Meaning." *Zeitschrift für Orient-Archäologie* 13: 300–329.

Raja, Rubina, and Julia Steding. 2021. "Production Economy in Roman Syria: New Views on Old Stones." In *Production Economy in Roman Syria: Trade Networks and Production Processes*, ed. by Rubina Raja and Julia Steding. Studies in Palmyrene Archaeology and History 2 (Turnhout: Brepols), pp. 1–8.

Raja, Rubina, Julia Steding, and Jean-Baptiste Yon. 2021. *Excavating Palmyra. Harald Ingholt's Excavation Diaries: A Transcript, Translation, and Commentary*. Studies in Palmyrene Archaeology and History 4. 2 vols. (Turnhout: Brepols)

Raja, Rubina, and Annette Højen Sørensen. 2015a. "The 'Beauty of Palmyra' and Qasr Abjad (Palmyra): New Discoveries in the Archive of Harald Ingholt." *Journal of Roman Archaeology* 28.1: 439–450.

Raja, Rubina and Annette Højen Sørensen. 2015b. *Harald Ingholt and Palmyra* (Aarhus: Antikmuseet Aarhus University).

Raja, Rubina, and Annette Højen Sørensen. 2019. "Historiography: Danish Research from Johannes Østrup (1893) to the Palmyra Portrait Project." In *Le tombeau des Trois Frères à Palmyre: Mission archéologique franco-syrienne 2004–2009*, ed. by Hélène

Eristov et al. Bibliothèque archéologique et historique 215 (Beirut: Institut français du Proche-Orient), pp. 59–64.

Raja, Rubina et al. 2020 (December). "Archive Archaeology in Palmyra. A New 3D Reconstruction of the Tomb of Ḥairan." *Journal of Digital Applications in Archaeology and Cultural Heritage* 19. https://doi.org/10.1016/j.daach.2020.e00164 [accessed 5 May 2020].

Rajak, Tessa. 1998. "The Rabbinic Dead and the Diaspora Dead at Beth She'arim." In *The Talmud Yerushalmi and Graeco-Roman Culture*, vol. 1, ed. by Peter Schäfer (Tübingen: Mohr-Siebeck), pp. 349–366.

Renfrew, Colin. 2000. *Loot, Legitimacy, and Ownership: The Ethical Crisis in Archaeology.* Debates in Archaeology (London: Duckworth).

Rey-Coquais, Jean-Paul. 1978. "Syrie romaine de Pompée à Dioclétian." *Journal of Roman Studies* 68: 44–73.

Ringsborg, Sara. 2017. "Children's Portraits from Palmyra." In *Palmyra: Pearl of the Desert*, ed. by Rubina Raja (Aarhus: SUN-TRYK), pp. 66–75.

Richmond, I. 1963. "Palmyra Under the Aegis of Rome." *Journal of Roman Studies* 53: 43–54.

Romanowska, Iza, Olympia Bobou, and Rubina Raja. 2021. "Reconstructing the Social, Economic and Demographic Trends of Palmyra's Elite from Funerary Data." *Journal of Archaeological Science* 33: 105432.

Römer-Strehl, Christiane. 2013. "Keramik." In *Palmyras Reichtum durch weltweiten Handel*, ed. by Andreas Schmidt-Colinet and Waleed al-As'ad (Vienna: Holzhausen), pp. 7–80.

Ronzevalle, Sébastien Joseph. 1934. "Sîma—Athén— Némésis." *Orientalia* 3: 121–146.

Rosen, Steve. 2017. *Revolutions in the Desert: The Rise of Mobile Pastoral Societies in the Negev and the Arid Zones of the Southern Levant* (New York: Routledge).

Rostovtzeff, Michael Ivanovitch. 1932. *Caravan Cities* (Oxford: Clarendon Press).

Rostovtzeff, Michael Ivanovitch. 1935. "Une nouvelle inscription caravanière de Palmyre." *Berytus* 2: 143–148.

Russell, Ben. 2013. *The Economics of the Roman Stone Trade.* Oxford Studies on the Roman Economy (Oxford: Oxford University Press).

Sadurska, Anna. 1988. "Die palmyrenische Grabskulptur." *Das Altertum* 34: 14–23.

Sadurska, Anna. 1991/1992. "Les rôle des femmes dans le culte à Palmyre (recherche iconographique)." *Vox Patrum* 11–12: 101–104.

Sadurska, Anna. 1995. "La famille et son image dans l'art de Palmyre." In *ARCVLIANA. Recueil d'hommages offerts à Hans Bögli*, ed. by Franz E. Koenig and Serge Rebetez (Avenches: L.A.O.T.T), pp. 583–589.

Sadurska, Anna, and Adnan Bounni. 1994. *Les Sculptures Funéraires de Palmyre* (Rome: L'Erma di Bretschneider).

Saito, Kiyohide. 2002. "New Discovery at the Southeast Necropolis in Palmyra, 2001." In *Proceedings of the International Conference Homs on Zenobia and Palmyra, During 19–21/10/2002 in Al-Bath University and Palmyra*, ed. by Al-Baath University, Ministry of Culture, and Directorate General of Antiquities and Museums (Homs: Al-Baath University), pp. 131–143.

Saito, Kiyohide. 2005a. "Die Arbeiten der japanischen Mission in der Südost-Nekropole." In *Palmyra: Kulturbegegnung im Grenzbereich. Zaberns Bildbände zur Archäologie*, ed. by Andreas Schmidt-Colinet, 3rd ed. (Mainz: von Zabern), pp. 32–35.

Saito, Kiyohide. 2005b. "Palmyrene Burial Practices from Funerary Goods." In *A Journey to Palmyra: Collected Essays to Remember Delbert R. Hillers*, ed. by Eleonora Cussini. Culture and History of the Ancient Near East 22 (Leiden: Brill), pp. 150–165.

Saito, Kiyohide (ed.). 2005c. *The Study of Funerary Practices and Social Background in Palmyra* (Nara: Archaeological Institute of Kashihara).

Saito, Kiyohide. 2016a. "Excavation of no. 129-b House Tomb at the North Necropolis in Palmyra." In *Palmyrena: City, Hinterland and Caravan Trade Between Orient and Occident. Proceedings of the Conference Held in Athens, December 1–3, 2012*, ed. by Jørgen Christian Meyer, Eivind Heldaas Seland, and Nils Anfinset (Oxford: Archaeopress), pp. 115–129.

Saito, Kiyohide. 2016b. "Palmyra. Japanese Archaeological Mission (Homs)." In *A History of Syria in One Hundred Sites*, ed. by Youssef Kanjou and Akira Tsuneki (Oxford: Archaeopress), pp. 349–354.

Salibi, Kamal Suleiman et al. "Syria." *Encyclopædia Britannica*. https://www.britannica.com/place/Syria [accessed 11 June 2020].

Samad, Bincy Abdul. 2020. "Civilizational Memory: The Transformation of Palmyra as a Cultural Patrimony of the West" (Unpubl. PhD dissertation, Bowling Green State University).

Sarraj, Bara. 2016. *From Tadmor to Havard* (CreateSpace Independent Publishing Platform) [in Arabic].

Sartre, Maurice. 1996. "Palmyre, cité grecque." *Annales archéologiques de Syrie* 42: 385–405.

Sartre, Maurice. 2001. *D'Alexandre à Zénobie: Histoire du Levant antique, IVe siècle avant J.-C.–IIIe siècle après J.-C.* (Paris: Fayard).

Sartre, Maurice. 2005. *The Middle East Under Rome*, trans. by Catherine Porter, Elizabeth Rawlings, and Jeanine Routier-Pucci (Cambridge, MA: Harvard University Press).

Sartre, Maurice. 2016. "Zénobie dans l'imaginaire occidental." In *The World of Palmyra*, ed. by Andreas Kropp and Rubina Raja. Palmyrene Studies 1 (Copenhagen: Det Kongelige Danske Videnskabernes Selskab), pp. 207–221.

Sartre, Maurice. 2019. "Dieux grecs à Palmyre: L'ambigüité d'un concept." In *Revisiting the Religious Life of Palmyra*, ed. by Rubina Raja. Contextualizing the Sacred 9 (Turnhout: Brepols), pp. 25–36.

Sartre-Fauriat, Annie. 2016. "Proche-Orient: Patrimoines en grand danger." *Anabases* 23: 139–156.

Sartre-Fauriat, Annie. 2019. "The Discovery and Reception of Palmyra" In *The Road to Palmyra*, ed. by Anne Marie Nielsen and Rubina Raja (Copenhagen: Ny Carlsberg Glyptotek), pp. 65–76.

Sartre-Fauriat, Annie, and Maurice Sartre. 2008. *Palmyre: La cité des caravans*. Découvertes Gallimard: Archéologie 523 (Paris: Gallimard).

Sartre-Fauriat, Annie, and Maurice Sartre. 2014. *Zénobie: De Palmyre à Rome* (Paris: Perrin).

Sartre-Fauriat, Annie, and Maurice Sartre. 2016. *Palmyre: Vérités et legends* (Paris: Perrin).

Savino. Eliodoro. 1999. *Città di frontiera nell'Impero romano. Forme della romanizzazione da Augusto ai Severi*. Pragmateiai 1 (Bari: Edipuglia).

Scarre, Chris and Geoffrey Scarre (eds.). 2006. *The Ethics of Archaeology: Philosophical Perspectives on Archaeological Practice* (Cambridge: Cambridge University Press).

Scharrer, Ulf. 2002. "Nomaden und Seßhafte in Tadmor im 2. Jahrtausend v. Chr." In *Grenzüberschreitungen. Formen des Kontakts zwischen Orient und Okzident*, ed. by Monika Schuol, Udo Hartmann, and Andreas Luther. Oriens et Occidens 3 (Stuttgart: Steiner), pp. 279–330.

Scharrer, Ulf. 2010. "The Problem of Nomadic Allies in the Roman Near East." In *Kingdoms and Principalities in the Roman Near East*, ed. by Ted Kaizer and Margherita Facella. Oriens et Occidens 19 (Stuttgart: Steiner), pp. 241–335.

Schlumberger, Daniel. 1933. "Les formes anciennes du chapiteau corinthien en Syrie, en Palestine et en Arabie." *Syria* 14: 283–317.

Schlumberger, Daniel. 1935. "Etudes sur Palmyre: I. Le développement urbain de Palmyre. II. Notes sur le décor architectural des colonnades des rues, et du camp de Dioclétien." *Berytus* 2: 149–167.

Schlumberger, Daniel. 1939a. "Les fouilles de Qasr el-Heir el-Gharbi (1936–1938): Rapport préliminaire." *Syria* 20.3: 195–238.

Schlumberger, Daniel. 1939b. "Les fouilles de Qasr el-Heir el-Gharbi (1936–1938): Rapport préliminaire." *Syria* 20.4: 324–373.

Schlumberger, Daniel. 1951. *La Palmyrène du Nord-Ouest: Villages et lieux de culte de l'époque impériale. Recherches archéologiques sur la mise en valeur d'une région du désert par les Palmyréniens*. Bibliotheque archeologique et historique 49 (Paris: Geuthner).

Schlumberger, Daniel. 1971. "Les quatre tribus de Palmyre." *Syria* 48.1–2: 121–133.

Schlumberger, Daniel, Marc Le Berre, Michel Ecochard, and Nessib Saliby. 1986. *Qasr el-Heir el Gharbi: textes et planches* (Paris: Libr. orientaliste P. Geuthner).

Schmidt-Colinet, Andreas. 1987. "Das Tempelgrab einer Aristokratenfamilie (Neue deutche Ausgrabungen in Palmyra)." In *Palmyra: Geschichte, Kunst und Kultur der syrischen Oasenstadt*, ed. by Erwin Maria Ruprechtsberger. Linzer Archäologische Forschungen Band 16 (Linz: Gutenberg), pp. 214–227.

Schmidt-Colinet, Andreas. 1990. "Considerations sur les carrières de Palmyre." In *Pierre éternelle du Nil au Rhin: Carrières et prefabrication*, ed. by Marc Waelkens (Brussels: Crédit Communal), pp. 88–92.

Schmidt-Colinet, Andreas. 1992. *Das Tempelgrab Nr. 36 in Palmyra*. Studien zur Palmyrenischen Grabarchitektur und ihrer Ausstattung. 2 vols. (Mainz am Rhein: von Zabern).

Schmidt-Colinet, Andreas. 1995a. "The Textiles from Palmyra." *ARAM Periodical* 7: 47–51.

Schmidt-Colinet, Andreas. 1995b. "The Quarries of Palmyra." *ARAM Periodical* 7: 53–58.

Schmidt-Colinet, Andreas. 1996. "Tessuti e decorazione architettonica a Palmira." *Asia* 7: 20–27.

Schmidt-Colinet, Andreas. 1997. "Aspects of 'Romanization': The Tomb Architecture of Palmyra and Its Decorations." In *The Early Roman Empire in the East*, ed. by Susan Ellen Alcock. Oxbow Monographs in Archaeology 95 (Oxford: Oxbow), pp. 157–177.

Schmidt-Colinet, Andreas. 2000a. "'Best Wishes from China,' Ancient Textiles from Palmyra: A Glimpse on Globalization in Antiquity." In *Das Spiel mit der Antike: Zwischen Antikensehnsucht und Alltagsrealität; Festschrift zum 85. Geburtstag von Rupprecht Düll*, ed. by Siegrid Düll (Möhnesee: Bibliopolis), pp. 280–289.

Schmidt-Colinet, Andreas. 2000b. "Ornamentik." In *Die Textilien aus Palmyra: Neue und alte Funde*, ed. by Andreas Schmidt-Colinet, Annemarie Stauffer, and Khaled al-As'ad. Damaszener Forschungen 8 (Mainz am Rhein: von Zabern), pp. 41–47.

Schmidt-Colinet, Andreas. 2004. "Palmyrenische Grabkunst ais Ausdruck lokaler Identität(en): Fallbeispiele." In *Lokale Identitäten in Randgebieten des Römischen*

Reiches: Akten des internationalen Symposiums in Wiener Neustadt, 24.–26. April 2003, ed. by Andreas Schmidt-Colinet. Wiener Forschungen zur Archäologie 7 (Vienna: Phoibos), pp. 189–198.

Schmidt-Colinet, Andreas. 2009. "Nochmal zur Ikonographie zweier palmyrenischer sarkophage." In *Lokale Identität im Römischen Nahen Osten: Kontexte und Perspektiven. Erträge der Tagung "Lokale Identität im Römischen Nahen Osten," Münster, 19.–21. April 2007*, ed. by Michael Blömer, Margherita Facella, and Engelbert Winter. Oriens et Occidens 18 (Stuttgart: Steiner), pp. 223–234.

Schmidt-Colinet, Andreas, 2013. "Thirty Years of Syro-German/Austrian Archaeological Research at Palmyra." *Studia Palmyreńskie* 12: 299–318.

Schmidt-Colinet, Andreas. 2016. "The Reconstruction and Distribution of Pattern Books in the Roman Empire. Some Archaeological Evidence from Palmyra." In *Intorno al Papiro di Artemidoro III: I disegni, Atti del Convegno internazionale del 4 febbraio 2011 presso il Gabinetto Disegni e Stampe degli Uffizi, Firenze*, ed. by Gianfranco Adornato (Milan: LED Edizioni Universitarie), pp. 129–146.

Schmidt-Colinet, Andreas, and Khaled al-As'ad (eds.). 2005. "Ausblick." In *Palmyra: Kulturbegegnung im Grenzbereich*, ed. by Andreas Schmidt-Colinet. Sonderbände der Antike Welt, Zaberns Bildbände zur Archäologie 27, 3rd ed. (Mainz am Rhein: von Zabern), pp. 73–76.

Schmidt-Colinet, Andreas. 2017. "Die antiken Steinbrüche von Palmyra. Ein Vorbericht." *Mitteilungen der Deutschen Orient-Gesellschaft zu Berlin* 149: 159–196.

Schmidt-Colinet, Andreas. Forthcoming. "Hellenistic Palmyra—a Fata Morgana?" In *The Oxford Handbook of Palmyra*, ed. by Rubina Raja (Oxford: Oxford University Press).

Schmidt-Colinet, Andreas, and Khaled al-As'ad. 2000. "Zur Urbanistik des hellenistischen Palmyra: Ein Vorbericht." *Damaszener Mitteilungen* 12: 61–93.

Schmidt-Colinet, Andreas, and Khaled al-As'ad. 2002. "Archaeological News from Hellenistic Palmyra." *Parthica* 4: 157–166.

Schmidt-Colinet, Andreas, and Khaled al-As'ad (eds.). 2013. *Palmyras Reichtum durch Weltweiten Handel: Archäologische Untersuchungen im Bereich der hellenistischen Stadt*. 2 vols. (Vienna: Holzhausen).

Schmidt-Colinet, Andreas, Khaled al-As'ad, and Waleed al-As'ad. 2008. "Untersuchungen im Areal der 'hellenistischen' Stadt von Palmyra. Zweiter Vorbericht." *Zeitschrift für Orient-Archäologie* 1: 452–478.

Schmidt-Colinet, Andreas, and Georg A. Plattner. 2001. "Geophysical Survey and Excavation in the Hellenistic Town of Palmyra." In *Archaeological Prospection: Fourth International Conference on Archaeological Prospection, Vienna, 19–23 September 2001*, ed. by Michael Doneus, Alois Eder-Hinterleitner, and Wolfgang Neubauer (Vienna: Österreichische Akademie der Wissenschaften), pp. 175–177.

Schmidt-Colinet, Andreas, Annemarie Stauffer, and Khaled al-As'ad (eds.). 2000. *Die Textilien aus Palmyra. Neu und alte Funde*. Damaszener Forschungen 8 (Mainz am Rhein: von Zabern).

Schnädelbach, Klaus. 2010. *Topography*, vol. 1, *Topographia Palmyrena*. Documents d'archéologie syrienne 18 (Bonn: Habelt).

Schörle, Katia. 2017. "Palmyrene Merchant Networks and Economic Integration in Competitive Markets." In *Sinews of Empire: Networks in the Roman Near East and Beyond*, ed. by Håkon Fiane Teigen and Eivind Heldaas Seland (Oxford: Oxbow), pp. 147–154.

Schörle, Katia. Forthcoming a. "Deserts and the Mediterranean—Border and Contact Zones," in *Mediterranean Studies in Antiquity—Setting the Agenda*, ed. by Rubina Raja (Cambridge: Cambridge University Press).

Schörle, Katia. Forthcoming b. *Long-distance Trade and the Exploitation of Arid Lands in Roman Times* (Turnhout: Brepols).

Schörle, Katia. Forthcoming c. "Organising Networks to Supply Mediterranean Markets." In *Palmyra and the Mediterranean*, ed. by Rubina Raja (Cambridge: Cambridge University Press).

Schörle, Katia. Forthcoming d. "Palmyrene Diaspora." In *The Oxford University Press Handbook of Palmyra*, ed. by Rubina Raja (Oxford: Oxford University Press)

Schou, Thorbjørn Preus. 2014. *Mobile Pastoralist Groups and the Palmyrene in the Late Early to Middle Bronze Age (c. 2400–1700 BCE): An Archaeological Synthesis Based on a Multidisciplinary Approach Focusing on Satellite Imagery Studies, Environmental Data, and Textual Sources* (Bergen: University of Bergen). http://hdl.handle.net/1956/10808 [accessed March 2021].

Schuol, Monica. 2000. *Die Charakene. Ein Mesopotamisches Königreich in hellenistisch-partischer Zeit* (Stuttgart: Steiner).

Seager, Robin. 2002. *Pompey the Great: A Political Biography*. Blackwell Ancient Lives, 2nd ed. (Oxford: Wiley-Blackwell).

Seigne, Jacques. 1989. "History of Exploration at Jerash: The Sanctuary of Zeus." In *Archaeology of Jordan II*, Vol. 1, *Field Reports, Surveys and Sites (A–K)*, ed. by D. Homes-Fredericq and J. B. Hennessy (Leuven: Peeters), pp. 319–323.

Seigne, Jacques. 1992a. "Jérash romaine et byzantine: Développement urbain d'une ville provinciale orientale." *Studies in the History and Archaeology of Jordan* 4: 331–341.

Seigne, Jacques. 1992b. "À l'ombre de Zeus et d'Artémis: Gerasa de la Décapole." *ARAM Periodical* 4: 185–195.

Seigne, Jacques. Forthcoming. *Gerasa of the Decapolis: Basilica and Civic Center*.

Seland, Eivind Heldaas. 2010. "Palmyra: Karavanehandel og geopolitikk i romersk Syria." *Klassisk Forum* 2: 54–69.

Seland, Eivind Heldaas. 2011. "The Persian Gulf or the Red Sea? Two Axes in Ancient Indian Ocean Trade, Where to Go and Why." *World Archaeology* 43: 398–409.

Seland, Eivind Heldaas. 2013. "Networks and Social Cohesion in Ancient Indian Ocean Trade: Geography, Ethnicity, Religion." *Journal of Global History* 8: 373–390.

Seland, Eivind Heldaas. 2015a. "Camels, Camel Nomadism and the Practicalities of Palmyrene Caravan Trade." *ARAM Periodical* 27: 45–53.

Seland, Eivind Heldaas. 2015b. "Palmyrene Long-Distance Trade: Land, River, and Maritime Routes in the First Three Centuries CE." In *The Silk Road: Interwoven History*, vol. 1, *Long-distance Trade, Culture, and Society*, ed. by Mariko Namba Walter and James P. Ito-Adler (Cambridge, MA: Cambridge Institutes Press), pp. 101–131.

Seland, Eivind Heldaas. 2016. *Ships of the Desert and Ships of the Sea: Palmyra in the World Trade of the First–Third Centuries CE*. Philippika 101 (Wiesbaden: Harrassowitz).

Seland, Eivind Heldaas. 2017. "The Iconography of Caravan Trade in Palmyra and the Roman Near East." In *Positions and Professions in Palmyra*, ed. by Tracey Long and Annette Højen Sørensen. Palmyrene Studies 2 (Copenhagen: Det Kongelige Danske Videnskabernes Selskab), pp. 106–114.

Seland, Eivind Heldaas. 2019. "The Trade of Palmyra." In *The Road to Palmyra*, ed. by Anne Marie Nielsen and Rubina Raja (Copenhagen: Ny Carlsberg Glyptotek), pp. 127-136.

Seyrig, Henri. 1932a. "Antiquités Syriennes." *Syria* 13.3: 255‒276.

Seyrig, Henri. 1932b. "Hiérarchie des divinités de Palmyre." *Syria* 13.2: 190‒195.

Seyrig, Henri. 1933. "Nouveaux monuments palmyréniens des cultes de Bêl et de Baalshamîn." *Syria* 14: 253‒282.

Seyrig, Henri. 1937. "Antiquités syriennes." *Syria* 18.1: 1‒4.

Seyrig, Henri. 1939. "Antiquités Syriennes." *Syria* 20.4: 296‒373.

Seyrig, Henri. 1940a. "Antiquités Syriennes." *Syria* 21: 277‒328, plates 29‒35.

Seyrig, Henri. 1940b. "Rapport sommaire sur les fouilles de l'agora de Palmyre." *Comptes rendus des séances de l'Académie des Inscriptions et Belles-Lettres* 84: 237‒249.

Seyrig, Henri. 1950a. "Antiquités syriennes." *Syria* 27.3‒4: 229‒252.

Seyrig, Henri. 1950b. "Palmyra and the East." *Journal of Roman Studies* 40: 1‒7.

Seyrig, Henri. 1971. "Bêl de Palmyre." *Syria* 48: 85‒114.

Seyrig, Henri, Robert Amy, and Ernest Will. 1968. *Le temple de Bel á Palmyre: Album* (Paris: Geuthner).

Seyrig, Henri, Robert Amy, and Ernest Will. 1975. *Le temple de Bel á Palmyre: Texte et planches* (Paris: Geuthner).

Shaheen, Kareem, and Ian Black. 2015 (19 August). "Beheaded Syrian Scholar Refused to Lead Isis to Hidden Palmyra Antiquities." *The Guardian*. https://www.theguardian.com/world/2015/aug/18/isis-beheads-archaeologist-syria [accessed March 2021].

Shapley, Fern Rusk. 1974. "Tiepolo's Zenobia Cycle." In *Hortus Imaginum: Essays in Western Art*, ed. by Robert Enggass and Marilyn Stokstad. Humanistic Studies 45 (Lawrence: University of Kansas), pp. 193‒198.

Shifman, Ilia Sholeimovich. 2014. *The Palmyrene Tax Tariff*, trans. by Svetlana Khobnya and John F. Healey. *Journal of Semitic Studies*, Supplement 33 (Oxford: Oxford University Press).

Shorrock, William I. 1970. "The Origin of the French Mandate in Syria and Lebanon: The Railroad Question, 1901‒1914." *International Journal of Middle East Studies* 1.2: 133‒153. https://www.jstor.org/stable/162437.

Simiot, Bernard. 1978. *Moi, Zénobie, reine de Palmyre* (Paris: Albin Michel).

Simonsen, David. 1889. *Skulpturer og indskrifter fra Palmyra i Ny Carlsberg Glyptotek* (Copenhagen: Th. Linds Boghandel).

Skowronek, Stefan. 2014. "Un trésor byzantin." *Studia Palmyreńskie* 13: 60‒64.

Smith II, Andrew Michael. 2013. *Roman Palmyra: Identity, Community, and State Formation* (Oxford: Oxford University Press).

Soderland, Hilary Allester, and Ian Ashley Lilley. 2015. "The Fusion of Law and Ethics in Cultural Heritage Management: The 21st Century Confronts Archaeology." *Journal of Field Archaeology* 40.5: 508‒522. doi: 10.1179/2042458215Y.0000000024.

Sokołowski, Łukasz. 2014. "Portraying the Literacy of Palmyra. The Evidence of Funerary Sculpture and Its Interpretation." *Études et travaux: Studia i prace. Travaux du Centre d'archéologie méditerranéenne de l'Académie des sciences polonaise* 27: 375‒403.

Soltan, Andrzej. 1969. "Ikonografia meharystów palmyrénskich." *Studia Palmyreńskie* 3: 5‒46.

Sommer, Michael. 2005. *Roms orientalische Steppengrenze: Palmyra‒Edessa‒Dura-Europos‒Hatra. Eine Kulturgeschichte von Pompeius bis Diocletian.* Oriens et Occidens 9 (Stuttgart: Steiner).

Sommer, Michael. 2008. "Der Löwe von Tadmor. Palmyra und der unwahrscheinliche Aufstieg des Septimius Odaenathus." *Historische Zeitschrift* 287: 281‒318.

Sommer, Michael. 2015. "Through the Looking Glass: Zenobia and 'Orientalism.'" In *Reinventing "The Invention of Tradition": Indigenous Pasts and the Roman Present*, ed. by Dietrich Boschung, Alexandra Wilhelmine Busch, and Miguel John Versluys. Morphomata 32 (Paderborn: Fink), pp. 113–125.

Sommer, Michael. 2017a. *Palmyra: Biographie einer verlorenen Stadt* (Mainz am Rhein: von Zabern).

Sommer, Michael. 2017b. *Palmyra: A History*. Cities of the Ancient World 1 (New York: Routledge).

Southern, Pat. 2003. *Pompey the Great: Caesar's Friend and Foe* (Cheltenham: History Press).

Southern, Pat. 2008. *Empress Zenobia: Palmyra's Rebel Queen* (London: Continuum).

Spoer, H. H. 1905. "Palmyrene Tesserae." *Journal of Oriental and African Studies* 26: 113–116.

Starcky, Jean. 1952. *Palmyre*. L'Orient Ancien Illustre 7 (Paris: Librairie d'Amérique et d'Orient).

Starcky, Jean. 1981. "Allath, Athèna et la déesse syrienne." In *Mythologie gréco-romaine, mythologies périphériques. Études d'iconographie*, ed. by Christian Auge and Lilly Kahil (Paris: Éditions du Centre national de la recherche scientifique), pp. 119–130.

Starcky, Jean, and Michał Gawlikowski. 1985. *Palmyre* (Paris: Librairie d'Amérique et d'Orient).

Stauffer, Annemarie. 1996. "Textiles from Palmyra: Local Production and the Import and Imitation of Chinese Silk Weavings." *Annales archéologiques arabes syriennes* 42: 425–430.

Stauffer, Annemarie. 2000. "The Textiles from Palmyra: Technical Analyses and Their Evidence for Archaeological Research." In *Archéologie des textiles, des origines au Ve siècle: Actes du colloque de Lattes, Octobre 1999*, ed. by Dominique Cardon and Michel Feugère. Monographies instrumentum 14 (Montagnac: Mergoil), pp. 247–251.

Stauffer, Annemarie. 2005. "Kleider, Kissen, bunte Tücher. Einheimische Textilproduktion und weltweiter Handel." In *Palmyra: Kulturbegegnung im Grenzbereich*, ed. by Andreas Schmidt-Colinet. Sonderbände der Antike Welt, Zaberns Bildbände zur Archäologie 27, 3rd ed. (Mainz am Rhein: von Zabern), pp. 67–81.

Stauffer, Annemarie. 2007a. "Antike chinesische Textilien als Handelsgüter im Westen." In *Unter der gelben Erde: Die deutsch-chinesische Zusammenarbeit im Kulturgüterschutz. Internationaler Kongress Bonn 2006*, ed. by Henriette Pleiger (Mainz am Rhein: von Zabern), pp. 189–198.

Stauffer, Annemarie. 2007b. "Imports and Exports of Textiles in Roman Syria." In *Productions et échanges dans la Syrie grecque et romaine: Actes du colloque de Tours, June 2003*, ed. by Maurice Sartre. Topoi orient-occident, Supplément 8 (Lyon: Maison de l'orient méditerranéen), pp. 357–373.

Stauffer, Annemarie. 2010. "Kleidung in Palmyra. Neue Fragen zu alten Funden." In *Zeitreisen: Syrien–Palmyra–Rom; Festschrift für Andreas Schmidt-Colinet zum 65. Geburtstag*, ed. by Beatrix Bastl, Verena Gassner, and Ulrike Muss (Vienna: Phoibos), pp. 209–218.

Steve, Marie-Joseph. 2003. *L'Ile de Khārg: Une page de l'histoire du Golfe persique et du monachisme oriental* (Neuchâtel: Recherches et publications).

Stewart, Andrew. 2016. "The Borghese Ares Revisited: New Evidence from the Agora and a Reconstruction of the Augustan Cult Group in the Temple of Ares." *Hesperia* 85: 577–625.

Stoneman, Richard. 1992. *Palmyra and Its Empire: Zenobia's Revolt against Rome* (Ann Arbor: University of Michigan Press).

Strobel, Karl. 1993. *Das Imperium Romanum im "3. Jahrhundert": Modell einer historischen Krise? Zur Frage mentaler Strukturen breiterer Bevölkerungsschichten in der Zeit von Marc Aurel bis zum Ausgang des 3. Jh. n. Chr.* (Stuttgart: Steiner).

Stucky, Rolf Andreas. 1973. "Prêtres syriens I: Palmyre." *Syria* 50.1–2: 163–180.

Stucky, Rolf Andreas. 2008. "Henri Seyrig—Engagierter Archäologe und Verwalter des Antikendienstes während der Mandatszeit." In *Das Große Spiel: Archäologie und Politik zur Zeit des Kolonialismus (1860–1940)*, ed. by Charlotte Trümpler (Cologne: DuMont), pp. 504–511.

Surface Survey North of Palmyra, April and May 2011. Preliminary report, prehistorical period (Bergen: Department of Archaeology, History, Cultural Studies and the History of Religions. University of Bergen, 2013). http://bora.uib.no/handle/1956/10476.

Swain, Simon. 1993. "Greek into Palmyrene. Odaenathus as 'Corrector Totius Orientis'?" *Zeitschrift für Papyrologie und Epigraphik* 99: 157–164.

Syrians for Heritage (SIMAT). 2020 (11 June). "A Report on the Confiscation of Looted Palmyrene Funerary Reliefs in Idlib." https://syriansforheritage.org/2020/06/11/a-report-on-the-confiscation-of-looted-palmyrene-funerary-reliefs-in-idlib/ [accessed March 2021].

Sørensen, Annette Højen. 2016. "Palmyrene Tomb Paintings in Context." In *The World of Palmyra*, ed. by Andreas Kropp and Rubina Raja. Palmyrene Studies 1 (Copenhagen: Det Kongelige Danske Videnskabernes Selskab), pp. 103–117.

Tanabe, Katsumi. 1986. *Sculptures of Palmyra*, vol. 1 (Tokyo: Ancient Orient Museum).

Tarlow, Sarah. 2006. "Archaeological Ethics and the People of the Past." In *The Ethics of Archaeology: Philosophical Perspectives on Archaeological Practice*, ed. by Chris Scarre and Geoffrey Scarre (Cambridge: Cambridge University Press), pp. 199–216.

Tarrier, Dominique. 1995. "Banquets rituels en Palmyrène et en Nabatène." *ARAM Periodical* 7.1: 165–182.

Taylor, Adam. 2015 (22 May). "Among Syrians, Palmyra Is Famous for a Different Landmark—Its Brutal Prison." *Washington Post*. https://www.washingtonpost.com/news/worldviews/wp/2015/05/22/among-syrians-palmyra-is-famous-for-a-different-landmark-its-brutal-prison/ [accessed March 2021].

Taylor, David G. K. 2001. "An Annotated Index of Dated Palmyrene Aramaic Texts." *Journal of Semitic Studies*: 203–219.

Teixidor, Javier. 1979. *The Pantheon of Palmyra*. Etudes préliminaires aux religions orientales dans l'Empire romain 79 (Leiden: Brill).

Terpstra, Taco T. 2013. *Trading Communities in the Roman World: A Micro-Economic and Institutional Perspective* (Leiden: Brill).

Terpstra, Taco T. 2016. "The Palmyrene Temple in Rome and Palmyra's Trade with the West." In *Palmyrena: City, Hinterland and Caravan Trade Between Orient and Occident. Proceedings of the Conference Held in Athens, December 1–3, 2012*, ed. by Jørgen Christian Meyer, Eivind Heldaas Seland, and Nils Anfinset (Oxford: Archaeopress), pp. 39–48.

Terpak, Frances, and Peter Louis Bonfitto. "The Legacy of Palmyra." Getty Research Institute. https://www.getty.edu/research/exhibitions_events/exhibitions/palmyra/ [accessed 27 July 2020].

Triebel, Lothar. 2004. *Jenseitshoffnung in Wort und Stein. Nefesch und pyramidales Grabmal als Phänomene antiken jüdischen Bestattungswesens im Kontext der*

Nachbarkulturen. Arbeiten zur Geschichte des antiken Judentums und des Urchristentums 56 (Leiden: Brill).

"Triumphal Arch in the News." Institute for Digital Archaeology. http://digitalarchaeology. org.uk/media [accessed 29 July 2020].

Trümpler, Charlotte (ed.). 2008. *Das Große Spiel: Archäologie und Politik zur Zeit des Kolonialismus (1860–1940)* (Cologne: DuMont).

Turner, Lauren. 2016 (19 April). "Palmyra's Arch of Triumph recreated in London." BBC News. https://www.bbc.com/news/uk-36070721 [accessed March 2021].

Ulf, Christoph. 2009. "Rethinking Cultural Contacts." *Ancient East and West* 8: 81–132.

UNESCO. 1954 (14 May). "Convention for the Protection of Cultural Property in the Event of Armed Conflict with Regulations for the Execution of the Convention 1954." The Hague. http://www.unesco.org/new/en/culture/themes/armed-conflict-and-heritage/convention-and-protocols/1954-hague-convention/ [accessed March 2021].

UNESCO. 1970 (14 November). "Convention on the Means of Prohibiting and Preventing the Illicit Import, Export and Transfer of Ownership of Cultural Property 1970." Paris. https://en.unesco.org/fighttrafficking/1970 [accessed March 2021].

UNESCO. 2017 (20 January). "UNESCO Director-General Condemns Destruction of the Tetrapylon and Severe Damage to the Theatre in Palmyra, a UNESCO World Heritage Site." https://en.unesco.org/news/unesco-director-general-condemns-destruction-tetrapylon-and-severe-damage-theatre-palmyra [accessed March 2021].

UNESCO. "Observatory of Syrian Cultural Heritage." https://en.unesco.org/syrian-observatory/ [accessed 28 July 2020].

UNESCO. "Observatory of Syrian Cultural Heritage. Damage Assessment: Reports." https://en.unesco.org/syrian-observatory/damage-assesment-reports?title=&field_institution_tid=All&date_filter%5Bvalue%5D=&field_report_tags_tid_1=&page=4&order=field_publish_date&sort=asc [accessed 28 July 2020].

UNESCO. "Safeguarding Syrian Cultural Heritage." http://www.unesco.org/new/en/safeguarding-syrian-cultural-heritage/ [accessed 28 July 2020].

UNESCO. "Site of Palmyra" http://whc.unesco.org/en/list/23/ [accessed 28 July 2020].

UNESCO. "Unite4Heritage." https://www.unite4heritage.org/en/unite4heritage-celebrating-safeguarding-cultural-heritage [accessed 28 July 2020].

UNESCO. "World Heritage List" https://whc.unesco.org/en/list/ [accessed 28 July 2020].

UNITAR-UNOSAT. 2017 (20 January). "UNOSAT Palmyra Roman Tetrapylon and Amphitheatre Damage Assessment." https://unitar.org/unosat/node/44/2537 [accessed March 2021].

University of Lausanne, "Project Collart-Palmyre: International Conference of Lausanne on Palmyra, 16 & 17 December 2019, Université de Lausanne, Amphimax 414. Program." University of Lausanne. https://news.unil.ch/document/1572960297244. D1575539872942 [accessed 29 July 2020].

University of Warsaw. "Life in Palmyra, Life for Palmyra" Conference, 21–22 April 2016. Institute of Archaeology, University of Warsaw. https://en.uw.edu.pl/conference-life-in-palmyra-life-for-palmyra/ [accessed March 2021].

van Berchem, Denis. 1976. "Le plan de Palmyre." In *Palmyre: Bilan et Perspectives. Colloque de Strasbourg 18–20 Octobre 1973, à la mémoire de Daniel Schlumberger et de Henri Seyrig,* ed. by Edmond Frézouls. Université des Sciences Humaines de Strasbourg. Travaux du Centre de Recherche Sur le Proche-Orient et la Grèce Antiques, 3 (Strasbourg: Association pour l'étude de la civilisation romaine), pp. 165–173.

van Wijlick, Hendrikus A.M. 2021. *Rome and the Near Eastern Kingdoms and Principalities, 44–31 BC. A Study of Political Relations during Civil War.* Impact of Empire 38 (Leiden: Brill).

Velestino, Daniela. 2017. "Rome and Palmyra." In *Portraits of Palmyra in Aquileia*, ed. by Marta Novello and Cristiano Tiussi (Rome: Gangemi), pp. 96–97.

Vermeule, Cornelius C. 1964. "Greek and Roman Portraits in North American Collections Open to the Public: A Survey of Important Monumental Likenesses in Marble and Bronze Which Have Not Been Published." *Proceedings of the American Philosophical Society* 108.1: 99–134.

Veyne, Paul. 2015. *Palmyre: L'irremplacable trésor* (Paris: Albin Michel).

Veyne, Paul. 2017. *Palmyra: An Irreplaceable Treasure*, trans. by Teresa Lavender Fagan (Chicago: University of Chicago Press).

Vincenti, Maria Cristina. 2012. "Culti orientali: Contesti e rinvenimenti tra Roma e i Colli Albani." In *L'Oriente nel collezionismo: Il collezionismo di antichità classiche e orientali nella formazione dei musei europei*, ed. by Beatrice Palma Venetucci (Rome: UniversItalia), pp. 553–567.

Visconti, Carlo L. 1860. "Escavazioni della Vigna Bonelli, fuori della Porta Portese negli anni 1859 e 60." *Annali dell'Istituto di corrispondenza archeologica* 32: 415–450.

von Gerkan, Armin. 1935. "Die Stadtmauer von Palmyra." *Berytus* 2: 25–33.

von Hesberg, Henner. 1992. *Römische Grabbauten* (Darmstadt: Wissenschaftliche Buchgesellschaft).

Vuolanto, Ville. 2019. "Children and Religious Participation in Roman Palmyra." In *Women, Children, and the Family in Palmyra*, ed. by Signe Krag and Rubina Raja. Palmyrene Studies 3 (Copenhagen: Det Kongelige Danske Videnskabernes Selskab), pp. 201–213.

Waddington, William Henry. 1870. *Inscriptions grecques et Latines de la Syrie recueillies et expliquées* (Paris: Librairie de Firmon Didot Fréres, Fils et Co.).

Watson, Alaric. 1999. *Aurelian and the Third Century* (London: Routledge).

Weiss, Thomas George, and Nina Connelly. 2017. *Cultural Cleansing and Mass Atrocities: Protecting Cultural Heritage in Armed Conflict Zones.* J. Paul Getty Trust Occasional Papers in Cultural Heritage Policy 1 (Los Angeles: J. Paul Getty Trust). https://www.getty.edu/publications/pdfs/CulturalCleansing_Weiss_Connelly.pdf. [accessed March 2021].

Weststeijn, Johan. 2013. "Zenobia of Palmyra and the Book of Judith: Common Motifs in Greek, Jewish, and Arabic Historiography." *Journal for the Study of the Pseudepigrapha* 22.4: 295–320.

Weststeijn, Johan. 2016. "Wine, Women, and Revenge in Near Eastern Historiography: The Tales of Tomyris, Judith, Zenobia, and Jalila." *Journal of Near Eastern Studies* 75.1: 91–107.

White, Richard. 2010. *The Middle Ground (Indians, Empires, and the Republics in the Great Lakes Region, 1650–1815)* 2nd ed. (Cambridge: Cambridge University Press).

Wiegand, Theodore (ed.). 1932. *Palmyra—Ergebnisse der Expeditionen von 1902 und 1917* (Berlin: Keller).

Wielgosz, Dagmara. 1997. "Funeralia palmyrena." *Studia Palmyreńskie* 10: 69–77.

Wielgosz-Rondolino, Dagmara. 2016. "Palmyrene Portraits from the Temple of Allat: New Evidence on Artists and Workshops." In *The World of Palmyra*, ed. by Andreas Kropp and Rubina Raja. Palmyrene Studies 1 (Copenhagen: Det Kongelige Danske Videnskabernes Selskab), pp. 166–179.

Will, Ernest. 1966. "Le sac de Palmyre." In *Mélanges d'archéologie et d'histoire offerts à André Piganiol. École Pratique des Hautes Études VIe section*, ed. by Raymond Chevallier (Paris: SEVPEN), pp. 1409–1416.

Will, Ernest. 1983. "Le développement urbain de Palmyre: Témoignages épigraphiques anciens et nouveaux." *Syria* 60: 69–81.

Will, Ernest. 1990. "La maison d'éternité et les conceptions funéraires des Palmyréniens." In *Mélanges Pierre Lévêque*, tome 4, *Religion*, ed. by Marie-Madeleine Mactoux and Evelyne Geny. Annales littéraires de l'Université de Besançon 413 (Paris: Les Belles Lettres), pp. 433–440.

Will, Ernest. 1992. *Les Palmyréniens: La Venise des sables (Ier siècle avant—IIIème siècle après J.-C.)*. Collection Civilisations U (Paris: Colin).

Will, Ernest. 1997. "Les salles de banquet de Palmyre et d'autres lieux." *Topoi* 7: 873–887.

Winsbury, Rex. 2010. *Zenobia of Palmyra: History, Myth and the Neo-Classical Imagination* (London: Duckworth).

Wisconsin Palmyrene Aramaic Inscription Project. http://digital.library.wisc.edu/1711. dl/WPAIPColl [accessed 25 July 2019].

Witecka, Anna. 1994. "Catalogue of Jewellery Found in the Tower-Tomb of Atenatan at Palmyra." *Studia Palmyreńskie* 9: 71–91.

Woltering, Robbert A. F. L. 2014. "Zenobia or al-Zabbā': The Modern Arab Literary Reception of the Palmyran Protagonist." *Middle Eastern Literatures* 17.1: 25–42.

Wood, Robert. 1753. *The Ruins of Palmyra: Otherwise Tedmor in the Desart* (London: Robert Wood).

Wright, William. 1872. *Catalogue of the Syriac Manuscripts in the British Museum* (London: Order of the Trustees of the British Museum).

Wright, William. 1895. *An Account of Palmyra and Zenobia: With Travels and Adventures in Bashan and the Desert* (London: Darf).

Yon, Jean-Baptiste. 1999a. "Les notables de Palmyre, Ier siècle avant J.-C. -IIIe siècle après J.-C.: études d'histoire sociale" (Thèse de doctorat en Histoire, Université François Rabelais, Tours).

Yon, Jean-Baptiste. 1999b. "La présence des notables dans l'espace périurbain à Palmyre." In *Construction, reproduction et représentation des Patriciats urbains de l'Antiquité au XXe siècle*, ed. by Claude Petitfrère (Tours, Université François Rabelais), pp. 387–400.

Yon, Jean-Baptiste. 2002. *Les notables de Palmyre*. Bibliothèque archéologique et historique 163 (Beirut: Institut français du Proche-Orient).

Yon, Jean-Baptiste. 2002–2003. "Zénobie et les femmes de Palmyre." *Annales Archéologiques Arabes Syriennes* 45–46: 215–220.

Yon, Jean-Baptiste. 2009. "La gestion de l'eau à Palmyre. L'exemple de la source Efqa." In *Stratégies d'acquisition de l'eau et société au Moyen-Orient depuis l'antiquité*, ed. by Mohamed al-Dbiyat and Michel Mouton (Beirut: Institut français du Proche-Orient), pp. 97–106.

Yon, Jean-Baptiste. 2010. "Kings and Princes at Palmyra." In *Kingdoms and Principalities in the Roman Near East*, ed. by Ted Kaizer and Margherita Facella. Oriens et Occidens 19 (Stuttgart: Steiner), pp. 229–240.

Yon, Jean-Baptiste. 2012. *Palmyre*, vol. 17.1, *Inscriptions grecques et latines de la Syrie*. Bibliothèque archéologique et historique 195 (Beirut: Institut français du Proche-Orient).

Yon, Jean-Baptiste. 2013. "L'épigraphie palmyrénienne depuis PAT, 1996–2011." In *Fifty Years of Polish Excavations in Palmyra, 1959–2009*, ed. by Michał Gawlikowski and Grzegorz Majcherek (Warsaw: University of Warsaw), pp. 333–379.

Yon, Jean-Baptiste. 2018. "Les tombes palmyréniennes étaient-elles des lieux de culte? Éléments de réponse archéologiques et épigraphiques." In *Constituer la tombe, honorer les défunts en Méditerranée antique*, ed. by Marie-Dominique Nenna, Sandrine Huber, and William Van Andringa (Alexandria: Centre d'Études Alexandrines), pp. 201–218.

Yon, Jean-Baptiste. 2019. "Palmyra and Its Elites." In *The Road to Palmyra*, ed. by Anne Marie Nielsen and Rubina Raja (Copenhagen: Ny Carlsberg Glyptotek), pp. 91-108.

Yoshimura, K., et al. 2016. "Inorganic Impurities in Teeth of the Ancient Inhabitants of Palmyra." In *Palmyrena: City, Hinterland and Caravan Trade Between Orient and Occident. Proceedings of the Conference held in Athens, December 1–3, 2012*, ed. by Jørgen Christian Meyer, Eivind Heldaas Seland, and Nils Anfinset (Oxford: Archaeopress), pp. 161–170.

Young, Gary. 2001. *Rome's Eastern Trade: International Commerce and Imperial Policy, 31 BC–AD 305* (London: Routledge).

Żuchowska, Marta. 2000. "Quelques remarques sur la Grande Colonnade à Palmyre." *Bulletin d'Etudes Orientales* 52: 187–193.

Żuchowska, Marta. 2006. "Palmyra: Excavations 2002–2005: Insula E by the Great Colonnade." *Polish Archaeology in the Mediterranean* 17: 439–450.

Żuchowska, Marta. 2008. "Wadi al Qubur and Its Interrelations with the Development of Urban Space of the City of Palmyra in the Hellenistic and Roman Periods." In *Proceedings of the 4th International Congress of the Archaeology of the Ancient Near East: 29 March–3 April 2004, Freie Universität Berlin*, ed. by Hartmut Kühne, Rainer Maria Czichon, and Florian Janoscha Kreppner (Wiesbaden: Harrassowitz), pp. 229–234.

Østrup, Johannes Elith. 1894. *Skiftende Horizonter* (Copenhagen: Gyldendalske Boghandel Forlag).

Østrup, Johannes Elith. 1895. *Historisk-topografiske Bidrag til Kendskabet til den syriske Ørken* (Copenhagen: Det Kongelige Danske Videnskabernes Selskab).

Index

Aglibol, 39, 44, 102–103, Fig. 39
agora, 37, 50, 51–53, 88, 120–121
al-Asaad, Khaled, 139
Allat, Sanctuary and Temple of, 39, 44, 46–47, 119, 121
al-Ṭabarī, 123
Antonine Plague, 85–86
Appian, 10, 94–95, 150n48
Arab invasion, 117, 120
Ardashir I, 106–107, Fig. 40
Arsu, Sanctuary and Temple of, 39, 44, 47–48, 98
art market,
  in the nineteenth century, 21
  and trade with objects from illegal excavations, 23, 58, 132–134, 142, 162n2
Atargatis, 39, 44, 98
Aurelian, Fig. 45
  provoked by Zenobia, 111, 113–115
  and the sack of Palmyra. See sack of Palmyra
  second rebellion against, 116
Aurelius Marcellinus, 116

Baalshamin, Sanctuary and Temple of, 44, 100, 119, 121, 142, Plate 4
  architecture of, 46, 55
  destruction of, 139, Fig. 51
  inscriptions about, 34, 46
  as tribal sanctuary, 39, 46 (see also tribes)
  See also sanctuaries
banqueting reliefs, 66, 82, Fig. 32
banqueting tesserae, 14, 33, 39, 44, 48, 88, Figs. 11a–h
banquets, 14, 28, 39, 43–44, 82, Fig. 9
Bel, Sanctuary and Temple of, 21, 121, Plate 3
  architecture of, 14, 38, 42–44, 49, 55
  destruction of, 7, 139
  as a fortress and village, 38, 124, 135, Figs. 46–47

inscriptions from and about, 39, 91, 170n43, 176n12
  as main sanctuary in Palmyra, 39
  used for worship of other deities, 44
  See also sanctuaries
benefactors, 14, 28, 81
  financing altars and cult images, 47, 100–102
  financing architecture, 33–34, 42, 45, 46, 122
  women, 13
  See also euergetism
Benjamin of Tudela, 20, 125, 154n125
bilingualism, 16, 27, 35–36, 71, 72–73, 88
burial practices, 14–15, 59–61, 69, 81–82, 122. See also graves

caliphs, 123, 178n58
Camp of Diocletian, 46–47, 58, 119–120
caravans. See trade
cessions texts, 27, 61, 66
children, 30, 102
  burial of, 60–61
  sculptural representations of, 31–32, 72, 76–77, 100, Figs. 10, 26
Christianity, 20, 121–122
churches, 20, 42, 121–122, 177n35
civil war (in Roman Empire), 10–11, 109
civil war (in Syria), 2, 21, 23, 24, 137–143
  See also destruction of cultural heritage
Cleopatra VII,
  during civil war, 11
  as model for Zenobia, 114
clothing, 31, 72, 78–79, 81, 88
  Parthian-inspired, 72, 78, 82, 84, 103, Fig. 32
Cohors XX Palmyrenorum, 92, 95
coins, 123, 175n140, Figs. 40, 45
  Palmyrene, 37, 113–114
  with Zenobia, 19, 111, 113–114, Fig. 44
collections, 21, 129–31, 134, 142, 154n129